Compassion and Self-Hate

Compassion and Self-Hate

An Alternative to Despair

by

Theodore I. Rubin, M. D.

with
Eleanor Rubin

DAVID McKAY COMPANY, INC.
New York

Compassion and Self-Hate

Library of Congress Cataloging in Publication Data

Rubin, Theodore Isaac.
  Compassion and self-hate.

  Includes index.
  1. Self-hate (Psychology)   I. Title.
BF697.R77   155.2   74–20325
ISBN 0–679–50474–5

MANUFACTURED IN THE UNITED STATES OF AMERICA
DESIGNED BY JACQUES CHAZAUD

ACKNOWLEDGMENTS

I cannot begin this book without thanks to Karen Horney, Nat Freeman and Paul Lussheimer, who are no longer with us, and many of my other former teachers and colleagues at the American Institute for Psychoanalysis. Particular thanks to Izz Portnoy, who more than anyone else taught me the true meaning of the word. I also thank my wife, my parents, my children, and my patients and friends. I thank Eleanor Rawson, the toughest, the most insightful and the best editor I have ever had.

Contents

x / Contents

If one is cruel to himself, how can we expect him to be compassionate with others?
—Hasdai, Ben ha-Melekh, ve-Ha-Nazer

PART I

An Alternative to Despair

This book was inspired by experience with myself and my patients.

Some years ago, as a result of what I felt as a great personal failure and consequent severely hurt pride, I suffered a very painful depression.

In psychoanalytic treatment, I learned a great deal about myself that I had no previous idea about at all. This included many emotional problems and confusions as well as much about good human substance, too. But despite these quite valid and important insights, my depression and despair went on and on and I began to feel that I never really would get better. I became aware that I was, in fact, psychologically beating myself unmercifully. I realized that much of the beating came from a false, perfectionistic, impossibly exalted image of myself. I felt that in falling from this image I had descended to considerably less than a subhuman status.

Despite myself, I could not turn the self-hating machinery off. My nights were particularly terrible. They consisted of either sleepless hours of self-torturing ruminations or were full of nightmares in which I once again saw myself as during periods when I felt most helpless, frightened and vulnerable as a child. Once again I relived the humiliating feelings I had when I was left back in the fifth grade. It was as if none of the development, evolving

3

and growth that had occurred in me since that time had ever happened. Despite myself I had no mercy for the somewhat confused child I had been and still obviously harbored within myself, and I had even less compassion for the young man I had become. The measure of my right *to be* was unfortunately based solely on accomplishment. One seeming failure was enough to upset this fragile, tenuous arrangement and to produce an almost incapacitating depression.

I was among the most fortunate of people. My wife, Ellie, never faltered in compassion and love and provided much insight too. My analyst, in addition to other human qualities, was also rich in both a fighting spirit and compassion. He employed both and fought valiantly against my self-hate. We won.

One night, after his own uncompromising compassionate outlook touched me deeply and I'm sure stirred my own dormant fund of compassion, a radical change took place. Before trying to sleep that night, I decided—not with my head but rather with my entire being, all my feelings—that I would "leave it all be," that I would simply let go, relax, stop berating myself, stop attempting to be in charge, to put it together—simply to let it go—to let be what would be. On a conscious level I felt as if a great weight had shifted from my chest. I was suddenly filled with a renewed faith in people, in the human condition, in the world, in nature and I suppose in all things some people feel as God. But this really represented faith in myself—myself—all of myself—sick and healthy. This represented both humility and self-acceptance and even more—compassion. It felt as though I finally knew that I was indeed smaller than the world I lived in, and this was humbling, relieving and good. And I liked myself this way. I could live with my virtues, assets, problems, limitations and failures, and without either subterfuge or horrendous self-hate. Though I didn't know it at the time, this was the beginning of a compassionate way of life. The battle was joined. That night I slept peacefully. In the morning my depression was gone.

❊ ❊ ❊ ❊ ❊

Each of us contains two opposing forces of enormous power and effect.

Compassion is the strongest human therapeutic agent in existence. Its potential for constructive growth and human creative possibility is almost limitless.

Self-hate is the strongest human antitherapeutic agent in existence. Its potential for destructive possibility is almost limitless.

To date, no culture has produced human beings exempt from this dichotomy. Division of the human psychic structure along this line is universal.

Despair is directly proportional to energy and substance used in the service of self-hate. Emotional well-being and relative freedom from destructive inner turmoil are directly proportional to energy and substance used in the service of compassion.

To those of us interested in human growth and enhancement of inner peace, it is vital to examine and to understand these forces. This is the only effective way to undermine self-hate, to potentiate compassion and to reduce internal despair. It is my belief that psychotherapeutic endeavors which neglect this area cannot succeed on a long-term basis. Any relationship, professional or otherwise, that ultimately reduces self-hate and enhances compassion contributes to a long-term and possibly permanent therapeutic effect. This process in turn makes self-growth, creativity and constructive relating possible. We invariably relate better to other people when we relate better to ourselves.

The first part of this book is devoted to a discussion of self-hate. In war it is vital to know the enemy and even without an iota of conscious awareness we are all participants in this intrapsychic war. For too many of us, the disastrous outcome is a foregone conclusion. Without the illumination of insight, hopelessness abounds and surrender is inevitable. Living with and nourishing an unseen and unknown but ever-present enemy destroys our inner resources, our vitality and our spontaneity. This produces emotional strangulation, deadening, loss of feelings and human despair. The first vital therapeutic step is to recognize and to understand the nature of self-hate.

In the middle section of the book I define and discuss compassion and the compassionate way of life. Compassion, as used in this book and as experienced in one's psychological life, refers to a very active and powerful force which must be understood in this highly specialized context. Some of its ramifications are intricate and complex but understanding them can be most rewarding and even life-saving.

Hopefully, it will aid in the active therapeutic process of reducing self-hate, enhancing compassion and obliterating despair born of intrapsychic surrender and hopelessness. The alternative is acceptance and growth of real self and a greater capacity for peace and happiness.

The final section of the book—"On Human Terms"—is devoted to a compassionate re-evaluation of our most important destructive cultural values. Understanding and changing these values must reduce self-hate, mutual hate and ultimately contribute to the construction of a more compassionate society.

PART II

Self-Hate

Self-Hate in Process

Hating oneself, one's actual self or any aspect or part of oneself is always part of an ongoing active process. If we hate our looks, the way we move, particular inabilities, culturally unacceptable characteristics such as jealousy, envy, possessiveness, fragility, vulnerability, duplicity, lying, stealing and even murdering, perversions, sexual and otherwise, we are engaging in the process. We engage in self-hate when we hate any aspect of ourselves and whenever we have feelings of self-contempt generally.

While feelings or acts of self-hate may seem isolated, they are always part of an ongoing continuous process. The process ranges from and includes mild feelings of discontent to contempt, disgust and abhorrence. It goes on to include sabotaging decisions, moves and activities against one's actual self and ultimately, suicide.

Actual self here refers to who we are rather than distorted versions of who we think we are or who we would like to be. These versions are in themselves a very important part of the self-hating process. Any distortion of self, either in degradation or idealization, must be viewed as rejection of actual self and is therefore self-hating. Thus, exaggerated opinions as to one's abilities are self-hating. Minimizing and ignoring one's abilities are no more, no less, self-hating. Rejection of reality as regards self, what-

9

ever form it takes, is always self-hating. Distorting reality, whatever form that distortion takes, always makes for destructive repercussions in terms of actual self.

Distorting reality may enhance a particular role we decide to play, but this must always occur at the expense of actual self. We can, for example, pretend to be all-knowing and incapable of a bad decision. This will feed the role of omnipotent superman. But it will demean the actual man, who, in being human, cannot be all-knowing, cannot predict the future and must make bad as well as good decisions. This kind of inhuman belief inevitably will lead to contempt and doubt about the limited but real abilities of the actual man. Later on we will find that many of our distorted beliefs are initiated by and linked to cultural misconceptions of the true human condition, some of which I will explore.

Any thought, feeling or action based on any combination of false beliefs, which in any direct or indirect way detracts from, depletes, denigrates or hurts that which is real and actual about oneself, must be considered as part of the self-hating process.

After childhood, the self-hating process has an autonomy of its own and unless active and, yes, heroic, intervention takes place, it goes on unabated in the same automatic, choiceless way as the heart beats. Often, what seems like the most passive aspects of self-hate can produce the most chronic and malignant effects. The effects of chronic self-hate and low self-esteem are insidious and pervasive even though they may not be immediately obvious. Generalized feelings of worthlessness and inadequacy invariably lead to a disastrous total life-style in all regards. Blatant self-destructive acts, on the other hand, may be obvious, but are often walled off and limited in the overall damage they produce.

I have a patient who invariably manages to destroy her vacation in one or another way. She hates herself for going on vacation because she unrealistically views herself as a nonfatiguing work machine. Thus, she gets sick on vacation; goes with "friends" whose close proximity she can't stand; has minor accidents—sprained ankles to cut fingers; brings the wrong clothes for a particular place or climate; and builds expectations that can't be fulfilled, which invariably leads to disappointment and unhappiness. But for the most part she otherwise lives a comparatively full and fulfilling life, has good relationships and is capable of sustaining reasonable happiness over extended periods of time.

I have another patient whose extremely low opinion and feelings about himself preclude the possibility of work or social encounters that would be appropriate to his real and considerable assets. This man's entire life is played out on a low-keyed, depressed, unfulfilled level. The same self-hating mechanism which forces him into a life just short of paralysis also prevents him from entering risk situations, which could lead to obvious self-sabotaging accidents. But even in this safety-enhancing position he is at a disadvantage.

My first patient, let's call her Betty, can readily see and feel the act and consequences relative to her self-hate. She can then meaningfully explore its origins. But John's total feelings about himself and their effects on his life are a much more ephemeral matter. They are not based on concrete situations which are easily discernible and do not lend themselves to easy observation and explorations.

His self-hate is not as apparent and on the surface does not lead to what we consider overt acts of self-inflicted pain, such as turned ankles and minor car accidents. *But* his self-hate is global in terms of himself and dictates an entire way of life. He is so permeated, inundated and totally identified with self-hate that *he* and *his self-hate* seem inseparable in making up the totality of the man. This is also why his self-hate was initially difficult to discern. I think of a total eclipse, in which the totality of the sun may be obliterated, versus a partial eclipse, where the sun's corona may still be visible along the edges. John's corona was barely visible when he came to see me. Actually it was only visible in the form of a strong but deeply buried feeling of "wanting to live" that was still alive in a tiny corner of himself. He called it a "yearning," though the chronicity and malignancy of his self-hate at first made it impossible for him to tell me or himself what he was yearning for. Betty's self-hate was visible. In fact, it was well delineated and easier to attack.

In any case, self-hate is always part of an autonomous active process, regardless of how little or much of a person's life it cancels out. While the connection between the process and its effects may not be at once apparent, they are always there and are invariably destructive. I shall have more to say about lack of awareness, or the unconscious aspect of self-hate, later on. In the next two chapters I want first to discuss the origins of self-hate and then how it is nurtured and sustained—that is, what feeds the autonomous process.

How Self-Hate Begins

As human beings we share a combination of unique characteristics that make us highly susceptible to the generation and continuation of self-hate. As members of our species we have the special ability to observe ourselves and to be critical of ourselves. We also have long memories. Unlike other creatures whose *present*, or *here and now*, is relatively short, our *now* is composed of a continuum of feeling and behavioral information which goes back to our earliest days. We are also exceedingly sensitive to receiving and registering information and influences from outside ourselves, especially at a very early age. Thus, we are less subject to, but also less protected by, inborn, biological, instinctual patterns.

This means that, unlike other organisms, we are capable of a great range of feelings and behavior and have a very large spectrum of adaptability. But this very ability to adapt and to be freer than other creatures from inborn primitive biological dictates also makes us particularly sensitive to influences from outside ourselves as we grow up.

When these influences are antithetical to what and whom a growing person actually is, i.e., *actual self*, the very vulnerable, fragile and highly receptive child develops hate for himself. What gives this process particular

13

impact is a child's extraordinary and very real dependence on the parent in early life. Initially the child probably feels like an extension of his parent. As such he or she is exquisitely responsive to a parent's own self-hate as well as to any manifestations that may be perceived as hatred for the newly developing individual. If hatred, as perceived by the child, as received from a parent, is particularly malignant, this makes matters worse in two ways. First, the child obviously develops more self-hate and a greater ability to reject himself. Secondly, as a result of self-rejection and lack of development of confidence in self, he feels that he cannot depend on himself. Thus, dependence on the parent is prolonged, as is his inability to differentiate himself from his parent. This further extends the period during which he will suffer parental onslaught, completing a vicious cycle from which it is most difficult to extricate himself. The process becomes particularly potent in the case of parents who have strong needs to comply with so-called cultural norms.

In this way, we have a baby who is utterly dependent on his parents for satisfaction of real needs and for protection against any danger he may be vulnerable to in his newborn state. His parents must, especially in a highly intricate and complex culture such as we live in, teach him rights, wrongs, permissions and prohibitions. Every baby must absorb a message which states that not all of his natural and immediate impulses or proclivities are acceptable. Therefore, even in the healthiest family environment, the baby inevitably learns to observe himself, judge himself and to reject certain aspects of himself. He also learns that "bad" aspects of himself bring on punishment. He, too, learns to punish himself for being "bad." This is the price we pay for culture and civilization. But in many cases, especially with apprehensive parents, "bad" unfortunately comes to cover much human ground.

Characteristics described by the culture as "bad," and viewed with particular abhorrence, include aggressiveness, passivity, jealousy, envy, hostility, anger, laziness, cowardice, fear, helplessness, etc.

Let me give a small example at this point. Let's say parents are dealing with Jill, one of their three children, who is three-and-a-half years old, *vis-à-vis* a bowl of cherries. Jill loves cherries, is eating them from the bowl and unless stopped at some point will happily go on to eat all of them. Her mother asks her to stop eating them. Jill objects, truthfully stating that she feels like eating them all. Her mother then says, "Don't be a selfish girl. Leave some cherries for your brother and sister." Jill's appetite is overwhelming and she keeps eating cherries. Her mother calls her a bad and selfish girl, slaps her hands and takes away the cherries.

Jill cries for a minute, stops and then goes on to play with a doll. But much has happened. Jill is of an age when she no longer feels she is an extension of her mother. But even though she is a separate, whole individual, she is still highly dependent on her mother and enormously sensitive to all things she perceives in herself, to influences from outside and to the impact of outside influences on herself. What her mother says and does, not only registers but is also permanently recorded, especially when it is repeated again and again. What did Jill hear and register? She heard more than her mother's words. The impact comes from mood, tone of voice, implied messages and action, if any, in this case, slapped hands. What then did Jill really hear? She heard that appetite is bad; that wanting all the cherries is selfish; that selfishness is a bad feeling; that a desire to share is a good feeling; that bad feelings bring on deprivation of love as well as consequent punishment.

Jill learns that aspects of herself are intolerable, that she must view them with suspicion and not like them, and in so doing she is not liking and rejecting part of herself. She also learns that when certain aspects of herself surface and are exposed, they need to be put down, hidden, depressed and that she may require punishment, eventually from herself, in order to do this. Of course this was a mild message. It could be harsher, more frequent and applied much too liberally to all kinds of natural human urges and proclivities. But it could be more compassionate, too.

Her mother might have said, "Of course you want all the cherries, Jill. Eating cherries makes us feel like eating more and more so that we forget other people want them, too, and we want to eat them all. The other children will want some, too, so I have to put some away for them." The important difference in this message is that it makes none of Jill's feelings pejorative. In effect it says, "You are allowed to feel any way at all and indeed you ought to have and own all your feelings even if you can't satisfy them." Thus, there is no repression of them and no inclination to punishment for having them.

Unfortunately, few of us as parents are geared to understanding the value of feelings, all feelings, and the need to prevent cutting them off through repression and inhibition. Feelings that are repressed become exaggerated, develop an autonomy of their own, and when they emerge, as they inevitably must from time to time, bring on a conditioned pattern of self-hate, often in the form of depression. Depression provides punishment, as well as an active process of putting oneself and one's feelings *down*. It provides a kind of anesthesia so that no feelings, including unacceptable ones, are experienced with any great intensity. Thus, *depression serves an important enough emotional economy to give it a most addictive quality,* and once used it is generally used again and again.

How Self-Hate Is Sustained

The ability most of us have to observe ourselves obviously can be most useful in the proper context. It can be a precursor to constructive criticism and to real growth. But it also contributes to a splitting of self or a kind of self-consciousness, which inevitably makes for at least some loss of spontaneity. This loss of spontaneity makes us that much more dependent on self-hate as a stimulus and guide in living.

Let me explain. There is a part of ourselves that, from childhood on, continues in the role of observer, evaluator, and censor, too. Unfortunately, what starts out as benevolent self-protection often, especially in all too common adverse circumstances, turns to tyrannical despotism. Standards begin to be imposed which cannot be met. Examinations are constructed which cannot be passed. Self-consciousness and observation turns to self-contempt and to an underlying ever-pervasive sense of self-defeat. Spontaneity and free behavior become confused with impulsivity and foolishness. In an effort to be safe from punitive aspects of this split-off hater of self, the victim becomes increasingly constricted and circumspect about behavior, feelings and even thinking. More and more he turns, as so many prisoners do with their jailors, to the tyrant in himself for direction and for a substitute sense of aliveness. This results in further loss of self-trust, a further sense of weakening in self and a further dependence on fixed and rigid rules and modes of behavior set down by the split-off, self-hating part of himself. There is then less and less practice and use of alive spontaneity in tapping one's *real* feelings, real thoughts, real assets and real possibilities.

Without any conscious awareness on the part of the victim, the tyrant has taken over and, for the most part, a self has been lost. Any small awakening of self, any threat of resurrection usually brings fast action on the part of the tyrannical side, to prevent conflict and possible victory of one's compassionate self. This usually takes the form of depression, which to me is often a signal that an individual still has hope and yearning to become alive and is feeling the beginnings of a constructive struggle. Without this yearning for a resurrection of spontaneity, we usually see abject, chronic *resignation* from the possibility of really feeling alive rather than just depression—a true withdrawal from life.

Depression is not only a result of the inner punishment we inflict on ourselves for daring to think of inner freedom. It is also the result of despair, born of the inner knowledge of disloyalty to self, and waste of one's self and one's real assets over a lifetime of capitulation to inner tyranny. Fortunately, as I shall explain when I discuss compassion, if the battle is engaged and sustained, spontaneity often wins out, because the great proclivity of most human beings is toward healthy growth, in the service of taking ourselves, our needs, our assets and our real hopes and desires seriously. Unfortunately, this is often not evident because we suffer from the pressures of an impossible cultural value system of which both we and our parents are victims. The combination of inner and outer pressures makes extrication from this vise extremely painful and difficult and requires considerable motivation.

But now, what about particularly destructive parents? Let me first say that most of us are the victims of victims and continue to victimize, unless real awareness, deep insight and constructive struggle to do otherwise intervene. Most people simply have no idea that they feed and help sustain the self-hating dynamism and also make contributions from it to their children as well as to an ongoing cultural morass. Parents, who through their own difficulties have lost spontaneity and behave in anxiety-ridden constricted patterns, will, of course, transmit many of their self-hating postures to their children. Parents who in one or another way reject the child or any aspect of him or of his natural proclivities are often, without awareness, engaging in the process of hating the actual child and are producing fertile soil for growth of self-hate. Again, it must be remembered that due to our great and prolonged dependence on parents during childhood we are particularly affected by how they feel about us.

The very young child, whose personality (his feelings about himself and himself relative to the world) and character structure (modes of behavior and relating to self and other people) are not yet formed, largely learns from his parents how to feel about himself. He automatically, without conscious awareness, applies how they feel about him to how he feels about himself. If they are grossly overpermissive and don't seem to care about him, then he feels he is a person not worth caring about. If they are overbearing and stifling, he sees himself as a fragile, vulnerable fragment of a person rather than as a separate, whole, capable human being. If they are excessively punitive, overbearing or worse—sadistic, he sees himself as a monstrous person who must not trust ordinary human characteristics and impulses, let alone individual differences and his own judgment. If they have little respect or regard for the person he really is, for his natural proclivities, desires, goals and talents, then he, too, will wish to be other than who he is. These parents may minimize his considerable and quite real assets while they extol the virtues of a mythical superman. This, plus pressures from an enveloping culture, replete with impossible standards, exaggerated notions and confusions as regards the human condition, will push the child into a self-idealizing process. He will aim for impossible goals of excess virtue, great power, ideal wisdom—all necessarily fraught with failure, frustration and hopelessness. These are followed by still more self-hate used as punishment for failure and as a goad to whip him on to further journeys away from his actual self and human possibilities and satisfactions.

Parents who are overly zealous and excessively stringent in meting out punishment and in establishing prohibitions produce overwhelming, castigating consciences in their children. Criminals, I believe, suffer from the most tyrannical consciences, which means that in order to survive with some feelings left intact and alive, they must totally rebel and deaden their menacing consciences. Overpermissiveness, on the other hand, does not preclude a parent being a despot while seeming detached. It is possible to suffer almost complete combinations of destructive influences from a single parent, as well as from a combination of both parents, and some cultural contributions. A single parent may herself suffer from considerable self-hate and active residuals of destructive pressures. The same parent may also contribute a large measure of compassion. This may seem incongruous and inconsistent, and indeed it is, but it is also characteristic of the human condition. We, each of us, are subject to both constructive and destructive elements in our development and in most cases we contain a plenitude of all possible elements. In any case, the question of ratio and degree are obviously of prime importance.

A stringent culture, combined with inconsistently destructive parents, who themselves contain little or no active compassion, will produce children who will be masses of self-hate. Fortunately, this is rarely the case, and with most of us at least some compassionate influence has been transmitted. Once the self-hating process has been set in motion, it becomes firmly entrenched and develops an autonomy of its own. It comes to be felt as more than just familiar. It is felt as the central core of one's identification. One sees oneself relative to self-hating values and ideas. Eventually, any feeling or idea about oneself that springs from whatever healthy self-esteem has managed to remain alive is felt as alien and threatening, and poses a threat to a process which, like all totalitarian processes, requires *total* subjection and compliance for survival. Therefore, *any* feelings of real self-esteem or any contribution to real self-esteem are quickly repressed. Sometimes, certain "shots in the arm"—such as momentary stimulation through sexual escapades, a good business deal, a windfall, going on a trip—are seen and felt as self-esteem. But they are frequently used to feed pride and grandiosity, and they represent further excursions away from actual self. Karen Horney described this process brilliantly in her work and I'll have more to say about this later.

To close this chapter let me describe a patient I treated

for several years. Bill was the only son of immigrant parents who were both profoundly insecure people preoccupied with the idea of "fitting in" to this culture and country by "always doing the right thing." They saw their son as the "perfect child," through whom the fact of their non-American births would be completely erased. From the earliest age Bill repeatedly demonstrated a considerable gift and desire to draw and paint. His parents' initial praise turned to discouragement and then to ridicule and finally to vindictive tirades by the time he was a teen-ager. They felt that "art work" was foreign, frivolous, feminine and the antithesis of whatever goals they could accept for Bill. Bill's initial attempts at self-assertion, and even rebellion, soon turned to complete capitulation and compliance. This was largely due to his being beaten and locked in the closet and, on several occasions when he vented his anger, having his mouth washed with strong soap. Bill says he became "a good boy" and a "nearly perfect student" in school. He also said that he distinctly remembered a day when he was fifteen when he "felt something die in me and I got into a kind of peaceful fog that I stayed in until now." This feeling, he recalled, occurred when he came home from school and told his parents that a teacher told him that he ought to consider transferring to the high school of music and art. Terrible recriminations and hysteria followed this announcement.

Throughout his childhood, Bill remembered his parents as being overprotective and tyrannical. He was constantly taken to doctors for all kinds of ills imagined by his mother. He was seldom permitted to participate in activities with other boys and could not have friends who did not dress and speak in a "proper manner." He doesn't remember ever being allowed to sleep over at anybody else's house or to go off on a trip with friends. He recalls his mother showing him off to neighbors as being absolutely neat and clean and showing them his almost perfect report cards. But this was always done out of his cognizance. Indeed, he only heard about these comments through the neighbors themselves. His parents never praised him, and, at most, only grudgingly approved of behavior they condoned, obviously feeling that marked enthusiasm would be a signal to him to let up on his efforts. "I felt that nothing I did was ever good enough and that I had to do better than anyone else I knew just to get by." He remembers his parents also frequently telling him "not to think you are too good" and "to aim for a good, regular job that you can count on because the world is really a jungle." Though teachers encouraged him to go to college, and he had the second-highest average in high school, his parents insisted he take no chances in getting started earning; college sounded frivolous to them. This meant taking a job as an assistant furniture designer in a well-known firm. He took the job, lived at home, socialized very infrequently and twenty years later, at the age of thirty-six became severely depressed.

Once again his mother intervened. She and Bill's boss consulted a local doctor who advised electro shock treatment. By this time, Bill was designing 90 percent of the firm's furniture but was still called "an assistant designer." He received 10 percent more than he had started with in salary and also parked the boss's car and chauffeured the boss and his parents around in his "spare time." Up to the time of his depression he incredibly had no feeling of exploitation, and as he put it later, "I wonder if I had any feeling at all." But he was extremely useful, and it was decided that ECT would get him back to full production faster than any other means. However, after two shock treatments, Bill suddenly asserted himself and refused to have any more, deciding on his own to see a therapist.

When he came to me he was severely depressed and agitated. Many early sessions were spent recounting countless events depicting tyranny, exploitation and choking off of any hope or aspiration. "I was a good boy and almost a complete emotional vegetable." Bill amply demonstrated the results of parental and cultural exaggerated pressures to conform, to make it, to be good, etc. He demonstrated massive self-hate of both direct and indirect kinds.

His concept of himself, his actual self, could hardly be worse, yet there were all kinds of goals of purity he felt compelled to fulfill. He saw himself as the selfless martyr par excellence, and his parents and boss helped feed this image. He was also a mass of rage and initially had no idea that he was angry at all. He feared anger terribly, equating it with madness and being evil. Thus, his anger at other people had been completely repressed out of awareness. Much of it had also been internalized, turned against himself, and took the form of chronic depression, resignation and deadening of feelings. Surrender to both inner and outer tyranny, the desire to give up the fight for self—which is the epitome of self-hate—was represented by the feeling that "something had died in me."

How did Bill become acutely depressed and what did his depression represent? How did chronic depression and years of smoldering rage become mobilized into severe, acute depression, which is too painful to be ignored? For countless people this never happens. Their actual selves have been reduced to ashes and no flame can be fanned up from embers that are all too dead. In these people, self-hate has triumphed completely. For many people chronic depression, inner emptiness and deadness have become a way of life and they no longer know that alternatives exist. Indeed, they don't even know that they are depressed.

I suspect that one of the big factors in Bill's life was his work. He was fortunate to get a job in furniture design (quite by chance, and fortunately his parents did not equate this work with artistic endeavor). While this work didn't begin to tap what eventually turned out to be a storehouse of considerable talent, it did give Bill some personal satisfaction and did keep a small part of himself alive and yearning. Several months after treatment began, when much of his rage had been vented (he realized he wasn't crazy after all), and his acute depression and agitation had abated, he told me something that he considered a deep and frightening secret. He was only able to tell me this because he trusted my interest and involvement in helping to bring his actual self into fruition and knew that I wouldn't castigate him. But when he told me—and this was at age thirty-seven—he was still quite obviously tremulous and fearful. The secret: That he locked himself up in his room periodically and painted a "small picture."

So he did manage to stay alive until a time came when two important events occurred. A very wealthy business-man, who manufactured furniture and who realized that Bill, without any of his own awareness, had become one of the most important designers in the business, offered to put Bill into business on his own. A new employee of Bill's firm fell in love with him, insisted on an affair and marriage, and encouraged him to go into business and to paint. He finally showed her one painting and she insisted that he spend more and more time painting, and set up part of her own apartment as a studio in order for him to be able to do this. Bill's parents knew nothing of the painting but thought the idea of his own business and the girl, too, were evidence of some kind of insanity which suddenly had taken over their son.

The pressure on Bill—both externally and internally— became intense. From the bottom of years of being pushed down almost into nothingness, his actual self fought its way up into awareness. Its yearnings for human satisfaction could no longer be ignored. Bill wanted the girl, the business, to paint, and to live. His self-hating side wanted him to go on quietly, to take no risks, to continue in a stunted existence and to sustain illusions of mythical grandeur through fantasies of glorious martyrdom and devotion to marvelous parents. Severe, acute depression was punishment for guilt felt for betrayal of the imaginary image and its rules, including the yearning for human satisfactions that brought with it the possibility of being "a bad son." He inflicted this punishment on himself in an attempt to whip himself back into his former position. It was also an attempt to anesthetize, deaden and to put down and away the entire conflict. But it also represented very real sorrow stemming from newborn awareness that years of good living potential had been wasted.

Bill initially raged at himself and was full of blatant and direct self-hate. He saw himself as a monstrous ingrate and as the equivalent of a parent-killer. This was followed by recounting years of self-neglect and various forms of indirect self-hate, which I describe in a later chapter. This included many delusions about his purity, sweetness, devotion, etc. He had no idea that his description was of an archangel and had little or nothing to do with the human condition. But actual self once heard from, really heard from, is not easily put down. Bill's choice of psychoanalysis over electro shock treatment was crucial. In this choice, he made the most important decision of his life. He had in fact decided to embark on a tough journey in search of himself rather than to execute himself by severe self-punishment and to resign once and for all.

Bill's treatment included much exploration, re-evaluation, education and painful struggle on his part. He came to realize how much of his confused feelings and thinking were part of an impossible cultural value system of which his parents were also victims. Self-hate was largely defeated in favor of compassion. Initial hatred for his parents turned to compassion and he eventually came to have a fairly mature, realistic relationship with them. Bill went into business and is currently very successful. His paintings have received considerable recognition and are now usually very large canvases.

Bill is happily married and has two children of his own, one of whom already demonstrates much talent in painting and receives plenty of parental encouragement. Bill did not marry the girl who initially encouraged him, however. He felt that she was too much like his mother.

Consciousness and Unconsciousness in Self-Hate

Self-hate often goes on consciously with the complete awareness of its victim. Unfortunately, unless it is a concomitant of severe and painful depression, it is seldom taken seriously. A severe depression cannot escape the attention of the victim and those close to him; it is manifested by self-castigation, self-derision, self-mutilation, starvation, even paralysis and actual inability to function. But short of painful depression, people will actively depreciate, demean and put themselves down generally, with almost complete ease and with little or no awareness of the destructive aspects and results involved. The same people may speak of feeling demoralized, depleted, weak, helpless, hopeless, frightened, vulnerable, fragile, incapable, or self-doubting, without making any connection at all between these symptoms and their own attacks upon themselves.

I had a patient, Jack, who simply never lost an opportunity to put himself down and also to blame himself for any mishap that occurred within miles of him. "I just can't do anything right. I guess I'm just stupid." "If I had known better my father wouldn't have made the investment and would have saved all that money." "I figured he must be right and as it turned out I was the one who was right all along. I know that he's much smarter than I am, I just can't understand it." "You tell me that I'm right and I just can't believe it. Are you telling me this just to make me feel good?" Jack was frequently tired, indecisive, unhappy, afraid of new situations and in most situations felt "damned if I do and damned if I don't." He was conscious of his self-derision but made no connection between his symptoms and obvious expressions of self-hate. Indeed, the very denial and lack of awareness of the connection is itself a form of self-hate, since ignorance beclouds the issue and prevents constructive change. It had to be pointed out to Jack again and again that he repeatedly expressed more contempt for himself and rejection of himself than anyone else inflicted on him. Indeed, much of his fear in new situations were projections of his own self-hate. It took much time before Jack realized that anticipated rejection from others had no realistic basis other than coming from feelings which had their beginnings in his own mind.

But most self-hate goes on unconsciously, that is, totally out of conscious awareness. It does not take the form of obvious verbalized self-derision and contempt. Its effects are more insidious, more pervasive and much more difficult to pinpoint and to fight against. This is a kind of emotional malignancy, a malignancy of the soul, in which we often feel badly and can't understand why.

In attempting to conform to cultural and to environmental pressures and to meet only values and standards which we have come to deem as acceptable, our ability to store away information about ourselves in a part of our unconsciousness that is not readily available becomes exaggerated. In other words, our ability to repress becomes too good.

We have the ability to remember and to forget. To clear

the road for the *here and now* business of everyday living, we forget for the moment material which is not necessary for immediate use. We can recall that material whenever we need it. *But there is much about ourselves, particularly all kinds of feelings, that we don't want to be able to recall or know about at all.* This is especially true of perfectly human feelings and characteristics which we have unfortunately come to view as inhuman or less than ideal. These may include anger, especially at people we love; selfishness; cowardice; very strong feelings; or, especially in men, softer feelings. Thus, we develop our forgetting ability to a highly exaggerated degree. We come to use it constantly and with extreme efficiency, so that much knowledge about ourselves and many feelings that we have are automatically pushed down and away (repression) without our knowing that we are doing this, without choice.

Another way of saying the same thing is that we *repress* a great deal and in so doing are constantly engaging in the process of adding to the unconscious part of ourselves. This process of anesthetizing, splitting, hiding ourselves from ourselves and deadening ourselves invariably has destructive repercussions. The feelings we push out of ready awareness cannot be selected at will, as we may think. When we repress one feeling we usually repress many others as well, and in so doing lose use of much that is of value in ourselves.

Also, feelings and information that are repressed don't just go away and die. On the contrary, they remain active forces in our minds and continue to produce all kinds of difficulties because once cut off from the main stream of consciousness they go on autonomously, often in a bizarre manner and with highly exaggerated force. Thus, *repressed anger may turn to severe depression* and to extremely morbid thoughts and fantasies. Repressed anger also often functions as a block to other feelings, so that *a person who is angry and doesn't know it very often cannot feel love or feel or express warmth.*

In any case, since exaggerated repression is a form of self-rejection, the process itself must be viewed as self-hating. The storehouse of potential aliveness we keep from our own use is evidence of self-hate. That many of us spend our lives choicelessly responding to inner dictates we know nothing about is further evidence of self-hate. Unlike conscious self-hate, unconscious self-hate is global and affects the total personality, life-style and all aspects of relating.

Self-hate provides much of the fuel necessary to the neurotic process and to the journey away from our actual selves. In this regard, we must view psychoanalytic therapy as compassionate, because its goal is to make conscious that which is unconscious. However, this process, too, must be conducted with utmost compassion if it is to succeed on a meaningful and sustained level. In other than a compassionate atmosphere and process, careless and uncaring revelation of hitherto buried aspects of ourselves often brings on massive self-hating onslaughts and further repression.

The solemn, deep promise to be gentle with ourselves must be invoked again and again, before and during any process of self-revelation. This is so because our culture dictates extreme harshness and punitive measures when violation of any of its dictates and standards of performance are revealed. I am reminded of Bill, who told me how he locked himself in the bathroom to avoid his mother's wrath over some minor infraction. She told him to come out and to confess, promising that the truth would save him punishment. When he did, she commended him for obeying her and yet beat him and washed his mouth with soap for committing the crime itself.

Most of us fear punishment from ourselves if we reveal certain truths. Thus, we keep the unconscious variety of self-hate going and resist revelation both in and out of treatment unless we promise ourselves compassion and keep the promise, absolutely refusing to engage in self-recrimination no matter what we encounter in ourselves. This can only be done with insight into both our self-hating and our compassionate processes.

Forms of Self-Hate: Direct

Self-hate consists of attacks on self whatever form they take. In *direct self-hate* there is nothing subtle about the onslaught. While its origin, motive, reason for being and its effects may be relegated to an unconscious level by the victim, identification as self-hate is usually obvious, with little need for interpretation. Simple observation and even the most primitive form of analysis readily reveals the self-destructive nature and intent of the process. Direct self-hate includes all active processes and also symptoms stemming from the processes, as well as signs and symbols of the processes, indicating that self-hate must be taking place.

The following are the commonest forms I've encountered, but there are numerous variations and any number of ingenious and unique inventions. Man can be enormously creative either in the service of constructive or destructive forces.

SELF-DERISION

This takes the form of thoughts and actual verbalizations to other people: "I'm stupid." "I'm no good." "I can't do anything right." "Look at me, I'm such a crass, clumsy oaf." In analysis, what is sometimes revealed is that each of us uses actual words and phrases repetitively and sometimes without any variation at all. These statements come forth on almost a conditioned-reflex basis, with what looks like an autonomy of their own and most often at times when the victim is about to do something worthwhile and constructive for himself. Many of these derisive, self-annihilating statements go back to childhood and sometimes they are the actual words, word for word, used by parents in conjunction to themselves, as well as to the current victim.

I had one patient who early in treatment never failed, often with what looked like superficially good humor, to refer to himself as "schmucky little Harry" whenever he was about to embark on a constructive venture. Another man, seemingly good-naturedly, called himself "a big crass oaf" in exactly the same circumstances. It soon became apparent that both men had very low opinions of themselves, and had designed constricted, self-effacing lives for themselves in order "to feel safe."

Both men recalled, with no small interest, their parents' skepticism with attempted new ventures and challenges as well as excess parental chastisement whenever they incurred failure. They were also both surprised that they engaged in maximum self-derisive name-calling whenever they were about to embark on a project which might in any way turn out to be truly self-enhancing. Not only had this kind of name-calling become a habit, an autonomous-reflex response, but it also served the entire self-hating dynamism of ever reminding its victims of the importance of not stepping out of line and of the dangers of becoming too successful and good to oneself. This was also a way of punishing for failure *in advance of failure*, hoping in this way to appease the self-hating mechanism so as to prevent much harsher self-hating punishment later on. It was also an attempt to satisfy the self-hating need for constriction so as to be permitted to enjoy life a little bit.

But both men were truly astounded when they recalled their parents using the exact derisive names, terms and phrases. Over the years they had completely forgotten the origin of these terms. This kind of evolvement is often quite evident in severely disturbed people who project their self-hate and imagine they hear other people calling them derisive names. This often takes the form of auditory hallucinations. I have interviewed any number of patients who heard voices calling them "bad names." In a good many cases they described the voices as those of their parents. Very often "the voices" call them "bad sexual names." While this may be related to sexual conflict and to self-hate related to having sexual feelings and "being impure," I believe that psychotic people who are extremely self-hating borrow from the culture in their use of self-hating terms. Thus, it has been most common for years for paranoid schizophrenic men to complain of voices which called them homosexuals and for women to complain of being called prostitutes. These, obviously, were the worst terms these people could extract from the culture's fund of pejorative conditions and terms to apply to themselves.

SELF-DERISIVE FANTASIES

These are very common and largely serve the same self-destructive purpose. The most common involve seeing oneself in embarrassing situations. Others involve being alone, forsaken, stranded and impoverished. Some become overtly and strongly masochistic and involve visions of powerful castigation. Many self-hating people are incapable of sexual stimulation and satisfaction, let alone enjoyment, without masochistic fantasies or overt acts against oneself. I know of one young woman who inflicted multiple superficial cuts on her legs. One man had to look in a mirror and call himself every disgusting term he could bring to mind. This kind of act and the fantasies serve two purposes. One is advance payment in the form of punishment for daring to experience pleasure which is antithetical to the self-hating tyrant. The other is to knock oneself down from a position of martyred purity to earthier levels where baser feelings, including sexual ones, can be felt.

SELF-VINDICTIVE CRITICISM

This is criticism with little or no constructive value. While the ostensible purpose of self-improvement may be used as a rationalization, the actual motivation is self-flagellation. The goal here is to demoralize and to paralyze one's actual self in the service of self-hate. This is often preceded by putting oneself in untenable situations and then following up with self-ridicule when extrication is impossible. This includes disastrous relationships and jobs, taking on impossible and multiple assignments, putting oneself into test situations that are designed for failure. Another favorite is the demand for absolute perfection as a passing grade.

I had one patient who suffered from perfectionistic standards that finally resulted in deadly fear of engaging in any kind of constructive work at all. His paralysis did not prevent him, however, from calling himself "stupid, cowardly, weak and inept." The man had been a highly accredited architect responsible for fine and well-received work. But the smallest adverse criticism, however benevolently delivered, brought down devastating attacks on himself by himself. When these, coupled with severe depression, became unbearable, he stopped working altogether.

On a conscious level he had no idea that his standards were beyond possibility. He had even less insight into the connection between these standards and his ensuing self-hate through recriminations, self-villification and depression, and fear of work and performance. Although he readily understood my explanation of the source of his suffering, his insight was largely intellectual and of very limited value until his free associations brought him very important, highly emotionally charged early memories. He began to recall onslaughts and punishment from his father for even the slightest deviation from absolutely perfect performance. This included getting 99 percent on a Regents' math examination. He was afraid to go home that day because his father regarded less than 100 percent as a failure, and failure was intolerable.

I viewed his paralysis and inability to function as a constructive rebellion against impossible and tyrannical standards. This was his way of saying that he wanted *out*. As these memories evolved, my patient exploded more and more in rages at the injustices committed against the innocent child he had been.

Eventually, he came to realize on a deeply feeling level

that his own self-punishment was, unfortunately, a contin-uation of his father's on an even more effective level than that had been. He also realized that his standards for human performance were absolutely Godlike, and a very hard struggle ensued to replace them with ones that were humanly plausible. These included acceptance of failure, not 1 percent failure, but real failure. Initially, he was amazed to find that he could fail (in a business venture) and survive without vindictive self-hate and depression. In short, he became compassionate with himself and involved in a life-long process of enhancing humility.

While this patient exemplifies a rather extreme case, nearly all of us in our own individual ways suffer similar though perhaps subtler manifestations. One of the princi-ple forms of vindictive self-berating is self-recrimination in the form of second-guessing. The signs and symptoms are common enough. These are a few of the statements we all hear and make and unfortunately take quite seriously, too: "Yes, but," "I should have," "I could have," "What if," "If I only had," "It's so obvious to me now." The self-recrimi-nation here takes place both as a response to a lack of perfection and an inability to predict the future.

If we demand wisdom after the fact, then in effect we assume an absolute ability to foretell the future and to make no mistakes at all. This results in our wasting energy and time in self-hate and in feeling badly to the point where any information we could possibly extract from these past mistakes is ignored and passed by. Self-recrimi-nation becomes the central issue and since this has no educational value whatsoever, and, in fact, produces anxiety, depression and fatigue, chances of more "mis-takes" are increased tenfold, thus completing a self-hating vicious cycle.

I had one patient who consistently made bad invest-
ments, then looked back with a multitude of second-guessing "ifs," hating and berating himself for "not knowing
better." He just couldn't understand why he didn't make
"better decisions." He kept talking about "paying my
dues" but refused to elaborate. After we worked together
a few months it became apparent what he really meant. It
was his belief that if he berated himself and suffered
enough, he deserved to succeed. He believed that his
self-created pain in some magical way should henceforth
guarantee prudent business decisions. We had to break
down enormous resistance to change before he really
understood, on a gut-feeling level, that his neurotic
emotional logic simply had nothing to do with reality.

(1) Self-hate and suffering do not make one deserving.
(2) However deserving we may be, just desert has little or
nothing to do with either accomplishment or rewards.
There is no big man up there who tallies it all up and sees
that the good person or the fellow who wants it most or
deserves it best gets it. (3) Self-recrimination, as a way of
expressing self-hate, and the endurance of the suffering
that ensues do not make a person more knowledgeable. (4)
Self-hate and suffering do not make a more perfect person
in any regard and do not confer the ability to predict the
future so that "future pasts" will be error free. (5) These
destructive forces *do* demoralize, fatigue and deplete,
increasing chances for further and even multitudinous
poor decisions and failures.

SELF-DIMINUTION

This form of self-hate involves the active process of
avoiding recognition of and neglecting one's real assets and

possibilities for fruitful development. This process is always linked to minimizing or completely negating any self-satisfying activity. The process here may be very subtle and can be overlooked by even highly experienced therapists.

The victim has often been so adept at putting down and hiding all kinds of valuable aspects of himself that he does indeed seem like a person who can barely feed himself, can barely make any decision and who really contains very few human assets and none of the energy necessary for potential growth. Such people often present both to themselves and to the rest of the world a façade of near-inarticulate helplessness and sometimes what seems like utter dependency on others. They almost inevitably turn out to have enormous hidden energy and as many human assets (intelligence, humor, human experiences and memories, feelings, warmth, strength, etc.) as their seemingly more capable confreres. Enormous energy is required to efface oneself and constantly to keep the most constructive aspects of self out of the conscious awareness of oneself or others. Such people often look and act exceptionally passive. But this passivity, in relation to other people, masks an extraordinary active process of diminishing and demeaning oneself, which leaves little or no energy for the so-called pursuit of happiness. Attempts by other people, including therapists, to point out obvious assets and constructive possibilities are usually met with a combination of suspicion, incredulity and embarrassment, followed by attacks of self-hate of a more discernible variety. "You really don't know me. I really am stupid. Like in the cartoon I once saw, I truly am inferior. I can't see how you can say that. You're just trying to make me feel good."

Prodding and urging self-diminishers to do something nice for themselves may bring on more overtly vicious attacks of self-hate and even severe depression. To be nice to a person who considers herself lower than dirt seems grossly inappropriate to the victim and engenders much guilt. Guilt and continuing self-denigration are a way of reminding oneself of low worth and insuring the continuation of the self-hating process. I have treated more than one patient who when they attempted to be "nice, good and constructive" to themselves met the attempt with vicious onslaughts on themselves. I have been fortunate when I've been able to divert some of their self-hate to me so as to avoid severe repercussions. During times of self-nourishment these people need the greatest support. They need no such support when they engage in familiar self-hating devices.

When I was much younger, I had a patient whom I urged to buy things for herself that she desperately needed and seemingly wanted, mostly clothes and a decent place to live. I remember at first being puzzled and confused when each move forward on her part was followed by periods of terrible self-castigation and depression. The same was true of situations in which I urged her to defend herself against people who were demeaning and destructive to her. Most of her relationships were designed to augment and promote self-hate and I asked her to terminate them. Very often, though, there is simply no way to avoid this initial confrontation with blatant self-hate *as a way of initiating self-compassion.*

It can be most useful in engaging the enemy once and for all if we point out the connection between the onslaughts of self-hate that follow acts of self-nourishment. Many people, after they have passed through early self-hating attempts to put themselves into a box, go on to state that they feel "confused, disoriented and just strange and not like myself." This is largely because they are in fact engaging in an unfamiliar process and way of life involving use of unfamiliar aspects of themselves. The fact is that in initiating a stand *against* self-eradication they are being *most* like themselves. But, unlike the situation with an infant, where confrontation with self is a slowly evolving process, exposure here can be sudden and explosive as well as massive. These sudden and huge exposures of self, antithetical and often opposite to a familiar life-style and understanding of self as a zero, that has gone on for years, can be shocking and frightening.

Some years ago a young man in his late twenties, Sean, came to see me because he said he was very anxious and depressed much of the time and couldn't understand why. Everything, according to him, was going well. He came from a working-class Irish-American family, never finished high school, but had had the same "fine job" since he was sixteen. His job turned out to be factory assembly work, where he stood in one spot for eight or more hours a day, joining three fittings together as they passed his station. The rest of his time was divided between drinking as many as twenty beers a night in a local bar hangout and sleeping. His mother worked as a domestic and his father was a sanitation worker.

Three brothers worked in similar jobs and a fourth, who was considered the brightest and most capable in the family, was a New York City fireman. My patient told me that none of the members of the family, including himself, thought they were nearly as smart as Tom, the fireman. Therefore, they never seriously thought of becoming firemen or policemen because it wouldn't be possible to pass the civil service exams. Also, two of them had never finished high school.

My patient was convinced that he was "the most stupid one in the family," "like my old man," and "can't concentrate," and could never have finished high school or "understood enough of the stuff to get a high school equivalency diploma." But he said he had no regrets, had a steady job, good beer-drinking friends, lived at home, "so I always have a couple of bucks in my pocket" and that's why he couldn't understand his symptoms.

He periodically became very anxious and had very rapid heart beats, cold sweats, nightmares and insomnia. He also frequently became "moody and melancholoy and felt like crying." He regarded the latter symptoms as very unmanly and "sissyish" and was quite embarrassed in revealing them to me. Early in treatment, he told me that at least several times, "a thought woke me up and then I kept thinking the same thing and just couldn't sleep and couldn't drive it out of my head." The thought was: "I wish I were someone else." This turned out to be a very important thought and in a way the key to his problem. The thought expresses the ultimate in total self-rejection and self-hate. It is an expression of revulsion for not just particular aspects of oneself but for all aspects of self—for the total self—which was confirmed and expressed by Sean in many subsequent sessions.

This young man soon uncovered and unleashed a remarkable fund of self-deprecating rage. He exposed an extraordinary fund of feelings of stupidity, inability, inadequacy, fear of sexual ineffectiveness—and on and on it went. The only area in which he had convinced himself of satisfaction was his work, since he decided that it was completely appropriate to his limited ability. But even in his vitriolic tirades against himself I picked up a superb ability to express himself, remarkable humor, occasional glimpses of deeper than usual understanding and had the feeling that there was indeed a hidden but considerable intelligence and creativity that was alive here, albeit in the service of self-hate. This was conveyed to me despite Sean's very limited vocabulary, limited general knowledge and generally poor sophistication.

It began to occur to me that Sean's thought, "I wish I were someone else," had a meaning additional to that of self-hate, as did his anxiety and depression. It conveyed the wish for expression and development of that other self, which due to socioeconomic, cultural and familial pressures had no chance at all for evolvement. In effect, this man didn't know it but he was screaming out to be given the chance to grow, and grow he did. He devoured information, books, experiences at a rate I've never experienced in anyone before or since. He turned out to be remarkably intelligent, perceptive, sensitive and creative, too. His talent for writing, learning foreign languages and psychological insight were more than one ordinarily encounters even in professionals.

At first Sean went through great suffering and trying times in himself, at work, in the bar and at home. His attempts at conversations with relatives, friends and co-workers about his newfound knowledge were met with derision and even sadism. He was called "crazy," "a homo," "a nut," and by his parents, "a useless fool." These tirades became particularly bad when he decided to go back to school. Interestingly, he was putting up the same battle within himself. As it became apparent that his development would proceed, whatever the struggle, his self-hate became almost intolerable. At various points he thought of "chucking the whole thing and staying put and shutting up." After all, how could he, Sean, who had long ago contracted himself to being "a simpleminded moron," aspire to richer needs and wants for "my soul and my heart." But he struggled both against his own self-hate and that of others who feared and envied any change in someone they knew so well. It soon became apparent that he would have to join a larger world, and as he left old friends he also gradually shed much self-hate, too.

Sean now has several degrees. He teaches in a major university. More than that, his life is enriched enormously. He treats himself well. He has a lovely wife, good friends, travels a great deal and enjoys music and the theater, all seemingly other-worldly twelve years ago.

TERRORISM

There are multiple devices we use to terrorize ourselves in the service of self-hate. Some are fiendishly ingenious and obvious evidence of unique and creative minds. Some are based on knowledge we alone have of ourselves and on our private fears and sensitivities and areas of our vulnerability that go back to early childhood. I'm reminded of George Orwell's 1984, in which Big Brother's henchmen knew and used whatever fears particular individuals had to break them down. In the case of the hero it was rats, which he had feared since early childhood.

A young woman patient of mine had a deathly fear of developing hair on her face. This fear, as it turned out, started in early childhood when she heard that nonfeminine, ugly women "developed the worst thing of all, hair

on their faces." Through the years she ascribed any
number of characteristics to femininity and developed
many confused notions as to what constitutes femininity.
Through the years, as her own self-hate deepened and
developed, taking on all kinds of painful elaborations,
doubts about her femininity grew to inordinate proportions. She was, by the way, exceedingly feminine by just
about any standards. But she consciously knew very little
of this until after she had been in treatment for a while. All
that she was actively and fully conscious of was the fear of
developing hair on her face. This fear never failed to
surface and to terrify her whenever and for whatever
reason she felt a surge of self-contempt or a "need" for
self-punishment.

Before long she made the fully conscious connection
between the deathly fear that she was finally developing a
beard and that she was "being bad" by failing some way in
her exalted image of herself. But this was not enough to
break the connection and to rid herself of the symptom.
This occurred only after a painful struggle, involving
clarification of her concept of femininity, her terribly
unrealistic demands on herself, her awful self-contempt
and compulsive self-hating activity, and after a great
increase in self-acceptance took place. This took several
years but at the end of that time she had changed
considerably. The hair obsession became an empty thing
that fell away because the self-hating energy that fed it
was no longer there. She was no longer plagued by her
misconceptions about what constitutes femininity; her
standards for it were not only clarified but it had taken a
realistic place in the hierarchy of matters of importance.
Most significant of all, she saw herself as important to
herself and as a human being worthy of care and

compassion. Initially, she had no idea at all of how cruelly and ruthlessly she attacked herself.

A reign of terror against oneself can be initiated and sustained through any number of psychological devices. These include nightmares; peculiar and disturbing thoughts, especially those including taboos—such as murder, incest, suicide, being crazy, helpless or homosexual; anxiety and panic attacks; unwarranted fears and phobias; ghoulish and paralyzing fantasies; terrifying hypochondriacal attacks; paralyzing, energy-depleting ruminations and any other device and combinations thereof that an ingenious human mind can devise in an attack on itself.

These "symptoms" are evidence of destructive relating to oneself. They are always evidence of anxiety. Often, they are attempts to obscure inner feelings or impulses that threaten to surface and make themselves known. But they never fail to indicate self-hate, to increase self-hate and to function as self-hating devices. The very act of using a psychological device or symptom or defense in an attempt to obliterate or to put down anything in oneself that is about to immerge into conscious awareness is a self-castigating, self-hating action.

Hypochondria is a particularly exquisite form of self-torture in that it serves two purposes at the same time. It usually diverts from and obfuscates the real source of anxiety and at the same time terrifies the victim with fear of impending death.

I had a patient in whom anger brought on terrible anxiety. He would develop fear of cancer whenever he got angry. By torturing himself this way he diverted himself from the original anger and anxiety and dissipated it by channeling it into this form of self-hate.

The struggle for a compassionate life includes nonjudgmental acceptance of all aspects of self, regardless of, and usually as a stand against, familiar personal and cultural value systems that are designed to obliterate pieces of ourselves. Unless we know and fight for our sacred human right to be human we invariably find that at least in some measure we live in a state of inner terror. Unfortunately, many of us have been terrorized for so long and so effectively that we no longer know what constitutes being human.

My patient Tom, who came to see me when he was in his early twenties, had reached an extremely pathetic condition. This is characteristic of people who have enough energy and talent so that the destructive job they do on themselves is particularly effective. To him, being human meant vast, confused fluctuations between two poles: utter omniscience, omnipotence and pure angelic martyrdom. He really believed that he was subhuman because "other people, really good people never get angry, love everyone, can always control themselves." He also believed that "real people," as he called them, were never afraid, never confused, never conflicted, could courageously assert themselves in all situations and always "came out on top." These were just a few of the values and standards he saw as par for people; he ascribed to the rest of us Godlike proportions and abilities. Anything less than these he considered subhuman and monstrous.

He was totally ignorant about the true anatomy of human emotions and our relating processes. When he measured himself against these quite *inhuman* standards he of course felt "like a worm that can be squashed out at any time." Small wonder Tom lived in a state of enormous vulnerability and fear. But he added to the terror with awful fantasies, self-prognostications of dire proportions, and had convinced himself that he could not be away from home and parents without "falling apart," whenever he was in any way reminded of, or in confrontation with, his "subhuman qualities."

Since he saw people as saints, he felt that his worst antihuman characteristic was anger, and, of course, he was loaded with an enormous burden of repressed anger. He tried to handle the emergence of angry feelings with denial—they just didn't exist and with obsessive ruminations in which he attempted to obfuscate his angry feelings by filling his mind with endless, boring strings of senseless thoughts, but these methods didn't work and only filled him with more rage at himself. At this point he would turn the anger on himself in any kind of terrifying way he could, telling himself he was crazy, had cancer and would die. This was actually an attempt to purge himself of "evil feelings" and to purify himself. Since this no longer worked, his next self-hating and self-anesthetizing act took the form of depression. When this became severe to the point of his becoming almost completely numb and paralyzed, he came to see me, and started on the long road back to strength and reality.

DEPRESSION

Depression serves multiple purposes, including welcome anesthetic relief. It is also a strong symbol of acute disharmony within one's inner psychic life, and is a way, though a poor one, of discharging accumulated anger. But the ultimate function and result of depression is to put oneself into a state of suffering. In this regard, depression is the agent par excellence of self-hate.

This multiple and often inconsistent and incongruous function of a human psychological device may seem peculiar and complicated, but it is nevertheless characteristic of human feeling and thinking. Dreams, unconscious processes, symbols and waking thoughts and actions, too, often have a vast diversity of incongruous meanings and motives. This is particularly true of depression, and the experienced therapist knows this and therefore treats this state of being with utmost respect and gravity.

People who are depressed usually need to be depressed, often as a respite from even greater suffering and sometimes to immobilize them sufficiently so as to keep them from taking their lives. But depression is always an indication of deep self-hate. Without self-hate depression is impossible. Yes, it is possible and, indeed, appropriate to be unhappy, sad and depressed about realistic tragedy. This kind of appropriate, short-lived feeling, however, basically is not the kind of self-hating castigation I speak of here.

However mild and chronic, or severe and acute, depression never fails to hurt, scare, destroy function and happiness, and to kill part of the limited time a human being has to feel happy on this earth of ours. Many people have been depressed for so long that they no longer know they are depressed. I've heard a number of patients state that they found out that they had been depressed when almost by accident they were briefly confronted with a little happiness for the first time in years. The contrast provided inescapable knowledge of long-standing depression.

But, of course, there are acute, devastating depressions in which people starve themselves, maim themselves, excoriate themselves and even paralyze themselves. These depressions often produce thoughts and language which describe bitter self-hate of many years' duration: "I'm no good"; "I deserve to die"; "I hate myself"; "I'm an ugly, ugly person." In speaking to very depressed people I have often had the feeling that they have been living in closest concert with a deadly enemy who has never let up in torturous occupation and castigation for even a moment. In fact, this is usually the case, because in severe depression the self-hating process has become malignant and sits there, split off from the healthy self, running its victim into the ground without permitting any relief whatsoever. During this period, many therapists are struck by the enormous resistance the patient puts up against reassurance of self-worth of any kind.

> THERAPIST: "But you are a decent person."
> PATIENT: "I'm a horror."
> THERAPIST: "You always worked hard and supported your family."
> PATIENT: "Only because I had to. I'm really lazy—a bum. I hate myself."

Of course, with the enemy of the self in charge—namely, self-hate—the therapist is addressing himself to the enemy and is engaging in a futile process. He must in fact outwit the self-hating component and reinforce the compassionate process. This is best done by a tenacious insistence on examination of the impossible standards and expectations imposed on the victim, by himself, for years before acute aspects of the depression became manifest. But a wily enemy cannot always be tackled head-on. His underpinnings and very basis for being must be undermined and destroyed.

SUICIDE

This is the ultimate self-hating device. But even in this ultimate expression of self-extermination varying degrees of self-hate are evident. People don't choose the particular way they kill themselves casually. Some will choose a relatively gentle and painless method, almost as a last consideration for even a much-hated self. Others seek nothing short of utter obliteration beyond recognition (e.g., dynamiting themselves). Some choose the most painful self-torturing devices possible (e.g., swallowing corrosive substances). In their self-hating zeal still others attempt to remove any trace that they ever existed. Artists and writers have attempted to burn all their works before destroying themselves. Parents sometimes kill their children as well as themselves. Some very disturbed people attempt to kill as many people as they can along with themselves.

Many construct elaborate fantasies and plans for world destruction. The entire human condition is detested by them and evidence of their own humanity produces intolerable revulsion. Some of these people, having murdered other people, welcome execution almost as a blessing and reward. Obviously, the depths and intensity with which we are able to castigate ourselves are just about limitless.

ACCIDENT PRONENESS, PSYCHOSOMATIC ILLNESS AND DANGEROUS SITUATIONS

These are largely functions of self-hate. These are what I have come to think of as the sneakiest methods of attacking ourselves. High blood pressure, asthmatic attacks, skin eruptions, repeated automobile accidents, accidents in the home, dangerous jobs, swimming out too far are always well masked, highly rationalized and most removed from their prime self-hating purpose. Indeed, they seemingly go on automatically, often on a physiological level, without even the smallest semblance of conscious participation or intervention.

This very direct form of self-hate, an actual onslaught on the physical well-being and existence of the victim, is usually evidence of extreme self-hate. Indeed, treatment of people suffering in this way is difficult for two reasons: First, it is almost impossible for the patient to connect his symptom with self-hate. Doesn't he present himself to the doctor because he wants relief from the symptom? Isn't this in itself an act of self-love? Yes, he would like relief, but the symptoms so thoroughly mask their origin and purpose that they often deeply complicate the process of revelation.

Second, self-hate strong enough to be converted to physical onslaughts that may result in death itself is extremely dangerous to tamper with. Precipitous insight may result in a catastrophic exacerbation of the disease or an accident of major and thorough proportions. It may also result in escape from self-hate into grave mental illness. Surgeons have unwittingly precipitated these situations. In some cases following surgical procedures for duodenal and gastric ulcers, ileitis, etc., the patient makes an uneventful physical recovery, shortly followed by a catastrophic psychotic reaction infinitely more incapacitating than his original symptom. This occurs because the physical lesion serves as a vehicle for both masking and dissipating self-hate.

Removing the lesion precipitously, often puts the patient into direct contact with raw and intolerable self-hate, which up to that point had been masked and dissipated through the physical affliction. Inability to tolerate the pain and anxiety associated with self-hate produces an attempted escape through psychosis. Many surgeons wisely insist on presurgical psychiatric consultation as well as postoperative psychotherapy at least for a short time in cases where psychosomatic conditions are involved.

Some years ago, I saw a twenty-six year-old woman (let's call her Rosalind) who suffered from an extreme form of skin disorder known as exfoliative dermatitis. Almost her entire body was affected. Her skin was a mass of inflamed, raw, weepy lesions and in many places the top protective layer of skin was missing altogether. To make matters worse, she was in almost constant burning, itching pain. When she said, "I suffer hell on earth," there was much truth in her statement.

From the first interview I picked up an ambivalence about her affliction. She detested it and herself for having it, but she also seemed to derive a kind of martyred glory as having been singled out to suffer in this way. From the first session, she conveyed the impression of a passive, easygoing person who never, "absolutely never, gave anyone a hard time." She immediately told me she had no memory at all of ever having been angry. This was particularly applicable to her parents, who felt that Rosalind had always been one of the best-behaved children in the neighborhood and who never failed to tell friends and relatives of their daughter's good nature and willing self-sacrifice in just about all matters.

Rosalind also told me, many times, that her parents were "saintly people" and that she had no memory at all of ever hearing a cross word between them. I asked her about human, anti-saint characteristics such as jealousy, envy, possessiveness, meanness, and avarice, and her reaction was combined shock and utter disavowal. These baser qualities simply never had invaded Rosalind's heavenly household.

But, at age eighteen, soon after Rosalind started a serious relationship with a boy, her skin suddenly erupted. At first it was diagnosed by the family doctor as "a minor rash which teen-age girls often get, which will go away by itself." The rash did not go away by itself nor did it go away at all, not even with the intervention of every conceivable kind of treatment. This included literally dozens of visits to dermatologists, endocrinologists, internists and famous medical centers abroad as well as throughout the country. Indeed, Rosalind told me that her skin and its treatment "occupied so much of my time and energy that I barely finished high school and soon afterward dropped out of junior college."

When I asked about the boy she had started to date, she told me that he dropped out of the picture, too, because "who, after all, wants to tie himself up to an invalid?" I asked her about sexual feelings regarding the boy, and with obviously painful embarrassment and shame she told me that she not only had feelings but also had petted and felt terribly guilty "because of my parents—what would they think?" Interestingly, nobody had asked her this question before.

The course of her rash was downhill and went on without relief or remission of any kind. Rosalind had long since taken to wearing gloves and high-button-neck, long-sleeve dresses whenever she went out, so that only her face showed. Fortunately, aside from some redness, her face (and she was quite pretty) was spared. Two years before Rosalind was referred to me by still another doctor, she became acutely depressed, and in a short time became depressed enough to stop eating, to lose thirty pounds and to stop getting out of bed. Her parents, a year-and-a-half before consulting me, on the advice of their internist, took her to see a psychiatrist whose sole treatment was electro shock therapy. He decided that the only treatment that would suffice would be a series of six electro-convulsive seizures induced by his shock machine. Rosalind was in no condition to object and so she underwent the "treatment."

A week after the "treatments" were over, Rosalind no longer felt depressed and her skin "miraculously started to clear until every sore was gone. In a few weeks I didn't even have a blemish. My skin was as pure and clean as it had been when everything was going so good for all of us." When I asked her how it had been "bad" for all of them she told me that her skin eruption also resulted in "eruption of the entire household, running to doctors, worrying, everyone miserable as possible. My parents never said anything, but I could tell how much I worried them. After the shock treatments things were actually back to normal—for a while."

The "while" was about three months long, and then all hell exploded. The rash returned with a vengeance, and this time it looked as though the disease would soon leave her with no skin at all. This time, it even attacked her face, but mercifully her face cleared after a few weeks. Though Rosalind "felt terribly disappointed," she did not become depressed. But her parents were distraught, "really devastated," and after frantic phone calls and consultations with the internist and the psychiatrist it was decided to have her undergo another series of electro-convulsive treatments.

At the last moment Rosalind balked. She recalls this as one of the few times, if not the one and only time, she refused to comply with a parental decision. She refused to return to the "shock doc," feeling that this treatment might destroy her even if it did save her skin. "I'd be a clear-skinned vegetable." Besides, she stated that she wasn't sure the shock treatment helped in the first place. "Maybe it was just a coincidence." But her condition got even worse. There were large areas of her upper arms, legs and back which were masses of raw, bleeding points. Once again the family was totally preoccupied with the girl's illness. Then her mother's brother, an uncle, a much respected member of the family, suggested that Rosalind see a psychoanalyst—not as a cure, but as a way of seeking a better adjustment. The uncle had become aware that "Rosalind had no life at all other than her skin."

Soon after she started to see me, it became apparent that Rosalind suffered from intense repressed rage directed mainly at herself "for being such a sweet, virtuous nothing fool" and at her parents, "who insisted on my being elevated to sainthood." Her anger and self-hate had been building for years, and the conflict between rage and saintly qualities became intensified with her first serious encounter with a young man. She soon "admitted" to me that she had in fact had very strong sexual feelings at the time, guilt in terms of her parents and enormous self-hate for permitting and enjoying petting. It was soon after a particularly heavy petting session that her "rash broke out." It also came out that in one petting session she had her first and last orgasm. What eventually became apparent was the cunning psychodynamic economy of her then newfound physical illness.

1. It provided enough self-punishment to mitigate her guilt.

2. It provided self-hate enough to push her sexual feelings, conflict and anger out of awareness and to drive her to further martyred purity and glory.

3. It made her unattractive enough, indeed, repulsive enough, so as to preclude further tempting sexual offers and possibilities.

4. It served to punish her parents and at the same time to guarantee an invalid's front-and-center privileged position in the household.

5. It offered safe and highly circuitous release of emotions through her skin, which in turn became red and angry; painful, itchy and excoriated; and wet and weepy. We even at times were actually able to correlate her feelings with specific skin manifestations because her rash did indeed change in quality, appropriate to specific feelings.

Interestingly, her face almost always remained in the manner of Oscar Wilde's Dorian Gray, placid, innocent and pure, while her intense and repressed feelings ravaged the rest of her usually covered-up body and the seat of sexual possibilities.

Feelings of severe depression actually signaled crises and an emotional crossroad. Self-hate had reached its peak, as did the need to break through and to face less than saintlike feelings and desires. Electro-convulsive treatment served as an even more severe form of punishment and functioned, too, in the service of temporarily putting down into deeper unconsciousness all conflict and potential rebellion against the self-hating aspect of herself, exemplified by the tyrannical need for sterile, saintlike perfection. But this kind of intrapsychic turmoil in a person with a great degree of health cannot be anesthetized out by electricity, and Rosalind suffered a massive exacerbation. Fortunately, her good health, self-preserving proclivities and the desire to fight for her life in terms of actual self precluded her return to electric punishment and total submergence.

As she acquired insight she also became better able to mobilize and to tap and express her feelings. The intensity of how she felt at times very nearly inundated her. Her rage at herself, her parents, and at times at me, created considerable discomfort in me, despite my experience and understanding. But it was more than worth it. In fact, I was privileged to witness and take part in a rebirth, in a process in which a woman was giving birth to herself, reclaiming her life and fighting for the right to be human—and winning!

As she was relieved of her venom and became increasingly self-accepting, her self-hate diminished very rapidly. At first, it was a shock for her to learn of her family's duplicity and of the false, idealistic dream world they had painted, and she raged at them. But this eventually gave way to understanding, and generated compassion for herself.

But the great bonus, especially for me—a psychiatrist who seldom witnesses or partakes in the joys of physical cures—was the amelioration of her skin condition. As she became a real and whole person and surrendered saintlike aspirations of purity and what she formerly considered "dirt" in herself, and ridded herself of self-contempt and the pus of repressed rage, her "dirty" skin cleared and eventually remained clear. I have treated a number of people with psychosomatic disturbances that resulted in unhealthy skin conditions, some, interestingly, who also had gone through the electro shock route. But Rosalind's recovery and evolvement as a real person was and is a high point in my life.

While this description of Rosalind and her life and treatment is somewhat sketchy, it nevertheless reveals the psychological base one often finds underlying a physical symptom. I was fortunate with Rosalind. She was young, well motivated and had a great capacity for psychological insight. Despite the severity of her symptom it was not nearly as complicated, involuted and ingrained as many I have seen. Indeed, this particular form, the somatic, or physical, manifestation of self-hate and consequent sabotage against oneself, is often one of the most difficult to pinpoint and eradicate.

ALCOHOL, DRUGS, TOBACCO AND FOOD

These are probably the ingredients most used in the service of direct self-hate. They are often used as sedative and anesthetic devices in an attempt to relieve self-hate. In other words, some people with unbearable hatred for themselves will use excess alcohol, drugs, tobacco and food to put themselves into a temporary haze in order to escape their feelings. But this becomes a way of inundating and drowning oneself in self-hate in order to escape self-hate. If an individual is beaten into insensibility, temporarily he no longer feels the effects of the beating. This device is also unfortunately and nearly always unconsciously used as a form of slow suicide.

The individual dies slowly, as he becomes increasingly incapacitated, until actual death takes place. Of course, awful deterioration and, still more important, degradation often precede death. In severe cases, the humiliation the victim visits on himself and inevitably invites from other people is itself a form of severe, blatant torture, often for "sins" long since forgotten or at least eradicated on a conscious level. I believe that so-called accidental deaths due to drug overdoses or auto mishaps of alcoholic origin or heart attacks and cerebrovascular accidents (strokes) associated with overeating are not accidental at all. These represent acute attacks on oneself due to feelings of unbearable self-loathing, precipitating the desire for vengeful punishment of self and permanent escape from the pain incurred. Though the immediate satisfactions derived from food and smoking are apparent and the destructive effects are not, the individual, nevertheless, does know of these latter effects. Unconscious self-hate sustains these habits. I have always been struck by the cause and effect between great eating binges and rage, especially at oneself. Getting fat and grotesque in a culture that abhors obesity is a certain means of sustaining chronic self-hate. Smoking in full realization of the terrible effects produced requires a ruthlessness born only of enormous self-hate.

USE OF PAINFUL MEMORIES AND LISTS OF CRIMES AND INDISCRETIONS

These are often used in blatant self-beating exercises. They are, of course, like all kinds of torturous ruminations, of a self-derisive nature, characteristic of depression. Murder is often characteristic of hidden depression, too. Indeed, it is difficult and often impossible to separate depression and all other forms of self-hate and self-punishment derivative of self-hate, largely because depression is almost always present at least to some small degree in self-hate. But remembering a list of "crimes" or less than socially approved, perfect behavior for the purpose of self-flagellation is often, like all other self-hating processes, an autonomous process.

This means that over the years we have developed a process, in this case calling up guilt-ridden memories, to flagellate ourselves. This process may after many years go on on its own, without any memory or feeling for its beginnings, origins or functions and sometimes without any connection to an immediate stimulus. In other words, it goes on because it has been going on, even without any *raison d'être*. Its survival continues largely because its victim accepts it as a regular part of himself and never for one moment even entertains the idea of asking himself about it, let alone intervening and stopping it. In this case, the list itself, and use of the list, is felt as an important and utterly familiar part of himself, without which some grievous danger to his very identification would ensue.

I had a patient who periodically, especially when she couldn't sleep, would torture herself with reiteration of her life's personal crimes. These included theft of a ten-cent comb when she was seven years old, hitting a smaller sister for whom she baby-sat, then lying to her mother about it, and not helping her mother enough with housework when she was a teen-ager. Of course, she suffered from insomnia not as a primary symptom but as a secondary one. I mean that her thoughts kept her awake; her keeping awake did not produce the thoughts. Nevertheless, her insomnia served a self-hating purpose too, and gave her still more reason to hate herself for not being able to sleep.

But the deleterious nature of these vicious cycles interested me very much. These were not the results or part of any recent or present difficulties or problems. No degree of probing satisfactorily linked them to the past either. While she suffered from all kinds of perfectionistic standards, these did not adequately explain chronic use and aliveness of her crime list. It was as if its original roots were buried, lost, and cut off in a part of the past that was absolutely unrecallable and even gone. The process had been going on because it had been going on and because nobody ever attempted to stop it.

In treatment over an extended period of time, her standards for self-acceptance became reduced to human levels as she gave up much of her perfectionism. But she still had to actively, and yes, even heroically, struggle against the recriminating autonomous process that had been going on for so many years. At first this was very difficult, but repeated attempts each time she became conscious of their appearance eventually resulted in success. Her awareness of the fact that she had never *attempted* to stop the self-hating process led to the *attempt*, the struggle and ultimately to victory over self-hate.

USE OF OTHER PEOPLE

Sometimes we pursue the insidious process of using other people to help us to hate and to punish ourselves.

Occasionally, we use people for this purpose whom we don't know at all, but who just happen to be handy for the infliction of an immediate dose of self-hate. This also includes forming all kinds of disastrous relationships of both short and long duration. Some of these relationships may be demeaning, boring, cruel, stultifying, frustrating or exploitive.

I remember seeing a patient who said she suffered from compulsive promiscuity. In searching for its roots she recalled an incident that occurred when she was a teen-ager. One afternoon she went to a movie alone. An older man sat next to her and soon had his hand on her vagina. He put his finger in while he masturbated himself and then he left. She hated the sensation and wanted to scream out, but she was "too embarrassed." "What would other people think?" In her present relations with men she was still "too embarrassed" to say no.

Promiscuity is less often due to sexual urge than the self-hating inability to say "no!" Under this heading, I also include what psychologists have come to think of as projection, in which we mistakenly imbue other people with our own feelings and believe that our feelings are coming from them rather than from ourselves. I include the extreme form of projection, namely, paranoia, in which we may feel that other people hate us, are plotting against us and are even doing things to hurt us, even though they may be completely oblivious of our existence. Under this heading I also include Karen Horney's concept of the process she calls *externalization.*

This process is similar to projection but is broader in scope. It encompasses projection but also subtler serious manifestations as well. Unfortunately we all externalize at least to some degree. In its fullest implication it alludes to the fact that many people feel that their lives are always in other people's hands and that their well-being is invariably determined by others. If other people like them, then they like themselves for the moment. If someone, anyone, rejects them, then they feel destroyed. As Horney explains, the center of gravity of *their feelings of identification* is felt as being in other people's hands. Of course, to the degree and extent that we externalize we are in the throes of self-hate and self-rejection. We come to view anyone outside ourselves as being a better helmsman of our lives and emotional well-being than ourselves.

Some of us who are particularly self-hating form relationships which in addition to being materially injurious and destructive on a practical level (bad business arrangements, terrible "love" liaisons) also serve to guarantee rejection, berating, vindictive assaults on ourselves, etc. It is as if the victim has so little self-esteem that he can't even accept his own assaults on himself as adequately self-hating and punishing. After all, how effective can punishment be coming from a "nothing person?" He, therefore, must find somebody, whom he respects enough so that the hate from him is meaningful. Yes, we can even develop pride in being martyred *nobodies* and then find ourselves needing a *somebody* to constantly remind us and beat us into a *nobody* status.

Unfortunately, many couples require this kind of sado-masochistic synthetic esteem for each other to sustain their mutual interest and their relationship. I should mention here that partners in these relationships usually keep changing roles. It's as if each must have his or her turn to receive a full dose of outside contempt to supplement his or her own self-hate.

In thinking of the exalted position of self-hate and

consequent self-eradication, I am reminded of an old joke. It is Yom Kippur, the Day of Atonement. The Rabbi and the Cantor are praying in front of the Holy Book. The Rabbi cries out, "Lord, I'm nobody, nobody at all." He prostrates himself. He tears at himself. He continues to berate himself and to convince God that "I am nobody, nothing, God, I am nobody and nothing at all." The Cantor hearing the Rabbi begins the same mournful chant. In a few minutes he is singing with consummate skill and strength that "Lord, I am as dust; I am nothing at all, nothing." In the back of the Temple, Moisha, the little janitor, who has been putting out prayer books for the day's services, hears his two superiors and he, too, prostrates and berates and belittles himself. In a tiny, reedy voice he also implores God to regard him as "a nobody, a piece of dirt, nothing at all, absolutely a nobody and nothing—nothing at all." Then the Cantor notices, listens to the janitor and with quiet derision pokes the Rabbi, points to the janitor and says, "Look who thinks he's nothing." Of course there are other ways we have of making ourselves feel like nothing, such as giving gratuitous information that can be used against us at a future date, excessive drinking, and talking against ourselves unnecessarily.

In all serious emotional disturbances—paranoia, the so-called schizophrenias and psychoses due to other than organic causes (actual brain lesions)—the missing ingredient is compassion for oneself. The combination of utter lack of compassion and extreme self-hate makes a withdrawal from reality mandatory. In paranoia, the projective dynamism is characteristic and obvious. Indeed, it is the prime characteristic of the disturbance.

In paranoid schizophrenia the individual has so little

regard and sense of self that in his feelings he extends his self to include other people. He then feels his self-hatred as coming from those people. In some cases he feels people are going to hurt him and he withdraws. In others, he attacks his imagined tormenters. If projections are strong enough, he may suffer from auditory hallucinations of a persecutory nature that may provide relief from unbearable pressures of internal self-hate.

Many people in the helping professions have felt that the substance of the hallucination is a clue to the illness. Thus, in our society, paranoid male patients, as we have mentioned, often have hallucinations in which they are called homosexuals. Women patients hear voices calling them "whores, prostitutes and promiscuous." These voices are often heard as coming from parental or other authoritarian figures in the individual's life. It was and is, therefore, believed by many psychiatrists that the basic problems involve repressed homosexuality and repressed sexual impulses, feelings and desires. But my own observation of these cases reveals more importantly as the base the presence of an unusually high degree of rage at imagined tormenters, and often generalized rage at the world at large.

Fantasies of world destruction are also a characteristic of various forms of schizophrenia. It is as if feelings of self-hatred are so great that they cannot be absorbed by projections to single persons but require fantasies involving complete destruction of the world. This kind of terrible rage, I believe, cannot be generated by any other mechanism than hatred for self. This is in large part expressed by the auditory hallucinations and delusions of persecution. The homosexual and prostitution content of these productions are mainly, if not totally, due to intense self-hate.

Cultural contempt for homosexuality and promiscuity and the individual's inabilty to accept these characteristics in himself and herself make for intense self-hate. But many people, suffering from self-hate from other sources entirely, use these name-calling terms because our culture makes them so degradingly effective. I believe the terms used in paranoid delusions and hallucinations will change as the culture develops other symbols and characteristics to represent degradation.

Paranoid patients are also known for developing and sustaining ideas of reference and ideas of influence. People, they believe, are always talking about them and pointing them out and ridiculing them. It is easy to see the projected self-hate here and also the sense of importance and megalomania linked to being a center of attention and contrived to compensate for feelings of inadequacy. People are also influencing them—controlling their thoughts and feelings. Intense, undiluted self-hate without any compassionate antidote leaves one feeling so dead and empty that only belief that others exert control can provide sufficient stimulus to function at all.

Some patients believe they are controlled by God, who gives them special messages: they feel that only divine contact can mitigate the paralysis of being reduced to nothingness by malignant self-hate. Nor is it accidental that some people believe they are controlled by machines. I believe these are people whose self-hatred flows over into terrible hate for the entire species and all aspects of the human condition. They prefer to trust the benevolence of remote, influencing machines.

As I mentioned earlier, some of the most bizarre suicides are concocted by paranoid-schizophrenic people who sometimes desire to obliterate themselves, all relatives, all works and residuals of themselves that may exist, and if it were possible, the entire species. Examples are people who throw themselves in front of a train, or mothers who kill themselves and their children. Adolph Hitler came as close to anyone in history in this endeavor; the suicides of most very sick people are not nearly as grandiose but may be particularly bizarre, grotesque and cruel in terms of self.

MURDER

Murder is to me the ultimate form of displaced and projected self-hate. Many people who have examined murderers closely find that just about all of them fall into one of three categories: (1) The criminal psychopath or sociopath. (2) The so-called normal neurotic who murders without a profit motive and most often without premeditation. (3) Psychotic people whose judgment is severely aberrated and who kill out of paranoid delusions (killing the supposed persecutor before he or she kills them), or as part of magical and ritualistic behavior (for example, in which killing may be seen as conferring magical power or Godlike attributes. "I kill to make the world holier and pure").

As with all other aspects of human behavior, here, too, there is much overlapping of the three groups. People are not, after all, born into well-delineated categories, and we invent and use them only in an attempt to understand the psychodynamics of human behavior a little better. Let me briefly discuss the first two broad categories.

For years people have believed—and still do believe—that psychopathic people are lacking in consciences because they commit acts against other people seemingly without evidence of either conscience or remorse. I believe that quite the reverse is true. People suffering from psychopathy—or sociopathy, as it is now called—and who commit criminal acts and even murder, do in fact have overwhelming, intensely self-hating consciences. As the self-hate escalates, the options of suicide, psychosis (paranoid schizophrenia) or acting out against society arise. This last choice has a twofold psychodynamic economy. It kills one's own paralyzing conscience and self-hate and displaces and projects self-hate onto victims who become representations of one's own conscience and of authoritarian figures in one's early life. Thus, shooting down an innocent victim may represent killing society, all authoritarian rules generated by society and convention, one's father and one's self-hate.

Neurotics who murder people other than themselves nearly always act out of rage engendered by hurt pride. Neurotic pride, as Horney so aptly described, is used to protect ourselves against contact with self-hate and diminutive feelings. The man who has great pride in masculinity is in effect protecting himself against much-feared feelings that he would consider evidence of femininity. The man who is terrified of feeling helpless takes great pride in being independent, resourceful and often omnipotent.

Any blow to neurotic pride exposes the victim to the very aspect of himself that he fears and hates the most and that generates maximum self-hate. Encountering precipitous hate for self is intolerable, and projection to the seeming generator of this hate, or to a person who characterizes similar hateful properties, or to a person who combines both aspects can result in passionate murder. Neurotic murderers often murder people who have hurt their pride, and in murdering people are in effect murdering representational parts of themselves. I think this also happens in capital punishment, in which society kills off aspects of itself that it refuses to accept as common aspects of the human condition. In murdering murderers we attempt to kill off murdering aspects of ourselves and thus protect ourselves from the possibility of becoming murderers.

I believe that all murderers are latent, chronically depressed people. Their depression sits there under wraps, held in place by a tenuous and fragile balance. If the self-hate involved would evolve out in the form of depression *as experienced by most of us*, this kind of emotional safety valve would probably prevent murder. But without this more usual kind of release, the explosive reaction that takes place is murder in the form of suicide or killing an individual other than oneself.

To further substantiate this thesis, many therapists who have worked with psychopaths will attest to utter lack of progress until self-hate is finally identified, exposed and felt. This almost invariably takes place in the form of severe depression. The psychopathic patient initially seems incapable of depression. Indeed, this is pathologically characteristic of the illness. But such patients fail to get well, to develop an ability for social judgment, social consciousness and human empathy until they encounter and go through the deep underlying depression that is invariably there and invariably covered up by all kinds of rebellious acting out.

Any discussion of murder would be incomplete without at least some mention of the little murders we inflict on ourselves on a daily basis. We "murder" ourselves when we invoke self-hating devices and when we annihilate our potential for enjoying life's realistic good offerings.

GUILT, ANTICIPATION AND EXCESSIVE AND INAPPROPRIATE WORRYING

These self-hating activities often have the special characteristics of being passed off as virtues. The victim rationalizes anticipation of disaster as prudence; anxiety in anticipation of such trials as exams and court appearances as practical rehearsals; guilt as a high sense of responsibility and morality; inappropriate worrying as human caring and great concern linked to martyred saintliness. But these are actually all devices working in the service of self-hate. They invariably destroy pleasure and happiness as well as efficiency and effectiveness in current *here and now* activities. They have a depleting, fatiguing, constricting effect and are ultimately destructive to self-esteem and to one's actual person. Of course, anticipatory planning can be of value, and guilt and worry can never be completely eradicated. But the inappropriateness of these activities when they serve self-hate is at once discernible. Indeed, what often becomes apparent is the utter lack of importance of the substance of the guilt or worry, as well as the rapid shifting from worry to anticipation to guilt. I've seen any number of people in treatment who torture themselves with these shifting devices and who can also shift worries from one subject to another, sometimes without any conscious awareness at all. It soon becomes apparent that the processes of generating guilt, anticipating and worrying are all important and that the subject matter used for these processes is of no consequence at all.

COMPETITION AND PERFECTIONISM

When we make excessive demands on ourselves to be perfect and to compete at all costs, we interfere with healthy motivation and growth. Perfectionism and over-competitiveness are disaster areas designed to promote personal discontent and unhappiness. Competition makes friendship with people impossible, but what's worse, it makes friendship with oneself impossible. Seeking impossible standards destroys any possibility of self-acceptance as well as any joy derived from current possibilities. *Now* becomes obliterated in favor of a future that somehow is never actualized. Perfectionism and driving to "get ahead" are used as terrible goads, making inner peace impossible and producing continuous hatred of one's actual self.

GAMBLING

Compulsive gambling is designed to keep the victim in a chronic state of deprivation and self-contempt. This is an addictive illness, not unlike addiction to drugs, alcohol and overeating. But the primary addiction in all these syndromes is to self-hate. While this may be covered up by a superficial veneer of a desire to win, this is never the case. The compulsive gambler cannot tolerate a state of personal dignity or success. Money, which represents both, creates great tension in him. He must get rid of it in order to satisfy his self-hating picture of himself. He plays to lose so as to reduce himself to the status of a dependent, supplicating, helpless creature for whom he himself has no respect. This momentarily leaves him tension-free in that it satisfies his self-hating dynamism.

POSTPONING DECISIONS

As I will discuss in Part IV, many decisions could, and even should, be postponed, but the process used in the service of self-hate is to put off decisions whose resolution will be no different at any time in the future. This is a sure-fire way to produce and sustain a chronic sense of imbalance and insecurity.

Most issues can be settled equally well with any one of a number of decisions. The nondeciding self-hater refuses to exercise chairmanship of the board. There is a constant chronic din heard from all board members and the chairman never calls for a vote. If a decision is arrived at, it is never sustained for any reasonable length of time. One of the board members invariably reopens the case without any real justification at all and the noise goes on, each time with increasing recriminations. The nondecider hates himself because he can't use all the alternatives at one time, which would obliterate need for a decision. He also hates himself for not being able to decide. And that is the principal purpose, to promote self-hate and to feed the self-hating process in all ways possible.

Indecisiveness over termination of disastrous relationships is a self-hating combination par excellence. The victim is victimized by self-contempt generated by his indecisiveness as well as by the deleterious effects of his destructive relationship, which goes on and on. For example: a sado-masochistic relationship in which two people maintain a "Who's-Afraid-of-Virginia-Woolf" kind of marriage, in which they tear at each other, destroy each other's morale, know they should part, but continue in their demoralizing, self-hating roles at all costs.

CHEATING ONESELF OF PLEASURE

People who are unhappy seldom derive pleasure from activities that should be fun, and yet often have no conscious idea of the energy and time they devote to self-hating mechanisms that make them feel this way. Cheating oneself of pleasure can sometimes be quite direct and blatant. Many people will invariably cheat themselves of attaining the very thing they want most—job, career, possession, relationship—just as they are about to attain it.

But this kind of simple symptom never exists in isolation. It is always evidence of an active, widespread self-hating process, however unconscious the victim may be of other aspects of the process.

I'm reminded of a patient who came to see me because of a "single isolated symptom." Throughout her married life she had suffered from periodic depressions. She also had a relatively easy and pleasurable time having orgasms. But about a year before she came to see me all this changed. She no longer felt depressed but no longer had orgasms either. At the exact moment she was about to come, worrisome thoughts would enter her mind and spoil it all. Of late, the major thought involved preoccupation with whether or not she would go on to have an orgasm. Of course, she didn't. Having destroyed her spontaneity with anticipated fear of not having an orgasm, she was of course unable to have one.

As it turned out, Mary had been a latent "pleasure-killer" for many years. She had been secretly suspicious of feeling too good over the years and had managed to spoil good times for herself. It was interesting that sexual pleasure and orgasms were areas left untouched by her self-hate for so long. But what precipitated things was her growing inability to tolerate her chronic intermittent depressions. Her solution was to make an unconscious pact with her self-hating enemy. She would give up orgasms and destroy her biggest source of pleasure in payment for relief from depression and other self-hating assaults. It worked, until she decided to look further into the very real machinations that made up the unconscious state of affairs in her mind.

HATING ONESELF FOR HATING ONESELF

Probably the most malignant form of direct self-hate is hating oneself for hating oneself. It is the mechanism that guarantees perpetuation of the self-hating process. The victim hates himself each time he discovers he hates himself or uncovers a self-hating mechanism. He must make every effort to conceal his self-hate and indeed to delude himself into believing that he is not self-hating at all. This completes the self-hating vicious cycle and/or prevents constructive revelatory investigation of self-hate. This process produces an extremely effective shield, protective of the self-hating totality. The only effective method of cracking the shield is by use of compassion, as I describe later on.

Forms of Self-Hate: Indirect

Indirect self-hate is chronic, pervasive, global, malignant, metastatic—and nearly always imperceptible—despite these dire characteristics. Unlike direct self-hate, which usually comes and goes in acute bursts, indirect self-hate is chronic and long-ranged in its effect. Indeed, it would be accurate to call it life-ranged, because it invariably affects us for an entire lifetime if not consciously stopped. It is pervasive and global because it affects every aspect of personality or character structure. It provides both fuel and form in the production and sustenance of neurosis.

Without self-hate, actual self flourishes in a friendly atmosphere in which happiness is rightly a prime goal. Neurotic states such as martyrdom, masochism, self-efface-ment, symbiotic and overwhelming dependency, grandios-ity, aggression, despotism, perfectionism, sadism, vindic-tiveness, withdrawal, resignation are all functions of self-hate.

Karen Horney believed that self-hate provides the fuel that drives people to the impossible and often conflicting goals inherent in each of the neurotic states just men-tioned. A person who experiences severe anxiety about his real self compensates by striving for glory through martyr-dom and perfect love. He will experience self-hate when-ever he asserts himself and thus fails the goal of martyrdom. In this way, self-hate propels him back to the glorious and neurotic goal of Christlike martyrdom.

I take no real issue with Horney. I agree with her almost completely. But I don't think it is necessary or expedient to separate self-hate and neurotic states. I think it is easier to understand and to fight self-hate by viewing any activity, illusion, belief, goal, symptom, neurotic state that in any way detracts from actual self at any given moment as self-hate.

Horney talks of real self, actual self, despised self and idealized self. Real self is who we are *potentially* if we were not neurotic. Actual self is who we are *actually*, health and neurosis included. Despised self is the neurotic way we see ourselves in the self-effacing position. Idealized self or idealized image is the shining illusion of impossible, glorious, goal fulfillment on every possible level. This image is used as a protective device against feelings of fragility. Failure to live up to this image produces self-hate, which, unfortunately, makes us feel fragile again and pushes us to glory once again. These various neurotic concepts of self include "shoulds" or inner, rigid laws that involve investment of pride in various illusions about ourselves.

From this "pride system" we also make claims on people and on the world generally. Thwarted claims and hurt pride identify us with despised selves and self-hate, and they produce rage at both self and others and a further try at "glory." Again, I agree with Horney and believe that her description of "the pride system" is one of the great contributions to understanding human neurotic behavior.

But my main interest and focus is hate and compassion for actual self. I feel that Horney's concept of real self has within it great dangers of idealization and impossible goals, producing feelings of failure, and thus may serve as a further generator of self-hate. For my purpose self-hate always applies to any destructive excursion we make against or away from our actual selves.

Actual self includes all aspects of ourselves at any given moment, both healthy and sick. Hating any aspect of ourselves, healthy or sick, is self-hate. Activity that leads to care of self and to greater inner comfort and happiness is the antithesis of self-hate.

Activities that lead away from self, in the form of compulsive striving for perfection, such as Godliness, purity, martyrdom, are self-hate. Neuroses, whatever form they take, are self-hate. Aberrations of reality in any form, since they must detract from actual self, are self-hate. This includes distortions involving oneself, other people, the world and any aspect of life and the human condition. I call this kind of self-hate *indirect*; it is usually very difficult to perceive it as self-hate because it is interwoven inextricably with every aspect of our lives and therefore is exceedingly difficult to separate out as self-hate.

For example, a man may be inwardly dying because of powerful competitive strivings. To a man who has been a competitor all his life, it is very difficult to see competition as a self-hating mechanism that is killing inner spontaneity, killing him physically and killing the possibility of joy through fruitful relating. Instead, he sees competition as a way of life, as a motivating force that keeps him going, and this concept is further enhanced by a culture that constantly speaks of the virtues of, and the necessity for, competition.

The fact that he really doesn't know where he is going or that he never questions where he wants to go or whether he wants to go at all does not enter his mind. Competition here deprives him of serious consultation with himself, and as such it is a self-hating device, because he is entitled to human consultation with himself. But the nature of the self-hate here is difficult to see, first because it is not a direct onslaught and second because its self-destructive quality is camouflaged by a veneer of virtue and worthiness. This kind of example multiplied many hundreds of times can give some idea of the global and metastatic, or spreading, nature of indirect self-hate. It is global because it takes over completely. It is metastatic because there is no area of living to which it fails to send colonizing branches. Fortunately, each colony does not have to be weeded out. Compassion, if used, is a powerful enough overall antidote.

Without the mitigating effect of compassion, the ruthlessness of self-hate is such that it reduces the individual to the level of a nunhuman automaton. Driven by self-hate, we have no opportunity to feel, to evaluate, to make choices or decisions or to grow. We are reduced to a slavelike status and must obey the commands of an implacable slave master.

Direct and indirect self-hate are always present in combination. They complement and supplement each other in keeping the victim in subjugation. Indirect self-hate is the dictatorial governing body, the tyrannical concentration-camp form of living. Direct self-hate represents the enforcing guards and executioners, the bullies, watchdogs and murderers. While we may become more adept at using some particular devices rather than others, use of one seldom precludes use of others. We almost always use all of them. Thorough examination of a single individual will usually reveal at least traces and aspects of all self-hating devices used in combination to pursue the war against self.

Much of what we perceive of self-hate is familiar because we all learn from each other, through imitation and identification. Also, despite ingenious modifications made by the human mind, with its great ability for diversification, sickness in any form is characteristically stilted, rigid, and unchanging. This is true of self-hate and the effects it has on people. As with all sickness, symptoms are usually characteristic and offer little variation, pushing the individual into rigid forms of behavior. The tubercular patient coughs; the patient afflicted with leprosy soon has a typical leonine facial expression; the cancerous patient eventually looks wasted; the self-hating person is depressed and full of illusions and functions at minimal capacity. Direct and indirect self-hate work in tandem to destroy individuality and produce an individual who is often recognizable as being generally self-hating.

Indirect self-hate is much larger than the sum of its parts. It represents a general pattern of sick behavior, a cloud under which we live, and a very malevolent one, which invariably destroys the possibility of sustained happiness.

The converse, then, is that health is characterized by individuality, flexibility and spontaneity. A person who is free to be whoever he is and really free to make choices based on free feelings is much more difficult to pigeonhole or to predict. The greater the degree of health, the greater the degree of individuality and possibility for free and creative behavior. Health leaves no diagnostic signs, no stamped-out characteristic symptoms of disease ravage.

Sick people often look alike as a result of having the same illness. Healthy people retain individuality.

ILLUSIONS

Most illusions probably have their earliest beginnings in modest childhood fantasies. These continue to be fed, sustained and to grow aided by a vast storehouse of material provided by the culture we live in. In describing some important aspects of our cultural value system in Part IV, I will demonstrate obvious connections between cultural standards and terms and the personal illusions described in this chapter.

Among the illusions that gladden the hearts of millions of children are the dreams of being the heroine, the good prince, the champion of champions, the scoutlike savior scoring all kinds of triumphs. As we grow up these illusions eventually are used to construct a host of feelings about oneself, other people, the world and the human condition. They form a matrix which strongly contributes to a malignant departure from reality. Self-deception, whether it involves ourselves, others, or life generally, weakens the actual self, making us less able to cope with real life, and eventually always leads to direct self-hate, usually in the form of depression and sometimes even suicide.

An illusionary matrix, examined carefully, usually proves to consist of a myriad of self-deceptions, many of which can be traced to the innocent fantasies and sweet imageries of childhood. To examine ourselves this way is not easy. We are almost always unaware of the self-hate inherent in the departure from actual self, and the consequent damage to self that is inherent in illusion. Equally, we have an enormous resistance to identify illusion with self-hate. Such identification is the beginning of the end of illusion, and our reluctance to surrender illusion is enormous. This is so because (1) illusion was initiated and sustained in the first place in order to compensate for what was felt as less than acceptable reality, or an intolerable life, and (2) having lived so long with illusion, it is felt that life without illusion would be hollow, empty, nothing. This effects a kind of personal blackmail that prevents us from consciously perceiving our illusions at all, let alone their damaging and self-hating effects. Since recognition of their existence would in itself shake the foundation of illusions, we largely relegate their existence to an unconscious level.

One of the greatest and most prevalent illusions is that we have no illusions. There are many people who take enormous pride in their ability to confront reality and who have no idea at all that their inner and outer perceptions are largely aberrated by illusion. Unconsciousness does not mean paralysis. Quite the contrary! The force of an unconscious belief or dynamism is particularly potent because it is cut off from the discriminating possibilities offered in consciousness. An illusion of which we are unaware has an autonomy that would not be possible if it were part of the mainstream of conscious feeling and thinking. Painful and even devastating repercussions from illusions that remain hidden in unconsciousness are quite common. Illusions are difficult to detect because they contain mixtures of reality, too. A merely good piano player may think of himself as a great virtuoso. A fine surgeon may see himself as a miracle healer. A good mother may feel that she relates to her children with saintlike perfection.

I saw a very depressed man some time ago who had recently lost a great deal of money. He could not understand why he was so depressed, because the money he lost, much as it was, represented only a small fraction of his total assets and did not affect him on a practical level in any way.

Soon after he became aware of the enormity of his self-hate he also became aware of an illusion about himself that he had unconsciously harbored for years. This illusion involved his infallibility. On a conscious level he saw himself as a relatively modest fellow to whom considerable humility seemed characteristic. But second-guessing and severe recriminations—"I am a fool"; "I should have known better"; "I deserve to have lost everything"—soon led to the realization that he really had an enormous illusion of infallibility, and this illusion was not confined to the world of finance.

The man's outward veneer of humility covered up an illusion of quite grandiose omniscience. It came out that he, in fact, had come to believe that "my judgment about people is always just about perfect. I guess this is what made me so good in business. I could read just about anyone a few minutes after I met them." It came out that this was pure illusion. More than that, it bordered on delusion. His understanding of people was very shallow and limited, largely because his relationships were almost nonexistent. This was largely due to distrust of people, detachment and withdrawal from them and fanatical and monomaniacal attention to business. The relationships he thought he had existed largely in his imagination and people he thought of as great friends turned out to regard him as little more than a casual acquaintance with whom relating was expedient to business.

His need for omniscience and omnipotence precluded his awareness of the reality of his superficial and narrow relating experience and poor judgment of people. It also kept him from being aware of the human fallibility to which we are all susceptible, no matter how wise. His illusion of his own infallibility reigned supreme until his particular fall from illusionary self-idealization took place. As it turned out, his financial fiasco was largely due to misjudgment of several people's ability and honesty as well as poor business judgment on his own part. Thus, the loss of money shattered a well-spread delusion on at least several fronts and brought on an onslaught of direct self-hate in the form of serious depression. The real purpose of the depression was not to teach him that he was fallible and to come down a few notches in his concepts and demands of himself. It was unconscious punishment, the same kind of punishment a parent inflicts on a wayward child, meant to teach him a lesson, and in this case also to push him back to repair the illusion and to take more care to maintain it in the future.

When I suggested he was treating himself too harshly, this came as an insult. Yes, for an ordinary man who had human limitations this would be harsh treatment indeed, like beating a dead horse. But for a man of omniscience his mistakes were unforgivable and deserved the harshest punishment. So, there, just below the level of the obvious pain and self-recriminations, the illusion and its concomitant vanity were still functioning and quickly reorganizing.

The man's early background was no great surprise. He came from a chaotic household in which there were many parental arguments and repeated crises about the shortage of money. The family moved about the country a great deal to accommodate to his father's attempt to make a living. But each "great promise of good fortune" failed, and his father remained an "economic failure." His mother in turn was a "tense, anxious, nervous woman" who seemed to get increasingly bitter as the years went by.

My patient felt that the great unhappiness of his parents and of his own childhood was entirely due to lack of money. He recalled very early fantasies in which he was a great business tycoon who came home to give his parents everything they ever wanted so that they would be happy, "especially with each other."

As with so many people in our culture, he saw life and human relations greatly simplified down to a matter of economic function and little else. On a not-so-unconscious level, he saw money as the measure of all things in life, including self-esteem. On a deeper and less consciously available level, what came out later was the strong feeling and belief that *only* money made existence worthwhile. He eventually admitted that he felt a man only deserved to exist at all if his financial attainments were commensurate with particular age levels. But at the time of this revelation, he admitted that this feeling only applied to himself and not to other people. He, like so many of us, was at least in some regards capable of much more compassion where people other than himself were concerned. They, of course, did not have to live up to his concept of omniscience and infallibility, nor did they suffer the hate he reserved specifically for himself.

This man, to no surprise, also suffered from the money illusion so many of us retain on an unconscious level. This one involves life itself. It is unconsciously believed that money is consistent with life and longevity. Many people, my patient included, harbor the secret illusion that enough money (usually a million or more dollars) attained by a certain age is virtually a guarantee of immortality. Indeed, many people are shocked when a rich man dies, while the death of a poor man is treated as an expected, natural phenomenon. In any case, my patient's loss, which to him meant only a small money loss on a practical level, represented a considerable symbolic trauma on an emotional and illusionary level.

1. It meant that he was not infallible about money or anything else. Shattering this illusion put him into immediate and traumatic touch with the tenuous nature of existence on all levels, including the possibility of what later turned out to be what he considered the ultimate blow to human dignity (really to neurotic pride)—death itself.

2. If he could lose a lesser amount of money then surely he could lose a larger amount, too. To him this meant that it was possible to find himself back where he had been in childhood—poor, frightened, vulnerable, helpless, and perhaps despised as a failure by his wife (a direct projection of self-hate), as his father had been despised by his mother. During this intense period of self-loathing and terror, it was impossible for him to accept and to use on a feeling level the fact that he was no longer a helpless child but a rather highly developed, multi-experienced, capable man. Telling him that his marriage was nothing like that of his parents had little or no effect. Rational arguments cannot stand up against powerful feelings of fragility that have unconsciously been nurtured and extended into many areas. Such unconscious meanings, feelings, influences and

illusions must be made fully conscious and brought into sharp, *full feeling awareness* before a fight against them on any kind of rational basis can have a significant effect.

3. He also, through this money loss, felt painful reverberations from an inkling, a beginning as it were, of what it would be like if he no longer had the making of money as the great motivating force in his life. This was experienced as a "feeling of a wave of emptiness," the source of which he could not define. This can go the other way, too. I remember another patient who had money-making as a motivation for living who became very rich—so rich in fact that further money-making had long since ceased to have real meaning. The fantasy that gave him the greatest stimulation and momentary happiness was one in which he would (through no fault of his own, so as to be spared hurt pride and self-hate) lose all of his money and then "could start all over again." This made him feel alive and would relieve a sense of futility and deadness. I'll have more to say about this man a little later on when I discuss the money illusion more fully.

4. Deep down, my first patient buried the belief that "the real truth is that I'm a replica of my father." Money, he felt, protected him from revelation of the "real truth." This "real truth" would, he felt, bring on complete loss of respect and even contempt from people around him.

It didn't take too much work on my part to reveal the contempt he was most afraid of. His potential for self-contempt was enormous and represented a much more terrifying possibility than the combined derision of all other people he knew, including his immediate family. This was well proved by his depressive reaction to the loss of an unimportant amount of money, and was further evidenced by many memories, conveniently forgotten up to that point, of sleepless, anxious nights and depressing mornings.

Many depressed people forget the depressing episodes in their lives. In part this is also due to self-hate. They expect and accept unhappiness and chronic, intermittent "small depressions" as a way of life. Eventually these "small depressions" are *felt* as depression only if some small awakening to happiness takes place, demonstrating the difference between happiness and sadness. Of course, what came out was the terror of losing a *lot* of money and losing all synthetic self-esteem, because, having so little compassion, he would have no defense against the enormous self-berating that would surely follow. His current depression, therefore, served as a stopgap against a more severe reaction by warning him against future mistakes and against deeper and more revealing identification with his "failure of a father."

5. My patient was using an extraordinary amount of human substance and energy to dedicate himself almost exclusively to self-hating processes and goals. His actual self suffered a chronic and continuous onslaught in which very little development and evolvement of innate resources and possibilities had taken place. He felt himself to be the money-making machine he had become and could envision little else for himself. As far as he consciously knew, at the time he began treatment, he was this money machine and nothing else. Therefore, any indication of failure in this one area of exclusive and total investment represented the possibility of a complete breakdown of the man's identifying characteristics. This means that he felt himself losing his self, feeling that he would no longer be,

that he would be alive only as an empty vegetablelike shell, a terrifying contemplation to be sure.

Our work together involved awareness of his very limited point of view as well as revelation of what turned out to be numerous self-hating devices. But this kind of work could only be constructive in an atmosphere of compassion. Attempting any deeper understanding in full view of accelerating and magnified self-hate could result in deeper depression and even suicide.

Eventually, our work involved a most important educational process. Inner and very longstanding yearnings were awakened for the first time in years. Once awake, a long-neglected, starved and tormented self wanted all kinds of nourishment, including richer relating to other people; derivation of pleasure from a multitude of earlier ignored interests and activities; development of new skills; and a general interest in discovering and using hitherto neglected inner resources. In short, the man had many areas of self that needed growing up and use. The resources were there and ready to be liberated and used in the service of relieving terrifying feelings of inner emptiness and deadness. It is interesting that as this man made progress in compassionately taking care of his real wants and needs, and began to fill up with a *real* love of himself, the nightmares of dying that he had suffered from for years disappeared completely.

ILLUSIONS INVOLVING SELF

The example we have just read about, of a self-illusion involving omniscience and omnipotence, is, of course, one of many possible self-illusions. All people who make use of a central overriding illusion invariably have many other illusions in use, too. All of us usually combine a number of illusions, some of which are directly contradictory to each other, causing much conflict, anxiety and confusion. The same applies to illusions involving other people and life generally. For example, some people are perceived as being all-knowing, while others are viewed as knowing nothing at all. Revelation in close relationships that friends and associates are actually combinations representing both knowledge and ignorance often produces shock and confusion.

In any case, illusion has more than a weakening effect on reality; it enhances fragility and increases the possibility of disappointment and direct self-hate. Illusions deflect energy and time from other activities and human possibilities, stunting inner growth and impoverishing actual self and the possibility for happiness.

Some of the most prevalent forms of illusion that are *very* important cornerstones of indirect self-hate usually exist in combination. They are all fed by self-hate, by each other, and by the confused cultural value system we live with.

It must be remembered that in the unconscious we have no need at all for consistency. Consistency, logic, and rationale are only necessary in conscious life and especially in dealing with the world we live in. The unconscious is not pressured by these societal needs. Seemingly utterly inconsistent dynamisms can operate in us without conscious awareness of anything other than painful symptoms of anxiety, depression and phobias. Thus, on an aware conscious level, I may think of myself as an easygoing, "nice," altruistic guy. On an unconscious level, I may have a need for being liked by everyone, which pushes me to "being nice," while I also have a need to dominate everyone and every situation I come into contact with. My conscious behavior will inevitably violate one of these two needs, and as a result, I may well be anxious and angry at myself a good deal of the time without understanding why.

Grandiose illusions involving mastery, perfection, bravery, courage, omniscience, omnipotence, great virtuosity, and invincibility are less subtle but no less destructive than self-aggrandizement gleaned through illusions of being martyred, benevolent, abused, self-sacrificing, pure, saintly, understanding, all-loving, all-caring, being the eternal nice guy, entirely free of jealousy, hypocrisy, envy, duplicity, possessiveness and dishonesty. The illusion of omnipotence and the illusion of self-sacrificing martyrdom, which lie behind feeling Christlike, are equally grandiose and are both departures from actual self, the human condition and human reality. The same is true of illusions involving what Horney called detachment. There are grandiose functions at work when we see ourselves as being noninvolved, utterly free from attachments, being above it all and actually superior to it all, and when we do not allow ourselves to be touched or to care. The same is often true of outward shows of contempt, disdain, cynicism and sadism. The foregoing are all illusionary attempts to feel better by escaping the view of actual self and the illusions of contemptible actual self. In other words, when we face actual self and reality, this may be insult enough to call for Grand Illusion, but illusions of a self-derisive nature (not apparent in the Grand Illusions) surely also call for escape to grandiosity. These grandiose illusions are self-hating attempts to destroy and obfuscate actual self.

The secondary onslaughts of direct self-hate following

the inevitable fall from grand illusionary heights make the Grand Illusion the parent of direct self-hate. Of course, much of the hate generated against actual self and reality, which starts us on the grand tour, is lodged in illusions about the human condition and world generally, leading to great disappointments, bitterness and cynicism.

And what about downgrading illusions regarding actual self, which make us see ourselves in such a poor light that we are forced to seek grandiose excursions away from reality in attempts at relief? These self-derisive illusions and feelings are, in treatment, often traceable to early environmental insults. They are often intimately linked to parental indifference, overpermissiveness and overprotection. The stifling effects of overprotection provide ample seed and root for future illusions of helplessness, incompetence and dependency. These in turn lead to compensatory Grand Illusions and subsequent disappointment when these cannot be fulfilled, followed by onslaughts of direct self-hate. All are departures from actual self and, therefore, represent hate of actual self.

The illusion of dependency is exceedingly common. I feel that it is extremely important to differentiate between *actual* helplessness and dependency and *the illusion of helplessness and dependency*. The illusion can keep us from adequately using ourselves and participating in life, and, thus, can be destructive in terms of our development, and can even make us somewhat more dependent than we are, which in turn adds still more to illusionary feelings of dependency. *But* there is still a vast difference between *being dependent* and having *illusions of dependency*. In my practice I have met many seemingly dependent people who turned out to be extraordinarily competent as soon as their illusions of dependency and superindependence and grandiosity were destroyed. The latter—Grand Illusions—added to a feeling of being relatively incompetent, and to childhood illusions about "inabilities," kept these people in a state of inhibition and even paralysis. Their *pseudo-dependence* invariably masked much ability, which needed release from crippling illusion.

Actual dependency and helplessness are quite something else. It takes very little experience or acumen to recognize the truly dependent person. These are people who never did grow up. In many cases this is due to severe and prolonged overprotection, which leads to a thorough and permanent stunting of just about all potential capacities. Even people such as these can grow, however, but not nearly as much as the person who has grown but who still suffers from the illusion of dependency or pseudodependency.

The pseudodependent person, in an effort to please, to lean on, to be safe, often takes on the coloration and mirrors the desires of the person she or he wishes to please. She or he may even seem at times to be an extension of that other person. She or he can then, if necessary, shift these imitative skills to another person. This is no small ability. It is only possible because the pseudodependent person can, like a good actor, tap areas in himself of mutuality and development. This is not usually possible in the truly dependent person who, lacking his own development, cannot *read* the wants, needs and sensitivities of others to whom he is relating. Pseudodependent people usually have a keen ability to manipulate other people to fulfill their own needs, while truly dependent people at best can only manipulate on the most infantile level.

I am reminded of a middle-aged woman I saw in consultation who was quite depressed following the death of her husband. She came from a very wealthy family that regarded girls and women as small, precious, helpless jewels, made to be loved, cherished, and, above all, guarded from the world's tougher realities. This woman married a wealthy man (discovered by her father) who had exactly the same outlook regarding women, and after a long life with him she did not suffer from an *illusion* of dependency. She *was* utterly dependent, and the treatment she required was quite different from that of a person suffering illusionary dependency.

This woman had been brought up and guarded by her parents and husband in such a way that her development as a real person coping in the real world was remarkably stunted. There was so much she simply did not know. Her lack of knowledge of the world ranged from ignorance of the simplest, practical financial matters to an utter naïveté concerning people and just about anything else that exists in most adults' information survival kits. She had relied on her father, and then on her husband, for absolutely all directives as well as opinions. She did as they said, felt as they said, voted as her husband told her to vote. She never bought her clothes without their direction, or, for that matter, did anything else without detailed guidance. She didn't know how to sign a check, pay the rent and much more.

People suffering from real dependency do not do well in psychoanalytic treatment unless they are fairly young, unusually resilient and potentially gifted. Analysis requires considerable strength and the ability to tolerate anxiety and frustration, which this woman could not. But even in cases where analysis can be used, truly dependent people require a very special kind of analytic treatment. In addition to learning compassion and going through the revelatory experience of what makes them tick, they also need much in the way of supportive direction.

I referred this woman to a therapist who in essence became a substitute for her husband and who functioned as a benevolent director. At the same time he slowly attempted to educate her so that she could at least to some extent rely on herself more.

By contrast, I had a woman in analytic treatment—let's call her Maxine—for several years, who had the *illusion of dependency*. She was thirty-eight years old and had recently parted from a lover with whom she had lived for three years. She had been divorced early in her adult life after five years of marriage, and this was followed by several moderately long, sustained love affairs.

She came to me because each parting was devastating and because she was convinced that she could "not go on alone," that "I'm not a whole person without him," that "I just can't take care of myself." The fact was that this woman had been taking excellent care of herself almost alone since early childhood. Not only that, but the men in her life were quite dependent and had leaned heavily on her, so that she took care of them, too. This was especially true of her husband.

Maxine was the antithesis of the older woman I had seen in consultation. She was the epitome of sophistication. She knew her way around in every conceivable area and was a top-notch business woman who enjoyed a superb reputation for competency and excellent judgment among her colleagues. *But* she truly believed "I am no one without a man."

From earliest times Maxine had been brain-washed and convinced that a woman without a man was without any kind of personal prestige, was exceedingly vulnerable, and would suffer from a very fragile sense of herself. She also believed that a woman without a man could not possibly take care of herself on a worthwhile, realistic level. These illusions persisted despite her efforts to dislodge them through identification with the women's movement and attendance at several consciousness-raising groups. Even more important, these illusions persisted despite the open, obvious reality that Maxine had, indeed, taken care of herself, and had done so very well, since childhood. The fact is that the men in her life were never as competent as she was in any area, and, realistically, largely depended on her.

Maxine also suffered from the illusion about love that nearly always is present along with the dependency illusion and which, indeed, contributes to its sustenance and continuation. The illusion is that love resolves all problems, destroys all pain and provides Heaven on Earth. This means that the quest for love and *the right partner* takes precedence over all other things in life.

Hooking herself to the right man meant to Maxine melding with his strength, his purity, his goodness, and no longer ever again being vulnerable to the onslaughts life occasionally delivers. Giving up these illusions meant giving up the possibility of Heaven on Earth, and giving up the idea of pain-free, problem-free, invulnerability. Like so many pseudodependent people, she believed that *oneness* was possible despite the biological fact of separateness, however close we ever get. But more than that, surrender of illusion meant self-acceptance to the point of recogniz- ing herself as a separate, complete, whole human being able to take care of herself. This was no easy matter, because it involved raising self-esteem in the middle of much self-hating, self-assault.

As with most pseudodependent people, Maxine had a secret, highly exalted image of herself that involved great nobility and purity and being endlessly loving and understanding. Since falls from these unrealistic standards were constantly taking place, she suffered from much direct self-hate and poor self-esteem. Her treatment largely consisted of giving up these inhuman standards, accepting her humanity, and deriving self-esteem from it, recognizing and blocking direct self-hate (a process I'll have more to say about when I discuss compassion) and giving up illusions and embracing reality.

In Maxine's case, the main illusion requiring surrender was that involving dependency and love, and the main reality to accept was that of her competence. The final block to acceptance of her competence was self-hate, fed by our traditional cultural ambiguity over competency and femininity, and the now-fading assumption that the two cannot co-exist. Maxine learned in analysis that she was ashamed of being competent and hid her abilities to cope as much as possible because she saw this quality as antifeminine, even masculine. This *confusion* existed despite the fact that Maxine was a superb example of what this same culture considers utterly feminine. She was graceful, beautiful, decidedly heterosexual.

Her consciousness-raising group helped her to realize to a certain extent that women can be both female and competent, just as men can be male and still enjoy gentle feelings. The group helped her to blast away many of the cultural myths she had imprinted concerning female and male characteristics. While this had some impact on her, mythical maleness or femaleness went on to plague her until her self-hate was markedly reduced and her compassion was enhanced. At this point much in her life began to make sense on considerably more than an intellectual, logical level. She began to "feel it all, deep down," and to enjoy much of what she felt.

In the beginning, Maxine was terrified to remember dreams, for fear of what they would reveal, and that they might bring on an onslaught of self-hate. "I'm frightened that I'll find out what's wrong about me that drove him away and I'll hate myself for it." Later on, as she saw herself as more and more of the complete and growing person she was, and was no longer the passive victim of self-hate, she looked forward to dreams "to find out more and more about myself."

Illusions involving perfect sex are extremely common and sometimes found in tandem with the love illusion and very often with the Heaven on Earth myth. This myth is found at least in part in just about all other illusionary manifestations. It is not too difficult to understand how an illusion regarding the total curative value of a mythical perfect sexual union is generated in a cultural milieu in which exhortations involving both sexual repression and total freedom run rampant. The propaganda about mythically perfect love and sex in movies, plays, songs, and in many novels and stories, makes for all kinds of illusionary material. Songs tell us that "what the world needs now is love, sweet love," that "lovers can live on love alone," that "love makes the world go round." We believe it! This illusion often destroys the joy in sex because of the gap between dream and reality, and because it tends to make its victims concentrate self-consciously on performance, thus killing spontaneity and creativity.

The illusion of perfect independence is just as prevalent as the dependency illusion, and they are not mutually exclusive. It must be remembered that the unconscious is full of incongruities. Therefore, the individual who craves perfect oneness with another person will hate himself because he also wants total freedom from involvement, too. Thus, he will constantly generate self-hate on the basis of one or the other illusion. He simply cannot *win*. The independence illusion involves the erroneous idea that one can live totally on one's own. The person who sees himself in this way is usually shocked and suffused with self-hate, anxiety and depression when he finds himself involved or about to get involved with someone on a serious level. I have seen quite a number of men trapped by this problem who go into a panic just prior to marriage.

ILLUSIONS INVOLVING SELF AND OTHER PEOPLE

Illusions about other people, especially those important to us—parents, teachers, leaders, mates, lovers and our children—can, if exaggerated, become huge repositories in which to bank bitter disappointment, hatred of others and self-hate. Such illusions are almost always projections of our self-idealizations and reveal much that is illusionary about ourselves. In therapy, patients almost invariably transfer many of these illusions and hopes for ideal relationships to their therapists. Examination of these ideas, beliefs and opinions about the therapist give much information about the patient, her expectations for herself and the people in her life and world. They can also make for considerable difficulty in treatment.

I remember one woman who knew nothing about me in actuality, but immediately on meeting me insisted that I was all-knowing, my every word and gesture was full of wisdom and meaning, my clothes were the very best, even though at the same time she believed that I cared not a fig about how I dressed, since "you have no vanity at all." I knew everything there was to know about everything; my wife was a great lady; my children were brilliant, talented and perfectly adjusted; my wife and I were the most charitable and altruistic people in the world and obviously had great charm, talent, charisma and the wide circle of brilliant friends "people like you deserve." Yes, she also believed that we deserved it all because we were undoubtedly special people, exempt from life's ordinary problems and vicissitudes.

These illusions were not confined to me. She readily applied them to a vast array of "special" people she never met. She also applied them to friends, but to a much lesser degree. However, here, too, gross unreality was involved and made for repeated disappointment, increasing bouts of bitterness, and attacks of self-hate and hopelessness. To combat these feelings, she had no idea that surrender of illusion was called for. Instead, she felt that she "related to the wrong people," and that if she "improved" herself maybe she could break into "the right crowd, where people are really nice and interesting and decent." But the "right crowd" eluded her and she continued to disappoint herself in her quest for achievement of status which would somehow grant her entry to the ranks of the beautiful people. In treatment, she eventually became aware of what "self-improvement" *had* meant to her and what it meant to me. For her it *had* meant greater self-idealization and becoming ever more glorious. For me it meant greater self-acceptance in terms of who she *actually* was. While some of us are not this extreme in our devotion to illusion, we nevertheless suffer ample self-hate proportionate to the illusions we inflict upon ourselves. My patient did well in treatment but not without great struggle and considerable pain.

Surrendering illusions can be most frightening and agonizing. Initial attempts to be one's real self usually bring enormous attacks of acute self-hate as a response from the self-hating part of ourselves in feeling seriously threatened. But the hitherto ill-used actual self blossoms forth and develops strength with considerable rapidity in an atmosphere of increasing compassion. The relief alone, like a dental visit, is easily worth the pain. Eugene O'Neill portrayed the agony and terror involved in destroying illusions in *The Iceman Cometh*. But he gave too little credit to actual self and the ability and desire for growth and health. My patient became aware of and struggled to surrender illusions and impossible goals and standards for herself. In doing so she also gave up many of the illusions she had projected onto others. Interestingly, I became increasingly human in her opinion as she gave up the quest for her own personal Godlike status.

A therapist of human proportions and limitations cannot help a would-be Goddess, but he can help a person of human-being proportions. How the patient sees the therapist is largely a measure of how the patient sees herself. Quick, early confrontation with a therapist whose humanity and limitations are evident can be very frightening to a person still fully identified with antihuman illusions. Confrontation later on can be very supportive, inasmuch as it promotes understanding and trust through mutuality of problems and common ground. I've found this to be true again and again in openly telling patients of depression and anxiety I've suffered from at various times in my own life.

Of course, illusions regarding children can be particularly disappointing and even devastating. Parents use children as projective screens for their own idealizations. In some cases children assume mythical Godlike properties so that parents stand off in awe. Adults sometimes seek and take the advice of utterly inexperienced young people whom they imbue with an illusory wisdom purely of the parents' own making. Idealization of children does not draw them closer any more than it produces real self-esteem. It contributes to a destructive family myth and to a broadening of the gap between generations, often destroying communications altogether.

ILLUSIONS INVOLVING SELF AND THE HUMAN CONDITION

An illusion that deserves special mention for its destructive ability in regard to *here and now* happiness is the belief that we can undo or make up for the past. Many of us refuse to accept a limited *here and now*, however good it may be, because it simply can never be good enough to undo the past. This dynamic can be particularly inundating and malignant.

I had one patient, Beverly, who destroyed the value of anything at all of current substance and happiness. She felt that her suffering in the past deserved a *here and now* that should produce nothing short of compensatory heavenly rebirth. One statement she repeated again and again that epitomized her position was, "I should be able to start all over again. This time it would be perfect." We can't start over again, and it wouldn't "be perfect" if we could. We can only continue. Beverly spent a great deal of time recalling each suffering moment of the past.

At first, I encouraged this process, feeling that it made for good, standard, psychoanalytic ventilation and catharsis. But then I realized that at least 60 percent of her time and energy had for years been spent in this kind of injustice-collecting activity. It destroyed her *here and now self* and many opportunities for happiness in the present, and was an all-too-effective self-hating device. Before too long I realized why Beverly did this. She had the unconscious illusionary, mistaken belief that somewhere, somehow, someone kept a big score card and that the road to alternate Nirvana and rebirth was paved with past suffering. Her reasoning was that if she couldn't achieve a complete compensation for a painful past, it was only because her proof of suffering was inadequate. She only needed to show further evidence of past injustices and wounds and, if necessary, to relive the past again and again in order to bring in a winning score card.

That perfect justice exists somewhere, somehow is a most common illusion. This, despite the fact that justice is not a spontaneous fact of nature or existence, but an entirely man-made invention. Each revelation of discrepancy between *just desert* and *actual result* leads to disappointment and a self-recriminating onslaught on an acute level. On a chronic level it leads to continuous injustice-collecting in an effort to prove to the mythical powers-that-be that justice has not been done and that suffering has been adequate to deserve perfect justice and what is appropriately deserved in the future.

Illusions regarding happiness are most common, as are

the invariable disappointments which lead to multiple attacks of self-hate and sabotage. For me, happiness is feeling good, nothing more than that. I know that feeling good, that is, feeling fairly comfortable and relatively tension-free, is no small matter and depends on the existence of many, many factors, most of which are not discernible, let alone controllable. Therefore, what I have come to view as happiness can only be sustained for limited periods of time, sporadically, and always on a relative level. Yes, even just plain feeling good is relative and cannot be perfect either in quality or duration. But illusions about happiness and ways of achieving it invariably destroy what happiness, however humanly limited, is possible.

The principal illusion is that happiness is an orgastic high, a fantastic continuum of peak orgastic experiences. This is not happiness! Such states of exhilaration almost always are related to depression and almost always are followed by depression. And even just feeling relatively comfortable is not a state that can be prolonged indefinitely. The sensitive and complex human psyche must experience wide fluctuations because life itself is tough and complicated. The illusions regarding the possibility of sustained, perfect happiness are multiple, often seen in combination, and usually are relegated to an unconscious level by their victim. Some of the most common are those involving money, achievement, love, possessions, power, prestige, marriage, sex, children, family and success.

Sexual fantasies in adolescence often stem partially from the sexual deprivation common in our complex society. Fantasy is used as a substitute for actual sexual satisfaction. But sexual daydreams often go way beyond the possibilities of future reality, which turns out to be disappointing by comparison. Even though the original sexual fantasy may be forgotten and buried in the unconscious, yearning associated with the fantasy may continue. This may produce a never-ending quest for impossible satisfaction.

Such fantasies sometimes also become linked to whatever else is felt as deprivation, and eventually become symbolic of potential satisfaction of all desires and needs. These fantasies and feelings about the exaggerated role of sex are incorporated into illusions of a perfect sexuality and harmony that will bring happiness in all other areas of life. Such an enormous burden on the role of sex can make for much anxiety about sexual function. If sexual activity must resolve all of life's problems, then that activity may be approached with trepidation at least equal to that incurred by any other unreal demand for perfect performance. This attitude, plus self-hate generally can make for all kinds of sexual problems, including impotence and frigidity. If sex must always be linked to utmost relatedness, love, the most blissful feelings possible, and must produce utter and sustained happiness, the burden on the individual in question may destroy sexual function altogether.

Deprivation through premature ejaculation, failure to get aroused, is immediately and directly pleasure-depriving and self-hating. Perversely, it also serves to prevent disappointment which must follow exorbitant expectation. Exorbitant expectation and disappointment are often markedly relieved when minimal function on any level is in question or even impossible. But the price paid for this kind of prevention of disappointment is chronic deprivation. As with the case of the legendary girl who could not

say "No," sex can be used as a direct form of self-degradation. Casual and frequent sexual activity by deeply moral-
istic people can be a form of self-hate. This may also be
true of so-called perverse sex activity such as masochism
and bestiality.

I have mentioned the danger in the illusion that money
brings happiness and resolves all problems forever. Yet it is
extremely prevalent and very difficult to shake in a culture
that constantly feeds and reinforces the myth. At one time
I had five self-made millionaires in treatment. They were
all depressed. Money had not resolved most of their
problems. Money had not made them happier. One man
said to me, "I was good. I did my part. I made it. I'm a
success. What's wrong?" What turned out to be wrong was
the awareness that all kinds of illusions related to money
had not been realized and that they never would be. Since
he now had the money, the illusions could no longer be
sustained. His anticipation that continuous happiness
would some day be his when he had millions was now
destroyed, because he had the millions and felt "there
doesn't any longer seem to be anything to look forward
to."

I treated one psychotherapy group in which there were
some very wealthy people and some relatively poor people,
too. Some of the poor people continued to harbor the
illusion that there would be complete resolution of their
problems and sustained happiness if only they had money,
despite the obvious unhappiness of their rich confrères. It
was quite revealing when, one evening, one of the poorer
people asked one of the rich men who had been quite
depressed for an extended period of time how he would
feel if he lost all his money. For the first time in months
Bill's face lit up and he looked positively joyous. His

immediate answer, and he said it with great joy, was, "I'd go out and make it all over again." It was apparent to everyone in the group that this would restore Bill's raison d'être.

The money illusion had robbed him of all other interests. If immortality and paradise can be realized through acquisition of money, then how can time be taken off for any other activity? This was the case with Bill. His entire life had been spent making money and all other areas and possible sources of pleasure had been neglected. He was bitterly disappointed because actualization of his fantasy had not led to promises fulfilled at all. Despite the acquisition of millions of dollars, he was getting older, his mother and father had died, and his children and wife had problems. Despite Bill's evidence of money being useful but not happiness-producing, most of the non-moneyed people in the group persisted in maintaining the illusion.

Illusions involving achievement, power and prestige are very similar to those involving money, in both prevalence and expectation. Unfortunately, they are all very often linked to desires and fantasies of great vindictive triumph and revenge. This is often projected to people other than oneself and to the outside world at large.

I remember one man, a former Swiss, whose life was taken up with "becoming important so that I can show them." He did in fact become quite important, eventually amassing money, prestige and considerable business power. His childhood dream came true when he visited his small Swiss village for the first time in many years. The trip was no casual matter and this was hardly a casual, light-hearted man. He planned everything in advance and made sure that former neighbors and friends were well apprised of his many achievements. Before he arrived, they knew that he had become a great industrialist, a financier, a well-known art collector, and also a man of many, many possessions including vast real estate holdings throughout the world.

As in a popular song of some years ago, "Jack, I'm coming back in my convertible Cadillac," this once-poor boy did in fact return to his village in a specially built, chauffeur-driven limousine. The awful part of the whole enterprise was that it produced the desired results. He was greeted as a great personage by everyone. Everybody was in awe. All the town officials were in full and great praise of him. Many former friends, enemies and tormentors were overtly uncomfortable, envious and jealous. There were dinners and testimonials given in his behalf. But all of it put together was not enough. When it was over his disappointment was enormous. He felt "dead and empty inside and like I'd been taken, duped, an enormous fool." This reaction was followed by a great deal of depression, guilt and self-recrimination. It felt like "there is nothing more to look forward to."

The fact is that my patient's achievements occurred *despite* desires for vindictive triumph and not *because* of them. Unfortunately, he really never had felt that he deserved anything that he accomplished or possessed. Since he felt that it was all done in the service of self-hate, and self-hate projected to others, and for vindictive triumph, the satisfaction he derived did not register on the side of compassion or self-esteem. It was all done as part of a vast illusion that, given a life-long enormous vindictive triumph coupled with the accumulation of power, prestige, accomplishment and possessions, he would enter a state of sustained and eternal comfort and happiness.

Instead, he was hit by utter disappointment. Not only

was he still mortal, but now he also felt the corrosive effects of years of self-neglect. Time and energy used in behalf of self-hate is corrosive, because when we are consumed by it we neglect self, which remains starved and wanting. Additionally, this man no longer had his fantasy of vindictive triumph to look forward to. The results had produced a vast disappointment, this despite the fact that "They all reacted just as I used to dream about and now it's all over. I guess revenge wasn't very sweet after all. I feel more taken than ever—a fool—an old fool."

Actually, he wasn't "old" at all. At that time he was forty-six. He felt "old" for two reasons: (1) His fantasy of vindictive triumph was indeed old, as it had existed since childhood; also, the energy poured into it made him feel old. (2) His disappointment and depression made him feel old, especially since one of his expectations turned out to be eternal youth. Yes, he really deep down, on an unconscious level, believed that great world success made for everlasting youth. This illusion existed and superseded the logic this man was famous for among colleagues and friends. "How could a man who owns so much get so old that he can't even enjoy it?"

The illusion of the power of possessions to overcome all problems is not uncommon among economically and emotionally deprived children, who view more fortunate children as living in a world apart, a protected world where eternal bliss reigns supreme. Of course, entrance to that world is seen as fulfillment of all illusions, especially illusions involving wealth. These are almost invariably linked to fantasies of revenge that originate as revenge against more privileged children, against parents who are felt to be unjustly limited, and against what is felt as an uncaring world. Of course, the greatest revenge would be *real* happiness and good living, *born of compassion and dedicated to the eradication of self-hate in all forms.* Had this taken place in my Swiss patient, many of his very real achievements would have been used in the service of enjoyment instead of providing fuel for more hate, self-corrosion and bitter disappointment.

Another patient, Jill, a forty-year-old woman, had just about every conceivable human asset with which nature ever blessed a human being. She was beautiful, multi-talented, enormously energetic, unusually intelligent, sensitive, sophisticated, knowledgeable, and very well educated. She had a wonderful sense of humor, considerable sex appeal, and was loved and adored by people who knew her intimately and by multitudes of people who knew her as a world-famous celebrity of many notable accomplishments. She had attained much, almost entirely on her own.

But on a deep emotional level Jill owned almost none of it. Her quest for ever increasing supplies of narcissistic gratifications in the way of still more proof of admiration was endless. Indeed, this quest left her with no time for real pleasurable gratification at all. She could never take time out to enjoy a simple conversation, a good meal, a good show or anything else. All energy had to be directed to more and more, and still greater accomplishments, in order to win more fame and praise and ward off feelings of intolerable self-hate.

This woman came to see me because even with her great energy and talent she could no longer tolerate the pace. Depression, and suicidal thoughts were beginning to take hold of her despite her outward veneer of poise and happiness. During the course of treatment it became apparent that her impossible quest was largely a reaction to a well-hidden, nearly forgotten, and repressed childhood, fraught with cruelty and terrible self-denigration. To this woman accomplishment became equated with self-acceptance, with a guarantee of total burial and repression of that unwanted, frightened and tortured child, and with the attainment of everlasting youth, life and Heaven on Earth to compensate for "those terribly mean times." Any time taken off from *the great quest,* as she and I came to call it, was seen as frivolous and foolish, and brought on terrible attacks of direct self-hate in the form of guilt, depression and self-recriminating mental beatings about purely imagined "crimes." After all, how could she tolerate a person— "herself"—who dared take time off from a quest for immortality, which she felt as being teasingly there, always just a little out of reach.

My initial attempts to instill compassion for herself in her were met with suspicion of my motives and considerable anger, because I, too, was viewed as someone who wanted to cheat and block her from entering Heaven. One of her worst symptoms, manifested during a period of great success in her career, was insomnia. Of course, a period of success and more than usual acclaim for great achievements was fraught with the danger of inability to sustain these peak experiences, fear of subsequent disappointment, and even greater fear of self-hating recriminations for inability to sustain an impossible "high."

Even more, so-called success in her imagination brought her still closer to the possibility of everlasting Nirvana. To fail to put just a little more effort into attaining this possibility, even though in actuality there was no effort spared, and even though Heaven still insisted on being a little out of reach, seemed "stupid" and even "criminal." For her kind of "criminal" there was no time off for good behavior and sleep was equated with time off. How could

anyone sleep when just a little more effort, just doing a few
more things still undone, would bring her perfect justice,
perfect rewards for all past hurts, perfect youth, everlasting life?

Understanding the roots of her problem helped mitigate
depression and anxiety to some degree, but this did not
relieve her insomnia. Remembering and going through
past memories of her mother's insatiable ambitions for Jill
and her mother's terrible accomplishment orientation and
pressure was of little help. Jill's sleeplessness had been too
much for even powerful sedatives and was beginning to
take a terrible toll. Malignant lack of sleep can produce
feelings of unreality, anxiety, depression and even hallucinations. Worse yet, a vicious cycle had been completed.
Jill's self-hatred prevented sleep and her sleeplessness
produced even more self-hate. "I approach my bed with
horror. I feel as if I am engaged in a terrible battle—my
fight with sleep. I spend the entire night recriminating
about my imperfections and going over lists of things
undone which I ought to be doing."

After considerable treatment Jill began to realize that
her sleeplessness did not produce the lists. Indeed, the lists
did not produce the sleeplessness. Her self-hate produced
both the lists and the sleeplessness. The entire process of
sleeplessness and "fighting sleep" (which was in itself
enough to keep her awake) was due to self-hating excursions away from self and in quest of impossible and
inhuman goals. To make matters worse, the sleeplessness
had become a well-ingrained autonomous habit which in
itself was extremely hard to break.

But Jill was a courageous woman, and on a reality level
wanted to live, really live. She realized that her fantasy
and quest would eventually kill her and she began a

serious fight against self-hating illusion. This, at first, as it nearly always does, brought on terrible anxiety. But she saw it through, and increasingly embraced the reality of her humanity and its inherent limitations. She then confronted the quintessential symbol of her self-hate head-on.

In addition to going to sleep at night, she attempted to take naps in the afternoon, too, a "luxury" that would have filled her with unbearable dread in the past. I suggested that she listen to music, that she ignore all thoughts, all lists, all recriminations and all observations involving sleep and sleeplessness—"just listen to music." For years she'd not realized that her "intrusive" thoughts actually could be ignored. This is one of self-hate's prime characteristics— the victim's total capitulation and ignorance as to the existence of any possibility at all of putting up a fight, let alone winning.

But she did it! She ignored all bombardment of self-hate from all quarters and in all forms, and made herself listen to music. She succeeded, and for the first time realized that she could block self-hate. This first active, direct, compassionate step paved the way for many more. She no longer fought sleep and the whole sleep issue ceased to be a measure of progress or failure. She listened to music and gently fell asleep. Her waking hours, too, became increasingly relaxed as the standards of performance she set for herself came down. As her self-measurement activity decreased, as her quest for immortality dissipated, and as her esteem became more a measure of total self-acceptance rather than a function of other people's approval, her need for the narcissistic supplies they gave her diminished.

"If I were only rich." "If I were only beautiful." "If I were only married." "If somebody really loved me." The illusion that the world and the human condition generally undergoes a radical change and a complete metamorphosis with so-called material security, love and marriage runs rampant. Our culture makes no small contribution in feeding illusions involving love, marriage and beauty. Songs, movies and television bombard us constantly with the importance and power of love and beauty and the extraordinary possibilities inherent in marriage. Many women not so secretly believe that beauty brings love and that love brings a great marriage, which represents a melding and produces a oneness which makes for a new identification, new feelings and sustained and continued happiness. Disappointment that stems from the gap between illusionary expectation and actuality often wrecks marriages that are fulfilling within realistic human possibilities.

Love can help communication and relatedness. Love can help self-esteem and self-acceptance. Love can make us feel better and at times pretty good. But vast illusionary concentration and expectation leads to cynicism and bitterness which destroys these limited but valuable possibilities. Marriage can be a most rewarding and enriching way to live. But it does not create a metamorphosis. People are still the same people after marriage. They are still individuals with individual needs, aspirations, frames of reference, feelings and problems. Marriage brings its own joys and problems, too. Young people who don't understand this are loathe to face any adjustment, problem or period and usually seek separation immediately after they discover their illusions are not being actualized.

Beauty, unfortunately, is often not even its own reward. I remember seeing an actress in consultation, world famous for her great beauty, who constantly felt ugly. She spent hours looking at the mirror trying to convince herself that she wasn't ugly after all. The fact that other people saw her as a great beauty wasn't at all convincing. The image of "a gawky, buck-toothed, awkward" little girl persisted, as did the illusions born of early childhood fantasies involving being vastly beautiful and "then liking myself and always feeling good."

Liking herself turned out to be much more complicated than the matter of looks. It was a function of literally every aspect of herself and much work and struggle was necessary in order to raise badly injured self-esteem. Only then would it be possible to *feel beautiful* and to believe that she looked beautiful, too. As self-esteem surfaces it becomes apparent to us that great beauty, great love, great marriage, great children, and all the great and superlative conditions in existence do not and cannot make for "always feeling good." Our species is much too complex, sensitive and vulnerable to feel good or to feel any way at all *always* or consistently.

I am also reminded of a forty-four-year-old man who, as it turned out, was terrified of growing old. His magical solution consisted of a compulsive quest for liaisons with young, beautiful girls. They had to be under twenty-four—that somehow was the magical number for him. He had convinced himself that relationships, and especially sex, with young girls would keep him young. *But* reality has a way of imposing on illusions. He continued to get older anyway, and increasingly more self-hating and terrified. Since he could not continue to relate to a girl once she got to be twenty-four, he was almost constantly between relationships and very lonely. One of his major complaints was that of late he was becoming very lonely *during* many of these liaisons, too. Beauty was no guarantee of intelligence or sophistication, and this, too, felt insulting to him. His own increasing wisdom, due to experience gained as he got older, further mitigated against his having much in common with his younger lovers, particularly since he broke up each of his relationships before the young woman in question had a chance to develop experience and knowledge approaching his own.

Awareness of the impossible demand for everlasting youth, coupled with the surrender of many illusions, as well as increased self acceptance made aging a less fearful prospect for him. Insight regarding his need for relationships with young girls helped, too. He eventually entered a relationship with a woman ten years younger than himself, which represented a radical departure for him. When I last saw him he was still living with this woman and she did not seem "too old" for him. He told me that they had much in common and that he was even thinking of marriage. This kind of commitment certainly represented a major change. When I questioned him further, he indicated that he was no longer preoccupied with the fear of aging, although he still thought about it once in a while.

Popularity is another famous area of great human illusion. Ah, the wonders and marvels that being popular is supposed to bring. To be known, liked and even loved and admired, this would be paradise indeed. This one is usually linked to other *ifs*. "If I were beautiful"; "If I were a great athlete"; "If I were really smart"; "Then I would be popular." The fact that some of the seemingly most popular people in the world have led unhappy lives, and even have committed suicide, does not dilute or mitigate the illusion of the importance of popularity. That individuality and uniquely constructive proclivities and assets are often ignored for the sake of popularity is seldom taken into account.

Illusions often produce an obsessional way of life that simply obliterates reality as well as many important aspects of ourselves. One of the most destructive aspects of the popularity illusion is the desire and need to conform. This is especially true of adolescents, who will literally destroy important parts of themselves in order to be popular with "the crowd." They will take drugs, use a stilted, impoverished language and generally engage in activities destructive to their well-being and development in order to be popular. Parents unwittingly feed this illusion by constantly bombarding children with the need to be liked by everybody. In fact, "being liked by everyone" is usually indication that one has obliterated oneself in favor of becoming a mirror image for everyone else. I have known teen-agers who hid their excellent vocabularies, abilities with language and intellectual interests in order to conform, to be liked, to be popular and to fulfill a kind of American success illusion.

Illusions involving "success" have little to do with human satisfaction and realistic aspirations. They have absolutely nothing to do with compassion for one's own humanity. They are the antithesis of the most important kind of success of all, *successful self-acceptance.* Success illusions may involve particular pursuits, such as vast business or professional success, or success as an ideal mother or wife. I had one patient who wanted to be nothing short of a "perfect mother" and who was convinced that fulfillment on that score guaranteed utter happiness and immortality.

Success is often equated with a generalized, vague

notion of entering a special realm. As Betty, a nineteen-year-old girl, told me, "I want to be with the beautiful people, the successful ones. You know, the important ones everyone looks at and wants to be. The people who have nothing to do with all the dull, small things plain people have to be busy with. 'Jet Set,' I guess they call them. Those people are always having fun. For them, the sun is always there. They never get sick. They're just special." This illusion is often coupled with a desire and striving for power over other people, which is felt as a way to compensate for hidden inner misery and weakness. I told Betty that I knew a number of people who had in fact actualized her fantasy. They were "the successful ones," "the beautiful people," and they still had all the human problems and limitations inherent in being human.

No socioeconomic status or influence over other people affects the chromosome count. We are still, all of us, human, and remain human biological entities. Whatever our status—and I include the youngest of us and the oldest, the healthiest and the sickest, the most successful of us and those people on skid row—we have infinitely more in common than we have apart. Indeed, some of the "most successful" people I've known have come to see me because of depression caused by disillusionment with success. Becoming famous did not save them from marital discord, problems with children, physical disability, aging and all other aspects of their quite real humanity. As a matter of fact, through the years I have seen a surprisingly high proportion of serious problems of attempted suicide, alcoholism and addiction to sedatives among those whom our culture calls the "successful" people. Linked to the power/success syndrome we often find a ruthless competitive drive that obliterates sensitivity toward self and others. This results in poor care of self on both a physical and emotional level, as well as very poor and impoverished relationships with others.

The illusion of living in a so-called successful Shangri-la world is often of such a compulsive and obsessive nature that it destroys all possibility of time or energy invested in pleasurable activity. When the individual finally does "get there" he has no idea that he has in fact "arrived," and has no ability left or developed to enjoy whatever it is he was striving for in the first place. To ward off ensuing feelings of emptiness he continues to drive on. When for some reason he no longer can keep driving uphill to nowhere, he feels terribly duped by the emptiness of his dream world and turns his remaining energy to savage attacks of self-hate.

THE GRAND ILLUSION

The Grand Illusion is the sum total of *all* our illusions. We have various ways of symbolically representing the Grand Illusion. I had one patient who saw himself becoming a knight on a horse, slaying evil dragons; another who saw himself living on a mountaintop and issuing bulletins which would resolve the major problems of a befuddled humanity, and still another who saw himself as "the universal seeder," a man who would make all women happy. Some symbols are not nearly so exotic or imaginative but nevertheless represent a vast complex of illusionary drives and the expectation of Heaven on Earth in fulfilling payment.

One patient, Charlene, often talked to me about "being

good." I learned that to her *being good* meant she would resolve all conflicts and fulfill all perfectionistic goals and standards, including contradictory ones, such as "telling everyone off in a huge binge of self-assertion," and at the same time "being universally loved." This would give Charlene "total peace, comfort, happiness and I will live happily ever after, making up for all the hell I suffered—justice and love forever." The latter was actually said as a rambling, free association in a joking mood, but very seriously represented her Grand Illusion. While the Grand Illusion can be tackled with some success head-on, serious dilution of it, let alone neutralization, is only possible with destruction of its many component illusions. I've listed the principal ones I've come across in myself and patients, but, of course, there is almost no end to human ingenuity and therefore there are many more illusions of a highly individual quality invented by all of us.

Delusion, to me, is a clinical term representing a state in which an almost complete surrender to an illusionary world of unreality has taken place. Here, the victim sometimes feels that in his illusionary world, his Grand Illusion, has indeed been fulfilled and he is no longer pressured by problems and limitations characteristic of ordinary people. Of course, delusions of grandeur, of being God, of being magically imbued with special extraterritorial powers are a function of extremely intense self-hate and a compensatory mechanism. Delusions involving persecution obviously are projections of intense self-hate. The latter are characteristic of psychotic states, in which the victim escapes to unreal worlds, feeling the human condition as he encounters it to be intolerably demeaning and painful.

IMPOSSIBLE STANDARDS, UNREALISTIC GOALS, EXORBITANT EXPECTATIONS

Impossible standards, unrealistic goals and exorbitant expectations are intimately linked to each other and to illusions, so that they are often impossible to separate and to differentiate. They also give birth to each other with great rapidity and profusion, filling the unconscious with considerable neurotic confusion and readily spilling over into conscious life, disturbing function in all areas, especially in how we relate to ourselves and to other people.

Illusions regarding self give birth to impossible demands on *ourselves*—unrealistic and cruel standards and goals. Illusions regarding other people, the human condition and the world at large produce exorbitant expectations of *others*. These transitions—from illusions to standards, goals and expectations and back to illusions again—are subtle and imperceptible. But the web of self-hate they weave around a person is anything but ethereal. Its tenacity and influence are overwhelming.

Illusions are loaded with emotional energy whose shock waves reverberate through the entire personality and character structure of the individual and his relationships with others. If a woman has the illusion of the perfect world that perfect love would bring, this must produce a standard for love that is nothing short of "perfect." It also motivates her to seek that goal through the attempt to be a perfectly loving and lovable saintlike creature. If the illusion extends to the wonders a perfectly loving partner can produce, as it surely will, then her expectation of her lover will be nothing short of perfect, all giving, all self-sacrificing and pure in his love.

The illusion of perfect justice leads to expectation of

utter fairness. Illusions regarding parenthood affect goals for self and expectations from children. These combined standards, goals and expectations produce a grossly aberrated view of reality. This, too, must affect function. The man with the money illusion sees and feels the world largely in terms of economic life, and as a consequence closes off his options to live a full social, cultural, emotional and intellectual life as well. He stunts his own development and evolvement and functions only as a partial person. The same is true of any of us who are flooded by the self-hate of illusory matter. The love victim is just as constricted and must, of necessity, also have a lopsided development and a lopsided view of life. Not only do many areas of self remain undeveloped and anesthetized but the world also seems terribly simplistic, since large aspects of it aren't seen at all and are simply blotted out.

The ultimate consequences of this kind of blotting out and of the combined forces of these indirect self-hating mechanisms is to produce an aura of impoverishment and shoddiness. The victim feels a continuing sense of deep deprivation and personal impoverishment. No matter what success or realistic fulfillment he achieves, he retains a sense of foreboding and the feeling of "being really poor inside, no matter what." He comes to see the world as bright and shiny only in flash moments of seeming illusory fulfillment. For the rest of the time, and this comprises nearly all of the time of his life, flash brilliance gives way to gray, shoddy impoverishment. The world seems dull and cruel as he plods on in search of sustained shiny lights. In relation to his unreal standards and goals, common, pleasant and enjoyable possibilities turn to dark, tortured insults.

In some forms of self-hate, constantly shifting and

changing goals are used by us as an instrument of torture. I had a patient who wanted to be a doctor until the week of graduation from medical school when "I realized I really wanted to be a journalist." What he did *not* realize was that he asked me in our first interview, "Why is it that everything I ever attain turns to absolute garbage? It seems great until I get it and then it turns to nothing at all." He didn't realize for a long time that he had been using shifting goals as a key process in his behavior for years. This was the prime method he used to drive himself on and away from himself, and away from the possibility of giving himself decent, human satisfaction. This was how he acted out his self-hate. He set goals that were achievable and then decided that they were the "wrong" goals after all.

Since this man was permeated with self-hate in just about all areas, his self-esteem was almost negligible. Therefore, any achievement or goal fulfillment on his part had to be seen as worthless. How could a worthless person achieve a worthy goal? Interestingly, he was only attracted to women who rejected him because, here again, any woman who cared for him and respected him must have been a fool indeed for being blind to his worthlessness.

In his perverse and destructive way he most respected people who were contemptuous of him. Somehow they always "knew the score." Since I realistically did see much merit in him, and I'm not sadistic, this posed a problem initially. I got around it by showing respect for who he really was and contempt for his self-hating stratagems. My contempt sustained him until he was ready to accept my respect.

Exorbitant expectations are destructive in several ways. Expectation of the self-hating variety, born of illusion, usually takes on a malignant anticipatory mantle. This means that the individual gives up *here-and-now* living for promises of illusory living in the future. His present, his here and now, is held cheaply and is seen and felt as having no importance except as link to an expected future which never arrives. He keeps waiting for the "Great Beginning," a term I heard used by a patient, which never begins at all. Each new *NOW* is discarded for a future *NOW* which is also discarded in favor of a life of anticipated beauty and wonder which never arrives. How can it?

The anticipations and expectations involve people and a human condition and world that are simply alien on this planet and utterly unattainable. Life continues to be tough. People look out for their own needs. Justice continues to be an imperfect expedient. Children grow up to have more in common with friends than they do with parents, and care more for their mates and their children than they do for parents. Friends are friends, meaning they are not 100 per cent loyal. Mates are not completely tuned in, understanding and self-sacrificing. People do get sick, age and die.

Exorbitant expectations involve a different kind of world entirely, a world of just desert in which everyone lives happily ever after. Sacrifice of the real world and the moderate rewards it offers for a millennium which never arrives is destructive enough to actual self in the actual world to bring on terrible attacks of self-hate, often in the form of serious depression. This process is bolstered as daily disappointments born of impossible expectations destroy constructive relationships and life situations that could lead to relative happiness.

If expectations are malignant enough, life as it is lived in the here and now becomes at best a gross insult and is felt as a totally unfair and undeserved onslaught on oneself. This leads to a continued state of feeling abused by an uncaring world, to feeling that others live an extravagantly better life, and to the belief that the real fault lies deep within and is connected to a kind of mysterious, sinful, personal flaw.

I have seen patients who have deluded themselves into believing that superficial "mistakes" of the past, and petty transgressions of no real consequence, in some mysterious way deprived them of realizing their expectations. They were unwilling to surrender this form of self-hate and preferred to think that some kind of "inner correction" would bring them, too, into Shangri-la after all. Since this is all illusion and delusion, disappointment and frustration continue unabated. This, combined with real impoverishment due to lack of involvement in the real world, and lack of satisfaction from what the world can in fact deliver to actual self, produces serious emotional starvation and painful feelings of emptiness, deadness and rage. This rage, largely a function of frustration and envy of others who seem to be able to enjoy simple bread-and-butter happiness, is thrust out at other people and at the world at large. It is mainly directed at the human condition generally, which is felt to be a fraudulent, duplicitous thief.

In terms of illusion and expectation, the victim has no problem constructing a logical argument to substantiate his belief and to justify his rage. But even as this goes on he still believes that failure is due largely to himself. "I'm just not good enough"; "I have to try harder"; "If I had lived my life differently"; and on and on it goes. This results in the major part of his rage being turned on himself, producing a bombardment from his direct self-hating devices, the sum total of which invokes a state of deep despair.

BOREDOM

I include boredom at this juncture because to me it represents a transitional form between direct and indirect self-hate. Most important, though, it definitely is a form of self-hate even though it is seldom perceived as such by its victims. Most of us feel boredom as a state of mind which is visited upon us by outside conditions. This is pure projection and is simply not the case. *Boredom is never imposed upon us by people or conditions outside of ourselves.* The following is a typical statement reflecting this belief: "Sure I'm bored, I have no money to really go out and do something I'd like. If I had money I wouldn't be bored for a minute." The patient who made this statement eventually did have money, and to her having money meant a great deal of money, and she was more bored than ever. Money simply had nothing to do with it. She was bored because she imposed a state of boredom on herself, and in this regard there is a direct self-hating quality to it. But the elusive *feeling* of boredom as self-hate makes it indirect.

In any case, boredom involves deliberate, usually unconscious, neglect and rejection of nondeveloped and yearning aspects of ourselves. Wanting the impossible and producing starvation by refusing what is possible is the substance of boredom. How did this woman achieve this state? She did so by refusing to nurture unrequited aspects of herself. Boredom simply cannot exist when we are actively engaged in the process of continuing growth through recognition and development of real resources in ourselves. But for this to take place self-respect is necessary. This means all aspects of self. Boredom represents rejection of one's proclivities and possibilities. It stems from neglect of real resources.

I saw a retired, wealthy man in consultation recently whose chief complaint was boredom. He described his current life as sitting around and doing nothing. During the course of our conversation, he recalled being interested in ichthyology as a boy. He then went on to recall a number of scholarly interests. During the course of his life he had pursued none of them. Business and making money became the central issue of his existence. He realized and revealed both to me and to himself the fact that "as a boy he had been embarrassed to be interested in such flimsy, esoteric nonsense." This embarrassment eventually grew to contempt and produced utter rejection and hate of those aspects of himself that he considered "esoteric" and not practical enough for recognition or pursuit.

We did not engage in a full and lengthy analysis. Our several sessions together were spent exploring and evaluating aspects of himself and early interests which had been despised, neglected and negated in the service of hate of actual self. It was not difficult for him to realize that there was nothing embarrassing about scholarly pursuits.

First, I had to help him not to be contemptuous about his early embarrassment and to have compassion for the young man he had been. This was easy. It was more difficult to convince him that those early interests were still alive in him and could even be brought to flowering passion. As we spoke it became apparent to me that the man had been yearning to realize these aspects of himself for years. In fact, it had taken great effort, time, energy and diversionary maneuvers on his part to subvert them almost, but not quite completely, out of his consciousness. He was really sick and tired and bored with his self-imposed, narrowly constructed starvation diet. He finally became convinced that a man of his age deserved scholarly nourishment at least as much as a young man.

The third and most difficult notion to combat was the question of involvement in activity which had little or nothing to do with money. Due to this man's background, full involvement in promoting apathy and doing nothing was acceptable, since this represented the dubious reward for having achieved financial success. But serious work without remuneration made him feel like a "damned fool." We explored his resistance to change for several weeks and found out that "feeling like a fool" was really a form of feeling guilty for nourishing his self, for daring to do something purely for self-delight, without the rationalization of doing it in order to earn money. Of course, the production of guilt in this instance as in all others is a very direct and destructive form of self-hate. We were able to clarify this issue and to stand up to the self-hating mechanism involved.

In the final weeks of a relatively short treatment course he was able to give himself what he really had wanted for years, simply because he wanted it. He became a serious student of ichthyology and pursued his studies with enough fascination and vigor to preclude any possibility of boredom. When we are in a state of development and are evolving and using our human assets and resources, the self-hating process, in which we refuse to give ourselves adequate emotional sustenance, resulting in emotional doldrums, simply cannot exist.

POLARIZATION AND SUPERLATIVES

Karen Horney long ago recognized that the black-and-white approach to life and to perceptions of reality is a neurotic manifestation. I want to emphasize that the use of superlatives and the view of life's issues as existing at widely separate poles is *more* than aberrated reality. This kind of viewpoint is a very definite form of self-hate.

The greatest, the best, the worst, the finest, absolutely right, absolutely wrong, all contribute to a world and to a sense of self which does not exist and which is, therefore, antithetical to the well-being of actual self in the actual world. But more than that, it contributes to standards which cannot be met, provides competiton which serves as a merciless goad, and is a major tool in constructing an inner world in which reality feels shoddy and worthless.

Having to be the greatest keeps us in a state of ruthless pursuit of the impossible. Having to be absolutely right makes us feel absolutely wrong most of the time. Polarizing people and issues into absolutely good and absolutely bad categories leads to grossly simplistic views of people and issues as well as to confusion, disappointment and attacks of direct self-hate. Refusing to accept the complexity of the human condition and its many shades and paradoxes precludes self-acceptance and acceptance of reality. People are not good or bad, clever or stupid, the most marvelous or the most horrendous, the most boring or the most fascinating, or the most cowardly or the most courageous. We are not mosts, bests, rights, wrongs. We represent vast admixtures of all characteristics. Each of us contains shades and evidences of all aspects of the human condition in all its diversity, and this is true of all institutions and endeavors devised by humankind too.

The human condition and human relationships are characterized by many contiguous incongruities. A man of high intelligence has blind spots a man of minor intelligence may be incapable of. A sadistic man may be capable of acts of significant kindness. An ugly woman may at times be beautiful, and on it goes. To be driven toward a personal condition involving any polarized superlative virtue or set of virtues, or toward a world of superlative *anythings*, or toward superlative relationships is itself self-hate and a guarantee of even more self-hate. It means going against the very substance of being human.

I had one patient who suffered from what I call "attacks of instant love" and "attacks of instant hate." This applied to people, ideas, ventures and propositions of all kinds. Of course, he was in constant difficulty with himself and others. His wife called him "the overboard man." He was always going overboard for someone or something. When I hear a patient say, "I just met the most marvelous man," or "I just got the most marvelous job," or "The neighborhood is perfect, absolutely perfect," or "I can't stand him, he's the absolute worst," I know that recrimination and depression aren't far off. I know that aberration of a view of self, distorted expectations of others, exaggerated competition and self-goading to unrealistic goals are already well in motion. Of course, this kind of viewpoint does not come into being, nor is it sustained, on its own.

My patient, "the overboard man," revealed in analysis that his instant judgments (and subsequent disappointments and recriminations) were part of an intense craving to find and to structure an ideal world of ideal people where he, too, would be ideal, special and specially cherished and safe. But this concept kept him in a state of turmoil sufficient to deprive him of what little realistic security our real world offers and the moderate but very real pleasures and satisfactions that are attainable in relative abundance.

SELF-HATE AS A WAY OF LIFE

Self-hate without activation and the heroic intervention of compassion *is* a way of life. This is so despite the fact that at least some compassion is active in all of us. If compassion is utterly lacking, life is untenable. We simply could not go on. All neurotic manifestations are in fact incarnations of self-hate. These include all those I've described plus countless other symtoms and self-destructive mechanisms:

- Compartmentalization, in which we keep different aspects of our lives separate as if we are separate people and only let parts of ourselves in on other parts of ourselves
- Fragmentation, in which we function as separate autonomous parts
- Inappropriate and excessive repression, in which we put down and out of consciousness our very own feelings, ideas and thoughts
- Deadening, in which we anesthetize ourselves
- Resigning, in which we pull out of involvement with life in its various manifestations

These and many others, including hysterical and psychotic manifestations in which reality is denied and aberrated as much as possible, are all forms of self-hate. While these mechanisms may have their earliest origins as attempts to cope with anxiety, they eventually, like

Frankenstein's monster, become the source of enormously exaggerated anxiety and misery in themselves.

The total fabric comprising self-hate is a way of life that tolerates no interference or dilution. It is despotic and dictatorial. Its attempt is to establish complete autonomy and control over all aspects of an individual's life, including his view of himself, what life as a human being is all about, his opinions in all matters, and his relationships with others. This results in many misconceptions and unreal simplistic notions full of wish-fulfillment fantasies having little or no relationship to the real world. In turn, this feeds the process of stultifying actual self, so that emotional paralysis takes place, further cutting off the possibility of knowing what it is to be a person and what can be realistically expected and enjoyed.

This automatic, autonomous, malignant process deprives us of the possibility of developing a psychophilosophy which strengthens us so as to be better able both to enjoy life here and now and to face the inevitable adversity we all meet from time to time and must be ready to handle. There is no question that the self-hating autonomy is a totalitarian slave master.

We can't escape our feelings and thoughts through linear motion, geographical change, new relationships or change of activity. Change can only take place through inner struggle. Without it, we remain small, starving children crying for impossible gourmet delights while we refuse to give ourselves readily available sustenance. Of course, resistance to change is enormous. Identification with self-hate makes us feel that little else exists in us. Without it, we fear a state of paralysis. "Won't the horse stop running if we don't flog it?" "Won't I go wild without a powerful conscience?" We are not horses and we won't go wild, and we can trust to both human spontaneity and good human judgment. Indeed, horrendous human acts are never the result of compassion, but always outgrowths of self-hating, overwhelming, castigating consciences. But the struggle to change for the better is very difficult.

Giving up a way of life is like giving up one's identity, and produces cataclysmic and very painful repercussions. This is especially so because self-hate as a way of life is also like a house of cards. As well entrenched and as all-permeating as it is, it is at best an artifact, a contrivance, and within its very core it contains the fragility characteristic of artifice. Therefore, any attack upon its structure is viewed with appropriate fear and abhorrence, and like all bullies under fire, a great show will be made, consisting of all kinds of terroristic maneuvers. However, following serious engagement in the struggle, people almost never fail to be surprised at the results. Despite our initial tendency to cling to self-hate as a way of life and despite initial terror and pain, the process once begun is a relatively rapid one. *This is so because both the direct intervention of concrete compassionate steps and the application of the compassionate philosophy to the intrapsychic life of the individual is in keeping with the healthy and natural human condition.* The fact is that we would like to be what we *really* are. We are hungry for reality *and only the compassionate way of life can give it to us.*

PART III

Compassion

Compassion in Process

Compassion is the only antidote to self-hate and the only human prerogative and alternative to neurotic despair.

Compassion is any and all thoughts, feelings, moods, insights and actions that serve the interest of actual self. These include all functions that protect, sustain and enhance actual self. These also include all functions which in any way diminish and destroy self-hate and which result in increased self-acceptance leading to greater self-esteem. Self-acceptance, here, refers to all aspects of self: feelings, thoughts, ideas, moods, insights, impulses, decisions and actions, without censorship, judgment value or moral equivocation.

Compassion is enhanced wherever and whenever consciousness displaces repression and unconsciousness and reality replace unreality.

Compassion, as with all other human entities, can only exist on a relative basis, but the battle for compassion is the most life-affirming endeavor of all.

Compassion is, ultimately, a state of mind in which benevolence reigns supreme and in which a state of grace is established with ourselves. This state of grace is antithetical to the promotion of self-hate. In this state of grace loyalty to self, in all circumstances whatsoever, is of prime importance in the human hierarchy of values. Being responsible for ourselves and taking good care of ourselves without guilt or other forms of self-hate take precedence over all other activities.

I have found that human efforts, struggles and insights (and I include psychoanalytic insights) are at best intellectual, superficial and of minimal value without compassion. At worst, they become perverted and used in the service of self-hate and misery. In a self-saving state of human grace, insight and struggle results in a gut response, understanding reaches a feeling level and activates the healthy growth of actual self. *Relative psychic peace can only exist in a compassionate emotional climate.* The stuff of humanity requires emotional nourishment and this is born of the struggle to be compassionate with ourselves against all inner and outside forces that dictate otherwise.

Origins of Compassion

I believe that it is the natural impulse and pattern of humankind to be relatively compassionate to ourselves and to others. When we act otherwise, it is only because we have somehow been subject to forces and pressures destructive to our natural tendencies. A human infant is born with a great capacity to like and to get along fairly well with himself. It takes considerable effort to divert him from his natural affinity for a compassionate life. People are not born prejudiced. As the song goes, "You have to be taught to hate," and this applies at least as much to self as to others.

The lessons learned in the developing, evolving child are crucial. As children we have little ability or experience to dilute or to fend off what we learn. Therefore, we are extremely sensitive, vulnerable and impressionable. That which is learned during childhood—our period of maximum flexibility and development—becomes part and parcel of our very substance and is never forgotten. Our memories of specific childhood *incidents* are not nearly as important as our *feelings* about those incidents and the attitudes and moods that grow out of those feelings.

The lesson of compassion is best learned in a compassionate household. This is one in which each individual is relatively compassionate to himself, invariably leading to compassion among the family members also. A child in a compassionate family will always perceive that his mother takes good care of herself with joy rather than with guilty repercussions that reverberate throughout the family. He will always register the fact that his father and his siblings are capable of a "good time" without self-recrimination or recrimination from other members of the family. He notes that feelings and expression of feelings, including less than purely altruistic ones (jealousy, envy, anger), but especially pleasurable ones, are characteristically accepted and praised in a household that respects and loves the human condition. He registers the fact that reality, including problems and human limitations, are accepted and even cherished rather than abhorred, diluted, and denied by flights of saintlike, illusional and even delusional fancy. In this household, a child perceives that while people care for themselves and each other, they can make decisions and reasonable moves, even those involving risk, without fear of self-hate or mutual recrimination should failure ensue.

A child incorporates into his very substance the experience of being cared for and cherished with respect and dignity, and without the stifling and really contemptuous effects of overprotection. If a child is respected and cherished for his own separate identity and individual needs and proclivities, he cannot fail to learn this lesson and to apply it in the service of compassion. The compassionate child has been encouraged to explore and to experiment commensurate with his experience and ability, without fear of recriminations for mistakes. He learns through encouragement, explanation and emotional support rather than through punishment and reward. He learns that human existence is tough and full of imponderables, uncontrollables, confusions and mortal limitations.

He learns that there is value and joy in everyday bread-and-butter existence, but that there is pain, too, and, not being Godlike, he is and always will be the recipient of both. In his family the happiness of daily living is not sacrificed for mythical future visions of Heaven. Feeling comfortable with oneself and just feeling good are considered of much greater value than rare highs and peak experiences.

Compassion does not exist in absolute form any more than any other human entity. Those of us who come from backgrounds in which our own natural compassionate substance was not distorted to any great degree are fortunate indeed. *But since human beings are inherently compassionate, compassion in them can be awakened and generated whatever their age and however horrendous their past experiences have been.*

Generating Compassion

Compassion, however dormant, can be vitalized, generated and sustained if motivation is adequate. Motivation is dependent on knowledge of the destructive influence of self-hate; on knowing that misery brings no rewards; on knowing that abject resignation and surrender to self-hate have taken place but need not continue to be a way of life; on knowledge of the constructive value of compassion and the fact that compassion can indeed be generated to the point of becoming a psychophilosophical way of life.

Most people, without full conscious awareness, have capitulated and surrendered to self-hate. The surrender has usually been so thorough and of such long standing that the combined self-hating modalities represent a way of life and are not perceived as self-hate at all. This includes even the most blatant forms of direct self-hate. The fact that fighting back is possible and that even victory is possible eludes most of us completely.

I remember one patient, Tim, who suffered from severe attacks of obsessive ruminating that would go on for hours, often preventing him from useful, let alone pleasurable, functioning. He told me that in all the years that this had gone on it never really occurred to him that he might try to arrest this process in an effort to stop the self-torture and to be compassionate to himself. Tim capitulated each and

144

every time and had no memory at all of ever attempting to do otherwise. Initial attempts at compassionate maneuvers or even thoughts of these possibilities can generate hope, but usually also bring on much anxiety and even terror. The well-ingrained self-hating autonomy does not simply roll over and die. It clings to life tenaciously and responds to threat with infliction of increasingly painful stratagems. My patient was so terrified of even worse retaliation from the self-hating part of himself that he never even theorized that the possibility existed.

He came to me "to feel better," to "function better," but not to rid himself of torturing ruminations. Interestingly, he didn't even tell me about them until we had seen each other for several months. Tim would not have revealed the process even then, but during several of our sessions I realized that he was terribly preoccupied and almost nonresponsive to what we were talking about, so I insisted on knowing what was going on. Fortunately, it did not take him long to realize that the substance of his ruminations had little importance or relevance.

The ruminating process itself was all-important as a function of self-hate and self-castigation. The thought, only the thought, of fighting this process was an enormous revelation, which at one and the same time filled him with hope and with dread. He almost immediately had dreams which combined symbols of warm, happy freedom and the infliction of terrible, dark, torturous processes. He was afraid "to feel too good," but didn't understand why. Of course, sustained "feeling good" without the leash of painful ruminations was unfamiliar enough to make him feel "like I'm another person." While this feeling eventually brings comfort and pleasure, it initially threatens one's sense of identity and may produce a great deal of anxiety.

This, coupled with repeated attacks by a now shaky self-hate system, produced anxiety bordering on panic.

My patient terrorized himself with awful waking thoughts and fantasies and terrible nightmares. But he stuck in the fight and these self-terrorizing attacks subsided with relative rapidity. Eventually, he was amazed that he actually could stand up to self-hating attacks, let alone obliterate them.

The process, once initiated, eventually gets easier. This is so because, as I explained earlier, the self-hating process is in the first place an artificial support. It is designed to cope with threatening, insecure surroundings born of an anxiety-producing family and culture. This kind of unnatural process requires enormous time, energy and dedication for its sustenance. Any depletion of energy immediately weakens the process because the human organism's natural proclivity is toward compassion and health. That which is natural makes immediate and maximum use of any effort at all made in its behalf. Unfortunately, in neurotic life, we find too often that minimum and nearly no energy at all is expended in the direction of health.

My patient characteristically felt that he would stop functioning entirely without the goad of self-hate. "Don't I need discipline?" "Don't people need a strong conscience?" "Without it won't I just stop doing things?" "Aren't you asking me to be selfish?"

People's "consciences" are almost always much too strong. We need freedom and the renewed ability to be spontaneous. The basic good of people and of human substance is a much better guarantee of satisfying behavior both in terms of self and society than the unrequited yearnings and frustrations produced by self-hate. Freedom "to be" invariably produces more constructive behavior than any kind of tyranny, either internal or external in origin.

My patient learned by example, through me and newfound relationships with others, and through insights generally, that he could trust himself "without my personal Nazi guards," that pleasure and "time taken off from ruminating and trying to be pure" was not wasted. He learned that he could stop self-inflicted punishment; that the primitive reward, punishment, pain and pleasure principles of learning were not nearly as effective or constructive as compassionate learning that takes place through emotional support and insight. He learned that self-saving, self-caring and self-support invariably make for better and less "selfish" relationships with others.

With Tim, and with many of us, it is helpful to look about and to look back at how we and other people relate to each other. We will almost invariably come to realize how much more compassionate we are to other people than we are to ourselves and how much more compassionate many other people are to us than they are to themselves. Usually it is not difficult to recall examples of "forgiveness" for mistakes among people as contrasted to long-standing self-vindictive punishment for "lists of personal crimes." More often than not, the problem does not involve, "Do unto others as you would have others do unto you," but rather: *Treat yourself at least as well as you treat other people!*

I knew that we were more than halfway home when Tim one day told me that he dreamed of "blossoming trees and a man who stepped into daylight from a dark dungeon." He said that waking up, in half sleep, he felt "there was something, someone, I was trying to find, to hold on to—I nearly had him but not quite—but I knew I would." "Something" and "someone" turned out to be himself, his actual self, and in the months ahead he became increasingly loyal to himself and compassionate in his battle against self-hate.

Forms of Compassion:
The Direct Way

Direct compassion consists of direct moves we make against direct self-hate in the service of actual self. Destroying the soldiers and guards inevitably causes havoc to the indirect self-hating hierarchy and weakens the entire self-hating structure.

There are three crucial steps and moves that make up direct compassion: *Recognition, Blocking* and *Surrender of Special Status.*

1. The self-hating mechanism must be recognized for what it is. The sooner recognition of any thought, feeling or activity as self-hate takes place, the more effective it is possible to be. The self-hating process usually produces characteristic maneuvers in each of us. With experience, these assaults become more easily discernible as self-hate. But since human beings are exceedingly clever in their efforts to maintain a neurotic status quo, switching to unfamiliar and increasingly sneaky and more subtle self-hating mechanisms usually take place under fire. Thus, a person who constantly uses recriminations and second-guessing to flagellate herself, and who readily diagnoses the latter as self-hate, may switch to psychosomatic manifestations or to the increased use of projections. People who have long suffered from a particular psychosomatic symptom may switch to another physical manifesta-

tion or to a phobia. In any case, *diagnosis of self-hate as self-hate is of prime importance,* since this step is an absolute prerequisite to going further.

I had one patient, Sally, whose principal self-hating device consisted of developing demeaning relationships in which she compulsively gave gratuitous information that the other party unfailingly eventually used against her. As Sally recognized, blocked, and virtually neutralized this mechanism, she switched to enormous overeating which produced serious gall bladder attacks and considerable obesity. Overcoming these self-hating mechanisms, she then went on to develop hyperventilating asthmalike attacks and asked, "Surely this, too, isn't self-hate?" But it was self-hate, and so were many other subtle manifestations she developed over the years. "I was feeling perfectly fine, really in a good mood. I don't know why but I suddenly felt like calling my Aunt Sarah, whom I hadn't talked to in months. You know, she's the one who never fails to remind me of all the family tragedy we've ever had. Sure enough, by the time I hung up the phone I felt wrung out. I could hardly breathe. My whole mood had changed. I really felt depressed."

Obviously, Sally did not recognize the urge to call her Aunt Sarah as the precursor to a self-hating move. She certainly did not recognize "feeling good" as a mood she deserved and should have cherished and protected. She did not recognize "feeling good" as a red flag and potential precursor to a self-hating attack. Because had the diagnosis been made in time, and "in time" could have been in anticipation of what would follow (she had ample past experience with depression following conversations with Aunt Sarah), she could compassionately have blocked her self-hate, compassionately preserved her good mood, and compassionately taken better care of herself.

I was fortunate that Sally did not use each discovery and recognition of "new self-hating devices" as a reason to hate herself still more. As I pointed out earlier, in the section on self-hate, hating oneself for hating oneself makes perpetuation of self-hate a certainty. It is one of the main blocks to diagnosis, since the victim rightly fears that each diagnosis will lead to a renewed recriminating onslaught. The individual gets anxious about being anxious, and depressed about being depressed, effecting a self-destructive snowballing and vicious cycle. Primary anxiety and depression, without this snowballing effect, are nearly always tolerable, however painful they may be. If this fear remains unconscious, the first crucial step, recognition of self-hate, may never take place at all. The victim will say, "Somehow I'm just not able to recognize that I'm doing it again until I've done a thorough job on myself."

The same is particularly true of people in whom a major cornerstone of neurosis consists of seeking glory through martyrdom and suffering. The psychoanalyst who recognizes the importance of establishing compassion must uncover these dynamics and make his patient aware of them if insights are ever to reach more than an intellectual level. The patient, in turn, must make a solemn promise to protect himself from self-hating aspects of himself, and this pertains particularly to hate engendered by the discovery of hate, as well as by the temptation to seek Heaven through martyrdom.

Sally and I eventually discovered that throughout her life two "peculiar symptoms" occurred whenever she was just about to become depressed. They would get worse and appear with increasing regularity a few weeks prior to depression. These were just like the early warning symptoms that signal onset of certain physical illnesses, such as sneezing before measles. Just prior to depression, Sally would misplace and lose things, and this included all kinds of valued objects. She would also spill food on herself "accidentally," especially on her most cherished and valued clothes. She eventually remembered a third warning symptom, or "announcement of depression coming in," as she called it. Normally a punctual person, she would come late to important appointments, antagonizing people, and in the process even losing several business deals. Recogniton of these symptoms as self-hate when they occurred might have been extremely valuable in preventing depression. In any case, Sally did eventually recognize these and other self-hating manifestations for what they were. She also, on a deep gut level, came to realize that they didn't just descend upon her. She, in fact, generated them and only she could block and stop them.

Arrogance, aggression, sadism, vindictiveness and pretense are always evidence of self-hate in ourselves. Knowing this provides a very valuable diagnostic tool. If we have just experienced an attack of vindictive rage against another person, this is proof positive that self-hate in ourselves has somehow been stirred up.

Pretentious behavior is a cover-up of actual self due to distrust and embarrassment involving actual self. If we take on "airs" and pretend to be other than who we actually are, it is because we hate who we are and feel certain that other people will hate us also.

Arrogance is certain proof of underlying insecurity, connected to feelings of unworthiness and fear of being found out. Aggression, sadism and vindictiveness are functions of feeling inner weakness, depletion and deadness. They are compensatory mechanisms designed to provide momentary feelings of synthetic power in order to relieve feelings of helplessness and impotence.

Any one of us who is open to the possibility of self-discovery and to embracing a compassionate life-style usually has little difficulty diagnosing and recognizing self-hate in its various manifestations.

This initial step of recognition is the most important one we can take in destroying direct self-hate. This is so for two reasons. Obviously, recognition of self-hate makes blocking and obliterating its roots a real possibility. But the second reason is even more important. Self-hate is like a foreign body in the eye or in the bloodstream, in which the natural physiological response is to reject and to extrude it. But unlike a physical foreign body, emotional abrasives cannot be defended against or rejected unless they are recognized and felt for what they are.

People often ask why simple revelation in analysis, that is, the simple business of finding out what is wrong, is so effective. Of course, struggle beyond revelation is necessary for solution to major emotional problems, but revelation in itself is an exceedingly powerful therapeutic tool. This is also true in many areas of medicine practiced on a physiological basis. The person who suffers from severe allergic responses is a total victim until he knows what it is he is allergic to. Knowledge of the allergen is no small matter, but represents a major solution to his problem. Knowing that his symptoms are due to allergy and then knowing what the allergen is make the rest of the battle, avoiding the allergen, a relatively easy matter. The same is largely true of emotional pain, too.

Knowing that pain comes from self-hate, knowing that one is actually despising oneself and inflicting hatred and pain on to oneself in a destructive way, is very valuable. Recognizing and diagnosing the ways this is done, coupled with a desire to be rid of despair, immediately start a crucial therapeutic process in motion. This is what occurs in psychoanalysis. This is the great value and power of the psychoanalytic process, in which unconscious destructive patterns and forces are revealed to the analysand in their true colors. This kind of revelation is the most powerful force in breaking through the paralyzing inertia characteristic of the entire process of contrived, wooden, self-hating living.

Following diagnosis and recognition, the next, second, or middle, step is *blocking*. To ignore self-hate following recognition, and to permit it to go on unabetted, is like trying to ignore a diagnosed case of cancer. Cutting off self-hate in whatever form it manifests itself is immediately ameliorative. This is true regardless of whatever form or method is used to dilute and to block the self-hating mechanism. If "bad memories" provide a fund for self-hating sustenance, then refusal to call painful incidents to mind can be an effective way to starve self-hate. If remembering pleasant and enjoyable incidents floods the mind with sensations of self-worth, then this, too, is a method of narrowing the stage for self-hate to play and feed.

Using a self-hating form of blocking, in an attempt to eliminate self-hate, is in itself a form of self-hate and constitutes what I call pseudoblocking. I had a patient who threatened to kill herself each time she became depressed. Another man beat his fists into bloody pulps to prevent obsessive ruminating recriminations. These are forms of blackmail and punishment and do not constitute *compassionate blocking*.

My depressed patient eventually learned that her depression was always linked to personal dissatisfaction with herself, to seeming "failures." She became aware that to block depression successfully she must realize first that she was depressing and putting down angry feelings and thoughts about herself and others. Blocking here largely consisted of permitting these feelings to surface so that she could cope with them on an open, natural level where she could exert much more control. She eventually also learned that her self-hate was connected to impossible standards, which required considerable reduction to realistic human levels and possibilities.

My patient who recriminated found that he could block his recriminations by engaging in either hard, mindless, physical activity or intellectual activity utterly removed from the substance of his recriminations, but totally involving. Step two, or the blocking of self-hate, is intricately linked to step three: giving up a false image of superhuman standards for oneself invariably leads to permanent blocking of onslaughts of direct self-hate.

Any stand against self-hate is invariably more effective when recognition, diagnosis and intervention take place early. Self-hate, especially of the recriminating variety, has a kind of conditioned-reflex autonomy that makes for a moving inertia that is harder and harder to block as it gathers energy to itself, steam-rolling everything in its path. Instant discovery and absolute blockage of any self-hating mechanism at its very inception is most effective. If one learns to control self-hate, it is possible to learn to block it in advance any time it starts to take over. For example, if you learn from previous experience that seeing certain people when you feel particularly vulnerable will be followed by self-deprecation and a bad mood, you simply block by not seeing those people at those times, whenever possible.

I had a patient who had been through a devastating love affair and who for a long time diligently avoided films, plays and books which depicted idealized love relationships, having learned that these filled her with self-recriminations which she could not yet control. This does not constitute avoidance of reality or denial of a problem. It simply, but very importantly, provides pain-free time in which to gather strength for constructive purpose.

I remember a period of time during which I felt particularly vulnerable. I studiously avoided news programs that were especially full of horror then because they demoralized me still further. Again, this is not sticking one's head in the sand ostrichlike. It is effecting a block to self-hate, and this or any other kind of block, especially of an early and even anticipatory nature, is a definite form of compassion and constructive caring for self.

It is also a block to self-hate to call a friend who has an uplifting effect on a drooping morale, or to seek distraction or help of any constructive kind, and generally to do for oneself whatever is possible to obliterate the self-hating dynamism as soon as even an inclination in its direction arises.

A patient of mine recently described going to Paris with her employer and his wife. All three are part of a clothing manufacturing concern, and they go to Paris periodically to look over styles and fashions. On the second night after their arrival, the three of them were to go to an elegant fashion party given by one of France's famous couturiers. While dressing for the party, my patient suddenly found herself thinking about the fact that she wouldn't have her own escort that evening. She immediately intervened before the self-hating process took hold. She knew from previous experience that this thought was designed to spoil her evening and that it contained the potential to destroy her entire stay in Paris. She had considerable previous experience with self-hate and fortunately also with involvement and enhancement of the compassionate way of life.

In the past this thought, lacking compassionate intervention, interference and blocking, would have led to thoughts involving severe self-criticism about her looks and dress (despite the fact that she was considered stunning by her confreres), "past mistakes in love affairs," the wisdom of being on the trip at all. Instead, she looked in the mirror, looked herself in the eye and said in a loud voice, "Mary, knock it off! Knock it off here and now! You are going to have a good time this evening and nothing, absolutely nothing is going to stop you!" She did have a good time, and her stay in Paris was fruitful both in terms of business and personal pleasure.

Another patient of mine was given to huge self-hating eating binges. When I first started to see him he weighed close to four hundred pounds. He was five feet eight. Each eating binge was followed by intense self-recrimination, which invariably led to depression and to another eating binge. Eventually, he came to realize that in the compassionate hierarchy of importance and in terms of the anti-self-hate process, dieting would be compassionate; to stop an eating binge after it had begun and to enjoy the food that had already been eaten was compassionate, too. To go through an entire eating binge, enjoy the food, and to block past recriminations also had elements of compassion and could permit control in the future to take place, since his moral was not weakened by recriminating self-hate. To eat, hate the food and himself as he ate, and to hate himself after he ate was lacking in compassion and guaranteed perpetuation of the destructive process.

The patient, Charles, started gradually to work through this compassionate hierarchy. From permitting himself to enjoy the food he ate, even during a binge, he stopped recriminating after a binge and eventually was able to interrupt a binge shortly after it had begun. In time, Charles was able to connect his eating to events leading to self-hate and to self-hating feelings generally, and control became possible. He was able to diet in order to save his life, which he began to view as worth saving.

Step three in direct compassion—*surrender of a false image that imbues one with special status or privileged position*—cannot take place in the middle of a self-hating storm. Therefore, steps one and two, and especially two—*blocking*—must take place in order to proceed to this vital end phase of direct compassion. This end phase, in turn, enormously enhances the first two steps and the entire, direct compassionate process. To help in detection, it is good to remember that seemingly inappropriate reactions of anxiety and rage are almost always due to recent attacks on a privileged position.

Another term I use for this end phase is *humility enhancement.* Humility is enhanced whenever privileged position is discovered and diluted, or better yet, eradicated. Humility is not in any way to be confused with humiliation. Quite the contrary, in a state of humility, self-esteem flourishes and feelings of self-worth insure self-care and self-satisfaction. The condition of relative humility is flourishing ground for human compassion and destructive to self-hate. Privileged position, on the other hand, inevitably creates a shaky center of emotional gravity and exposes us to great vulnerability and the possibility of steep descents from illusionary antihuman heights and onslaughts of devastating self-hating attacks.

For our purposes, the third step in direct compassion is seeking out our hidden thoughts and feelings about privileged position and wherever possible surrendering it. Finding it can be as difficult as giving it up. Once exposed, logic and even moderate contact with reality usually make at least some dilution possible, and with repeated exposures and dilution we eventually can eradicate it. Finding it is made easier if we know that it is usually connected to our immediate self-hate and is part of a process we have repeated many times. This kind of constructive and ultimately compassionate procedure and evolution cannot take place if one does not realize that the search for unreal privileged position is taking place, that it is the enemy of *actual self, and part of the self-hating nucleus,* and that exposure is vital to real self-care and self-enhancement.

At this point, let me give two examples to demonstrate the three-step direct compassionate process, which actually is a relatively simple one. Yet, simple as it is, the three-step process contains not only the power of immediate relief from emotional pain and the enhancement of function but also provides the groundwork for *indirect compassion,* which is more intricate and of still greater compassionate force as a psychophilosophy and a way of life. It is all-important.

First example: 1. I find myself feeling increasingly moody and anxious. Then I start recalling mistakes I've made in the past and begin a second-guessing game of how I could have avoided those mistakes by doing things differently—I recognize the process as an onslaught of direct self-hate.

2. I immediately take whatever steps I can to block the process, to stop it going any further, to refuse to indulge in the memory of so-called mistakes, recriminations, *could have beens*. I call up a friend and make an appointment to see a movie. In the meantime, I go on a long, vigorous bike ride. While riding, thoughts of "past mistakes" intrude. I am the "chairman of the board" and have a lot to say about how I use my time, energy and thinking process and so I refuse to recriminate. Instead, I think about past pleasantries, past satisfactions, current satisfactions, like the movement of my muscles as I pedal, the trees I pass, the faces I see. I anticipate the pleasure of seeing the movie and talking about it later with my friend. I refuse to indulge in self-hate. I refuse to feed it even the smallest morsel.

3. Later on, perhaps the following morning, I try to recall what preceded my attack of self-hate and its earliest symtpoms—the moodiness, the anxiety, and the general feeling of being out of sorts with myself. Let us assume that I've had at least some experience with myself along these lines in the past.

Did I make any decision in favor of myself?

Did I do anything that represented completely loyalty to *me*, only *me*, which in the past I might have considered as an act of selfishness and which only of late I've come to see as an act of self-rescue? I recall that I did, in fact, make a very difficult and, I might even say, tortured decision.

I had a patient, a physically very sick man, who had to go into the hospital. I promised myself to visit him in the hospital that day. Then, realizing that I did not feel like visiting him, I decided not to do so. I'd either put it off to another day or wait for him to leave the hospital and come to see me when he got out. No, I wasn't particularly fatigued, and I have no phobic feelings about hospitals. If I could have leaned on these artificial devices, it would have been superficially easier but would not have represented true loyalty to myself. I decided against visiting him, not as an act of cruelty to him but as an act of kindness to me. For whatever reason, I did not feel like visiting him, and I made and carried out that decision. I did not visit him.

But then the self-hate began. Where was the position of privilege? Where was pride, invested in an effort to become more than human, which in reality made me less than human to myself? The answer was soon evident. I had attacked my privileged position of being saintly.

My privileged position consisted of one in which I was all-caring for other people and self-sacrificing. This, in turn, was linked to a larger position of martyrdom, self-abnegation and feelings of utter and pure responsibility toward others. In short, this was a facet of a very grandiose self-concept of being angelic and saintly. If indeed I had been the pure saint I aspired to be, then there would have been no conflict in the first place about wanting to go or wanting not to go to the hospital. There would have been no sense of duty or self-sacrifice either. There simply would have been a pure desire to go to the hospital and I would have gone with no feeling of self-deprivation at all.

But I am not pure. While I have a sense of responsibility toward others, this was not an emergency situation, and I do care about myself. Therefore, my self-hate was an effort to promote pretense, the pretense of being something I am not, the pretense of being a mythical, superior, self-sacrificing saintlike type. Uncovering this pretense is not easy. Obviously, direct self-hate intervenes and must be deleted and blocked. When other people do this for us by wounding our pride, and we are confronted with real self, and our self-hate is then projected onto them, an unconscious effort to restore the position of privilege to ourselves can ensue and be murderous. Many murders are committed out of rage stemming from this kind of hurt pride.

Now that the area of special status has been exposed, a struggle must ensue to give it up. I had to deepen my realization and conviction that indeed I am not and in fact don't care to be a participant in a ruinous hoax, a hoax which has been immediately and demonstrably chronically destructive to me. I made every effort to surrender special status of "nice, all-caring guy." Why should I continue to make this terrible imposition on myself? I eagerly accepted the fact of my humanity, including self-serving feelings, desires and multiple responsibilities—especially toward myself.

Second Example: My patient, Jean, found herself becoming increasingly depressed as she began to think that everyone led a more interesting and worthwhile life than she did. For the moment her attention was focused on a particular girl friend, Cynthia. Cynthia went to parties, was invited all over, everyone seemed to want her. She was never turned down in anything she wanted. Why couldn't Jean be more like Cynthia, accepted and wanted by everyone? Things weren't bad enough but she also lost out on a position she had been applying for that involved extensive tests and interviews. "Other people seem to have what it takes. Cynthia surely would have been chosen for the job." Feeling depressed, she called "a friend" and made a date. The friend was a man she saw on and off for several years, who never rejected her but who invariably denigrated her and made her feel bad. Each encounter with him began relatively well and wound up leaving her dazed and further demoralized and self-hating.

Jean did not immediately recognize the self-hate involved in her projection to Cynthia and in her increasing depression. Initially, she believed that her feelings about her impoverished position relative to that of Cynthia were valid. Later on she did say that she had a few thoughts about diffiiculties that Cynthia had encountered in the recent past but "had somehow pushed out of her mind." Of course she said this in the service of self-hate. It would not have served her self-hating comparison to Cynthia to comfort herself with the reality of any of Cynthia's difficulties. This immediately would have put her in touch with the fact that neither Cynthia nor anyone else was "accepted and wanted by everyone." This would have made at least some small contribution to reducing her self-hate by making her realize that Cynthia—and she— were as human as anyone else.

Recognition and diagnosis of what she was doing to herself—and that *she* was in fact doing it to herself, not the world, Cynthia or anyone else, but that *she,* Jean, was busily setting up a hate campaign for Jean—dawned on her following the call to her so-called friend. The self-saving signal went off loud and strong.

She was immediately flooded by many memories of "feeling awful" and of inflicting all kinds of self-hating attacks on herself following seeing him. At this point she realized that her increasing depression as well as the projective construct she was developing *vis-à-vis* Cynthia were self-hating devices. She had made the diagnosis! She slowly became aware that she had been engaging in the process of injustice collecting, which in the past always led to cynicism, bitterness, a sense of hopelessness and further attacks of self-hate, mostly in the form of depression.

2. She immediately called her "friend" and broke the date. She then began to entertain thoughts about Cynthia's status and, more important, thoughts about her own. There had been good and bad times in both their lives. She not only recalled the jobs she *did* get but also those in which she had succeeded admirably. She decided that she really didn't feel like being in anybody's company and instead pored over vacation material she had gathered some months earlier before she decided to try for the new job. She concluded that she "still needed that vacation" and immediately came to a decision about a trip she would take within the week. She said that she "felt a bit bruised" and decided to "take some good and loving care" of herself. On a pragmatic level she had effectively blocked her self-hate.

3. Investigation and self-examination later revealed a rather subtle but very important privileged or pride position. Jean realized that her reaction was due to being turned down for the job.

But investigation of her projection to Cynthia demonstrated an important, much deeper and more pervasive ramification. Her demand on herself consisted of attaining a position in which rejection would never take place and would be impossible. She demanded immunity from rejection, and this demand was made on the world at large, on all people offering jobs or providing potential social situations that might interest her in any way. This condition simply does not exist for anyone on this planet. It is contrary to the human condition. No matter who we are, no matter what our position, rejection is at times inevitable. Of course the need for total acceptance is a reaction to a history of self-rejection, *but it becomes diminished as self-acceptance is restored.*

As with most self-abnegating pride positions, the need for total acceptance from others can go on autonomously even after enormous strides have been made in the area of self-acceptance. This happens on almost a conditioned-reflex inertia basis. In short, the need for total acceptance becomes a habit and is felt as a genuine need even though it actually has become an awful burden leading to a great deal of unnecessary pain. Jean at one point asked, "Who am I, after all, that I should never be rejected?" This is not a demeaning question. It is a practical and human one and deserves a practical answer.

The answer is that Jean is a human being. As a human being she must be free to engage in encounters in which she may either be accepted or rejected without recriminations of any kind. She came to realize that she had to fight to give up her special position status. She had to struggle for the human right to be rejected. As I shall describe later on in Part IV, fear of rejection is augmented by our culture, which demands and feeds the notion of total acceptance. Jean had relatively little difficulty realizing that she could survive rejection very well. Actually, after surrender of a privileged pride position survival becomes much easier.

When the self-hating autonomy can still blackmail us and we fear the onslaught of a self-hating attack, we feed the illusion that life will not go on unless we sustain the antihuman position of privilege. Not only can it go on but it can do so on a much simpler, easier and happier level, but only if the compassionate fight against self-hate is engaged. I "learned" repeatedly that being a mythical virtuous angel *was not* only not vital but actually destructive to my existence, and Jean learned that living with rejection was entirely compatible with human existence. She realized that this indeed constitutes the compassionate position and enhances the position of humility.

Repeated application of direct compassion does much more than provide immediate relief, function and the possibility of pleasure although these in themselves are of vital importance. It contributes to a general pattern of humility production, and the process gets easier and is initiated with increasing rapidity until it becomes spontaneous. The terrible onslaughts of direct self-hate—phobic attacks, anxiety attacks, depressive reactions, obsessive ruminating—cannot exist in the face of real humility. Humility is after all the essence of the real self-esteem that is essential to being a real person. This is the very opposite of blown-up, synthetic self-aggrandisement, in which we are burdened and stultified by the antihuman characteristics we attempt to arrogate to ourselves to ward off attacks of direct self-hate. This process of direct compassion also provides fertile ground for indirect compassion and for the budding and growth of a state of grace with ourselves as a way of life. As "the enemy's" soldiers are destroyed, the growth of new and healthy human substance can take place.

That Jean could take a vacation at a time of rejection, not using success as a blackmail criterion to justify her needs, was most constructive. To recognize that she was bruised and to decide to care for herself in whatever way possible without *I deserve because I won, or because I feel hurt* as necessary rationalizations but rather as a function of *I want* (of which I'll have more to say later on), demonstrates considerable progress in the struggle for compassion.

Forms of Compassion:
The Indirect Way

Indirect compassion comprises all moves designed to neutralize any and all forms of indirect self-hate. It includes any process that hampers, limits and destroys the neurotic structure and frame of reference.

DESTROYING ILLUSIONS

An integral part of one's move toward compassion is the destruction of illusions. To initiate the struggle we must first understand and accept the fact that illusions exist in us. Illusions are more than *representations* of departures from self. They *are* departures from self, and as such are antithetical and destructive to actual self. The desire to change, to grow and to engage in the necessary struggle with them must be a conscious one. Such a desire is often signaled by a painful emotional reaction commonly called a nervous breakdown. Of course, nerves haven't broken down at all. I prefer to call these reactions nervous break-ups, and a more accurate term would be neurotic break-up. What is happening is usually a sudden or acute *dis*illusionment, which, momentarily, at least, is causing a break-up of the entire neurotic pretense structure, consisting of all the devices designed to take the individual further and further away from actual self.

Severe emotional reactions, however, are not *always* necessary to initiate the process. Many people with awareness of chronic unhappiness enter psychoanalysis precisely to initiate this kind of investigation, even though their pain is neither acute nor different from what it has been for many years. Psychoanalysis is useful. The objectivity of the psychoanalyst and his training, experience, and hopefully compassionate support can accelerate and make the process easier. But the compassionate work eventually *must be done by ourselves, regardless of whether or not we seek help outside ourselves.* The compassionate process ultimately depends on establishing benevolence and a state of grace with and within ourselves, and this only we can do for ourselves.

Discovering and giving up illusions has a great deal in common with step three of direct compassion, in which a false image of privileged position is surrendered. One process is often part of the other and sometimes they are hard to tell apart. The real difference is one of sweep and magnitude. Giving up a pride position often involves a particular moment and a particular issue. Many pride positions linked together form an illusion or a series of them. Illusions then sweep through a person's entire character structure, color the world he perceives, and shape the self into other selves. Let me reverse this explanation for the moment, using myself as an example.

I had a vast illusion involving my goodness and the rewards that goodness would bring when I suffered my own depression. This "goodness" of mine contained many Christlike tenets and many needs. One of the great needs I had was to be universally loved. My illusions masked a great deal of arrogance (because I was in fact arrogating to myself characteristics that did not really exist), much pretense, and a great deal of rage, since I felt abused by both myself and others. The very grandiose aspect of this stance was hidden from conscious view, as I demanded recognition and even adulation for my remarkable saintliness. When adulation and recognition were not forthcoming, this created rage. A would-be saint must repress rage and must suffer the consequences of this kind of repression, which leads to depression, anxiety, psychosomatic aches and pains from increased muscular tension (clenching one's jaws produces a jaw ache), and any number of self-hating devices and consequences.

This is a bird's-eye view and a very simplistic explanation of the pervasive and sweeping quality of illusion. Of course, illusions about other people, about the world, plus exorbitant expectations and other indirect self-hating dynamics, go along with such a state. My reaction to not going to the hospital to see my ill patient, which I described earlier, could not have taken place had I not had an unrealistic illusion of goodness. When my direct self-hate was revealed in that instance I followed up by blocking it. I had started the process of discovering and especially *giving up the pride position of saintliness*; I was chipping away in this fashion at my overall illusion. Repeated chipping away in this way eventually undermines the illusionary process and makes collapse of the illusory structure possible, if not imminent. As we struggle, eventually we identify more with reality than with illusion. This means that our total perception of ourselves, other people, life and the world generally is altered in the direction of that which is real rather than imagined.

We discover illusion each time we *discover a pride*

position in ourselves. We give up some of that illusion each
time we struggle and succeed *to any degree* in giving up
that pride position. Eventually such an ongoing struggle
leads us to discover reality. I speak here of much more
than an intellectual discovery. I speak here of *a profound
gut feeling of change and discovery in ourselves,* something
that cannot be contrived. With time and struggle we
become aware of the sweep and feel of the entire illusion
and eventually we feel its collapse, as compassionate
reality sweeps in.

As an analogy, I am reminded of an experience I had
when I went to Switzerland to study medicine at the
University of Lausanne, in the French part of that country.
I had studied French in the United States for six years
during high school and college. But those six years of
French seemed almost entirely wasted when I first arrived
abroad. I say "almost" because I could make myself
understood, but I could understand almost nothing of what
others said to me. I picked up a word here and there, but I
couldn't put them together. I "heard" and understood one
word and missed ten others. Then I went through another
period where all the words jumbled into one. The people
spoke too rapidly for me to comprehend. The words
combined together into long jumbles which I could not
separate into individual words. Studying more vocabulary
and grammar was pointless. I had already done that for six
years.

My frustration and increasing desperation went on for
about three months. I'd sit at lectures and would "hear"
only one in ten words. Then I started going to movies
where I heard only French nearly every night, and
suddenly, six months after my arrival, it happened. The
words suddenly separated into place. My mind's ear had

learned the rhythm. I could understand the language. While this seemed *sudden*, it wasn't so at all. Indeed, it would not have been possible without the preceeding six years of study and six months of struggle to "hear." The process of discovering illusion is much like this.

"Hearing" illusions can be of enormous value. Tuning in on ourselves in an attempt to pick up any "sounds" smacking of illusion is invaluable. But this "tuning in" cannot be forced and must not be converted to pressured intellectual ruminating, which is the antithesis of the compassionate position.

Periods of great emotional pain offer special opportunities for self-evaluation. Freud said that the dream is the royal road to the unconscious. Anxiety is surely the royal road to discovering illusions and, eventually, to achieving realistic disillusionment. When we feel bad, any tracing back that we do to the illusion that has been jolted momentarily is of value. The same is true of any re-evaluation we do *vis-à-vis* ourselves and the outside world, but only if this does not lead to recrimination, moral equivocation and harsh judgment of ourselves.

Discovery of illusion can be followed by almost spontaneous surrender of illusion. When unwanted and unexpected forces strike us and cause disillusion, then direct self-hate follows and a struggle for compassion and surrender of illusion must ensue. For example, you recall the case of my patient, the businessman who lost some money. His disillusion about his omniscience followed. This was followed by depression and recriminations and these were finally followed by realistic awareness of his unrealistic illusion about his powers and his omniscience and omnipotence. This was followed by painful struggle to surrender these illusions as he made the effort to become a

compassionately realistic human being. In his case the
entire process was initiated by unforeseen circumstances
(though even in his case and others like his, I'm sure a
certain readiness and even craving to be his actual self
existed), and began in a state of acute and direct self-hate
and warfare with himself.

"Disillusionment" that is initiated consciously, in the
pursuit of compassionate reality, can proceed along a
much less stormy course. A re-evaluation based on wanting
to help oneself, and initiated in an atmosphere of peace
with oneself, rather than in the middle of a siege of pain,
can also reveal illusion. A compassionate and realistic
atmosphere creates a climate that makes it easier to tap
our resources and to see the world realistically.

Had my patient quietly and with dignity (toward
himself) and at a much earlier stage started the process of
self-revelation, he might have come to the knowledge of
his omniscient illusion much earlier and with considerably
less pain. Without the battering of his autonomous self-
hate, which was generated by his loss of money, he might
well have been in condition to realize the pervasiveness
and unreality of his illusion and might gently have begun
to surrender it.

Self-willed, constructive re-evaluation for the purpose of
therapeutic disillusionment or illusion eradication is always
painful and always involves a struggle, but in varying
degrees. Compassionate motivation and a compassionate
atmosphere can reduce trauma and pain enormously and
produce an open invitation to reality, making the struggle
less arduous, as illusion is spontaneously replaced with
reality.

One test of how well we are doing with giving up
illusions is how we feel about aging and death. The illusion

of being able to live forever often produces enough fear to preclude any thought of death. The ability to envision death, to feel it as an absolute certainty, to know that the word *forever* is antithetical to the human condition, is only possible if we can see ourselves as finite creatures. This is only possible if we are relatively illusion-free and as a result have developed considerable humility. The relief involved in knowing that "I am a person, a person doesn't live forever, can't accomplish and experience all things" can be significant.

We are, for the most part, illusion-free if we can comfortably and happily, but without resignation, picture our current here-and-now condition as being the one we will live with, without vast changes in the future. That is not to say that change and growth are not certainly possible and often desirable. But compassionate, nonillusionary, realistic change and growth are invariably connected to good feelings about *here and now*. Envisioned changes, dreamed up in hatred of a current life in the here and now, are usually full of Heaven-on-Earth illusionary embroidery and are never satisfactory. If you like here-and-now living and if the finite facts of life and death are neither insulting, disgusting nor terrifying to you, chances are excellent that your illusions on all levels have indeed been significantly neutralized.

LOWERING STANDARDS, LIMITING GOALS AND REDUCING EXPECTATIONS

Destroying grandiosity and reducing addiction to stimulation and the compulsive need for narcissistic support are not humiliating and do not detract from actual self. On the contrary, destroying these processes is self-enriching and life-enhancing. As people, we can only be and live as people. This means living and enjoying living within the realm of *human possibility*. The search for standards, goals and expectations consistent with human possibility not only prevents self-hate but also makes satisfaction and feelings of inner peace and strength attainable.

I don't suggest that we reduce our standards, goals or expectations to unrealistically shoddy levels. This would be self-hating, too; those I have dealt with who have had standards that were disproportionately low turned out to be persons of little or no humility. Their surface shows of modesty concealed inner standards of such extrahuman and extraterrestrial proportions that it became easy to understand their inhibitions and paralysis. As we have seen, impossibly high goals and expectations prevent our acting on and attaining goals and relationships that are humanly possible and satisfying. To achieve human satisfactions we must be aware of the limits of human reality, we must not give way to illusion, we must be in touch with the limits of human possibility to reach a compassionate level of life.

It is *not* self-deprecating to fight for the right to enjoy the commonplace. The commonplace is what is commonly found in being alive as a person and, if we don't deprive ourselves of the right to it, offers a constant source of satisfaction. The richness of everyday life must not be damned by pejorative terms such as "mediocre," "everyday" or "nothing." We must guard zealously against the need for "highs" and must be very wary of success for its own naked sake. Addiction to success inevitably leads to profound self-hate and depression. Like any addiction, success too often becomes an inner demand on self for "what have you done for me lately," as each success becomes a coercion for still more success.

I recall seeing a patient who earned fifteen thousand dollars a year. He told me at the time that earning twenty-five thousand a year "would seem like Heaven" to him. I warned him, to no avail, of the many other kinds of exorbitant goals he harbored and told him that unless his complete outlook changed he would never feel that he earned enough.

Within a relatively short time his earnings increased enormously. But his quick appreciation for these rapid increases turned as rapidly to contempt. His living expenses soared with his income and so did his appetite for all kinds of things he never knew he needed before. These included very high insurance policies, a larger house, better clothes, private schools for his children and many more of "the good things of life."

When he was earning twenty-five thousand dollars a year he told me that he really was only feeling the satisfaction that came of earning five thousand a year. This was considerably less satisfaction than he got from the fifteen thousand he earned when he first came to see me. This was so, he told me, because it now cost him "twenty thousand-plus a year just to get by, my basic needs." This left less than five thousand to do what he wanted with. He was also angry because he had to pay so much in taxes. I reminded him that he once told me that he would "love to earn enough money so as to have to pay plenty of taxes. I should only be in that position."

He went on to earn over a hundred thousand and his financial and emotional condition became even worse. My intervention became almost negligible because while his earning ability brought less and less satisfaction, it never-theless increased his very real self-hate and arrogance. He was loathe to investigate any possibility of examining standards and expectations, let alone lowering them. He was caught in a self-grinding, ever-escalating goal enter-prise, which was utterly ruthless in its pressure on him. To complicate matters the expectations he had of his children were being thwarted in some ways by his affluence, too. His daughter had taken up with a private-school crowd that experimented with drugs. He really had believed that money and affluence would prevent such things, that if he gave his children the best of everything they would be immune to "crummy things."

My patient finally had a heart attack. It was a mild one and he recovered. He then began a serious re-evaluation of his standards, goals and expectations. Fortunately, it was not too late. He was among the lucky ones. He had to relearn the value and joy involved in taking a walk, looking at a sunset, good conversation, a decent meal with friends. But it took a heart attack to initiate a humanizing process. How much less painful and less dangerous it is to conduct this kind of investigation of ourselves, and ourselves *vis-à-vis* the world, before self-hate nearly destroys us.

I remember my patient in his pre-heart attack days, objecting when I told him how much less other people could be happy with, really happy. He did not want to hear about other people. Identifying almost completely with self-hate and with rejection of what is really human, he viewed other people with contempt and arrogated to himself dimensions beyond "ordinary people." But at-tempting to fill these dimensions very nearly destroyed him. Of course, his terrible drive was due in large part to underlying feelings of being less adequate than the very people for whom he expressed contempt.

Actually, I find I can learn much about myself by listening to other people. Listening to their "disappointments" invariably tells me much about their expectations and makes me think of my own. Listening to their "satisfactions" also often tells me much about my own exorbitant expectations and reminds me of the work needed to reduce them. I have found it invaluable to think in terms of excessive standards, goals and expectations nearly every time I've suffered emotional pain following some decision or act.

I remember feeling quite depressed after we bought our first house. Later on I realized that my pain was largely due to unrealized and unrealistic hidden expectations about how it would make all our lives different. The house was comfortable and adequate in every way, but it was not a palace nor did attaining it provide a solution to all the problems I ever had. Following the realization of my exorbitant expectations for what it would do for us to have it, I felt enormously relieved. I have found this process repeating itself nearly every time I've had undue anxiety preceding an activity.

I remember a point in my life when I became extremely anxious, almost to the point of combined agitation and paralysis, before I gave a lecture or a paper to a large group. I finally asked myself what it was that I expected of myself, of my audience? It was most revealing and eventually relieving. I learned that I expected much more than comprehensive delivery on my part and fair understanding by a good percentage of the audience. This expectation would have been *more than ample* for a compassionate person.

The answer came through loud and clear: I expected a *great* performance on my part, although I am not an actor, and a *great* emotional response on the part of my listeners, even though they were participating in the intellectual exercise of simply trying to understand some scientific material. Not only did these expectations deprive me of satisfaction from work well done but they also inflicted upon me a state of terror, in which I couldn't sleep and overate enormously to the point of nausea, days before a lecture. Self-examination resulted in a humane lowering of my goals and expectations so that giving lectures in recent years has become a genuine source of human satisfaction and pleasure to me.

THE MOVE AGAINST BOREDOM

It is just about never too late to go back to books, to take courses, to attend lectures, to develop a latent interest. To make compassionate use of our assets, through a compassionate evaluation of our resources for growth and our yearnings that are being ignored, is anti-self-hating and opens us up to satisfactions that are realistically attainable. This is so much more satisfying and life affirmative than pursuing evanescent, unreal peak experiences and then suffering the terrible emotional mood drops between "highs."

In the attempt to mitigate boredom I find it of great value to remember that *involvement precedes interest.* We must risk at least a minimum degree of involvement in any activity or enterprise before interest can be generated. Waiting for an interest to strike us before we take steps to become involved may well keep us in a state of relative boredom for a lifetime. Actually, the process of waiting for interest before involvement is an unconscious way of prolonging self-hating boredom and is linked to neurotic expectation of interest without the participating experience that is necessary. In a real move against boredom, the primary goal is pleasure through *involvement and evolvement rather than achievement or accomplishment.* Self-hating, perfectionistic goals must not be invoked.

COMPASSIONATE SHADES OF GRAY

We must, if we observe the human condition at all, realistically realize that the composition of our emotional lives is characterized by inconsistency, incongruity and many subtle shades of all kinds of feelings. We are, all of us, exceedingly complex creatures and do ourselves a service in regarding ourselves as complex. Otherwise, we live in a dream world of nonexistent, simplistic black-and-white notions which simply do not apply to human life. There are none of us who are all good, all bad, all wise, all stupid or all anything at all. We are vast combinations of every kind of characteristic possible. As I said before, we all have more in common than we have apart, and the world we affect is full of subtle and blatant incongruitites and complex shadings, too. Viewing ourselves and the world in this antipolarizing, antisuperlative way mitigates to a considerable degree the kinds of illusions and expectations born of simplistic notions.

It is of considerable value to hear people, and particularly ourselves, think and talk. The superlatives a person uses—great, sensational, marvelous, very brilliant, extraordinary, tremendous, fantastic—are not casual or meaningless. If they were, their use would be innocent enough. Like other symbols, these words derive from very real ideas, intrapsychic dynamics and cultural characteristics. When I hear a young patient say "marvelous" repeatedly, I usually find that he or she has a desperate need for marvels and for things to be marvelous, and a tendency to depression when things are just "normally all right."

Superlatives very often indicate perfectionistic drives of ruthless magnitude. Fortunately, they can serve as signposts in giving us insights about what we demand of ourselves and others so that we can constructively re-evaluate. I am tired and frankly chagrined when I hear politicians speak of greatness and say that "America must be great." It is much more important to be "human." It is much more important for America to consist of people who struggle and who accept human possibilities in all their ramifications. The business of "being great" is invariably linked to some of the worst aspects of self-hate, the kind that generates arrogance and contempt for one's actual self, for others and for the real human condition generally.

Compassionate Psychophilosophy

COMPASSION AS A WAY OF LIFE

By *psychophilosophy* I mean a philosophy which has the power to change a person's psychology, or way of feeling and thinking about himself. The compassionate psychophilosophy can contribute immeasurably to establishing inner benevolence and a state of grace in relating to oneself. This psychophilosophy makes up the essence of the compassionate frame of reference and life. It has the capacity to affect all aspects of one's life in constructive and healthy living commensurate with the human condition on a reality basis. It is the very substance of acceptance of actual self on all levels and the antithesis of self-hate in any form—particularly that expressed by repression, deadening of feelings and extension of unconsciousness and unreality. This philosophy is neither ethereal nor highly theoretical. It is essentially pragmatic and practical, and in my own case is born of my personal and clinical experience, and readily lends itself to practical application. It easily replaces any gap left by the eradication of self-hate. Spontaneity is enhanced as this philosophy replaces inner tyranny and despotism.

In the following pages I describe in detail the principal

181

components of the compassionate psychophilosophy that has been most helpful to me in helping myself and my patients. As the compassionate struggle goes on, each individual discovers concepts particularly useful to himself as he adds to his own compassionate philosophy and psychology.

I AM BECAUSE I AM!

I am because I am! means I exist because I exist *and need no justification whatsoever for my existence.* The fact of my being is enough. I require no terms, conditions or permits from myself or anyone else. I live, and in living I am fully entitled to go on living. My life, my existence, my being is not predicated on standards, values, achievements or accomplishments. *I am,* not because of books I write, money I earn, degrees conferred, children I have—*I am* with or without these accouterments. These *things* and *people* are not *me!* I do not exist *because* of them. Relative to my life, they exist *because of me.* While they may give me satisfaction, *they in no way justify my existence.* In my life's frame of reference, *I justify theirs.* They are a function of me. I am not a function of them. This psychophilosophical fact provides the central kernel of my relationship to myself and to the rest of the world. It mitigates against the inner blackmail of self-hate, the pressures of other people and the pressures born of inhuman cultural standards and values.

"How do I feel?" is a very important question as applied to people, issues, myself and especially as to my state of well-being. If I feel good, that's good. If I feel bad, then is there anything I can do to make myself feel better? Am I involved in any way in a self-hating enterprise? Most important, do I feel bad because I haven't accomplished enough? Achieved enough? Conformed enough? This is blackmail and antithetical to my philosophy. I must fight to give myself the right to feel good about myself and to feel good mood-wise, regardless of any accomplishment or nonaccomplishment whatsoever. This in no way mitigates against enjoying accomplishments, but it relegates them to a proper sense and place and proportion in the scope of things. It replaces compulsivity with spontaneity. "Things," "events," "tasks," "accomplishments" are never more important than I am and are not permitted to destroy my well-being. Do I feel badly because of destructive relationships? Then I must break them!

I don't wish to imply that it is not worthwhile to struggle to attempt to sustain a relationship that has many good ingredients. But if a relationship has turned out to be predominantly destructive, then it well serves all those concerned to terminate it. Too many destructive relationships are sustained only because of convention, lack of energy and resignation.

As the Beatle song goes, "I've got a ticket to ride." The fact of my human life and existence *is* my ticket. I need pay nothing more for it. My choices, decisions and actions are not based on the need to justify or to reinforce my existence. *I* would *be*, with or without them.

To the extent that this belief exists and permeates me, I am free of inner and outer coercions and can make choices free of neurotic need and based on actual desire and healthy spontaneity. This, in large part, frees me from the self-hating need to be universally loved, universally admired, always nice, always helpful, totally independent,

all-knowing, all-giving, all-powerful, the best, and any
other unreal demands that put me in a self-enslaving,
antihuman position.

I am because I am is identical with utter benevolence
toward myself. This means regarding myself with dignity,
the antithesis of pretense, and with seriousness and loyalty.
Of course, this does not preclude humor, which is so often
a way of lightening the load of adversity that must come to
all of us at times. But taking myself seriously and being
loyal to myself are of prime importance. It means that I am
a person worthy of consultation and good treatment. I
listen to me and I regard what I hear as serious and
important in terms of my own life. I learn about me and
my requirements. I take good care of myself and take
healthy satisfaction in that care.

Some time ago I was physically ill. A patient of mine
worried about me and my health, but seemed very
embarrassed about it. I finally got him to admit that he was
primarily and realistically worried about his own welfare
should anything happen to me. As he developed a
compassionate and healthy sense of proportion, he realized
that his primary concern for himself was human and in the
healthy service of self-care. My thoughts, feelings, ideas
and opinions are important because they are mine and not
because I have achieved any special status in this world.
They are important only because they come from a person,
the most important person in my life, my person.

In a state of grace with myself, I do not abandon myself
when the going is tough or should others find me
antithetical in any way in their frames of reference.
Loyalty means care and kindness at all times, and particularly when they are needed to reduce the pain of difficult
times. I never, absolutely never, side with anyone who is

against my welfare. I aid nobody who detracts from my dignity, who makes me feel less than human either through subhuman onslaughts or superhuman demands. I fight or avoid people whose effect is ultimately destructive to my validity as a person, or who in any way dilute my ability to take myself seriously.

I readily consult with other people in making important decisions. But I approach them only after I have first approached myself and I consult myself again for my own decision after all consultations with others. In my life *I* must be the final authority, whatever expertise I choose to get from others.

Meaningful consultation with another and a relationship with another can only be real and worthy if two *whole,* actual *selves* are relating. Relating between oneself and a mirror, or between two mirrors, produces infinite reflections which in no way contribute to actual self. Knowing this, I bring my actual self to relationships as free as possible from the need to conform or to overpower. Thus, relating when I am contributing my actual self invariably has an enriching effect on both my partner and myself. This *"compassionate contribution"* to the human relating process is no small matter. It ultimately leads to treating other people with increased compassion and dignity.

I am because I am becomes a habit, a very special habit, inasmuch as it contributes to spontaneity. This is so because the habit and process of loyalty to actual self work against rigidly designed inner dictates of autonomous self-hate. The habit of seriously listening to myself gives me ever-increasing skill in listening to myself. Like a fine musician, I become more skillful in discerning self-hating discordant sounds and in hearing harmonious sounds coming from the real substance of my actual self. My skills in the process grow, and as they do I am able to feel more, know more of what I feel, and to use more of what I feel in the service of myself, all of which constitute alive spontaneity, characteristic of the myriad shades, nuances and currents of life itself.

I AM I

I am I is the essence of self-acceptance. But it is not passive or selective self-acceptance. It is active, loud, strong, and, if necessary, heroically aggressive. It applies to all aspects of self. It is dictated to only by the highest regard and dedication to individuality, however that individuality may conform or depart from what are commonly regarded as "cultural norms." This includes all thoughts, ideas, feelings, desires, decisions and eventually actions. *I* includes *all* that *I am.* Judgment value, moral equivocation, cultural and conventional values, the ideas of others do not cause me to deaden, repress or attempt to cut off parts of myself. *I* includes all that the culture may see as assets, liabilities, limitations, resources, insensitivities, cruelties, neurotic, good, bad, sensitive, wise or stupid in me.

While *I am I* does not preclude change, it is indeed the only condition that can lead to change. If *I* am not *I* how can *I* change *I*? How can *I* participate in real self-examination and real choices in order to change? If I am a conforming mirror, change can only be a synthetic, confused reflection of what I *believe* other people desire. Real change involves a real *I*, an *I*, who is accepted in all my manifestations and ramifications. This *I* is dedicated to the belief in myself and in all my individual self-identifying characteristics and proclivities. Change for this *I* involves *choice,* not *compulsion.* I do not change myself because others consider me *bad* or *perverse.* I change only because *I* have determined that *I* want to change. *I* have decided that change is good for me. Otherwise, I retain my status quo however perverse any of my particular characteristics or attributes may be judged to be within our cultural frame of reference.

I am I, as a self-accepting force is a great self-integrator and is antithetical to self-fragmentation. If we actively cherish all aspects of ourselves and learn to stand up to inner and outer chastisement, *however and whatever is revealed,* then deadening our inner selves does not take place. Cutting off feelings, dichtomizing, anesthetizing and extending the unconscious, thus destroying real conscious autonomy, does not take place when we are loyal to ourselves. As consciousness is extended, various aspects of myself come into focus and come under the jurisdiction of my full awareness, that is, of me, as a fully conscious person. *I* become a real chairman of the board. *I* bring all aspects of myself into a unified whole as *I* apply myself to any and all facets of living. No member of the board goes off in his own direction because he has been ostracized or hidden. All members have been heard from. The chairman brings all opinions into integrated focus and acts accordingly.

Real self-acceptance precludes the scattering and fragmentation characteristic of repression which produces compartmentalized, autonomous pieces of self which send up confusing messages from hidden corners of the unconscious. Self-acceptance is the essence of integration. All aspects of oneself are heard from and choices are made by a unified, fully awake, responsible person. Since fragmentation is the result of great repression, due in turn to self-hate, fragmentation must be regarded as a child of self-hate, a perpetuating device of self-hate and is in itself the essence of self-hate. *I am I* is then, as an integrating instrument, one of the key nuclear forces in the compassionate process. Integration permits us to tap the totality of ourselves, to make choices and decisions—real choices based on actual self rather than on drives toward impossible goals.

I am I is one of the most important forces in establishing benevolence and that all-important state of grace with myself that I've been talking about. The struggle to be *me* in all my ramifications and manifestations, to accept all aspects of myself without equivocation, against all inner and outer forces that would dictate otherwise, against realization of illusory flights of fancy and those born of cultural ideas of perfection, is a struggle for self-respect and dignity. This struggle dignifies the *I, I am*. It indicates that the *I, I am*, rather than a pretentious *I*, deserves my time and energy. This dignity contributes to a state of benevolence and grace within myself, in which I categorically refuse to embark on flights of self-hate for any reason whatsoever.

I treat myself as I treat a child I love. In respecting him, I dignify all aspects of the human condition. In observing him, I eagerly expect him to demonstrate much that is human. How can it be otherwise since he is human and *all* that he *is* must be human, and I respect that which is human. I bring no harsh judgment to him. In accepting all that he is, he need not fear me. I love him because he is who he is and I will not and indeed cannot hurt him. Thus, we exist in a state of grace, in a state relatively free of the tensions and fears born of chronic impending destructive judgment, criticism and castigation.

I am I also makes an important contribution to alive spontaneity, as opposed to wooden mechanical behavior, born of the need to comply stringently with inner and outer dictates. Since nothing in myself is demeaned I do not deaden any aspects of myself. Therefore, all of the substance of my resources is available for being, feeling and acting with natural, spontaneous aliveness. Energy and time are not diverted, dissipated and wasted seeking illusionary fulfillment. They are not wasted in useless rituals imposed by a tyrannical self-hating martinet. They are free to be used in the service of the actual everyday *I*, in the service of *my* feelings, *my* ideas, *my* proclivities.

My self-acceptance prevents self-hating criticism. If I criticize it is criticism without a sting. It is benevolent criticism whose only aim is to make me feel better about being me. I, therefore, have little or no need to expend myself in pretentious acts designed to protect myself from self-hate. In being myself, I tap myself, as I am, without fear of castigation, freely, this is the essence of alive spontaneity.

I NEED, I WANT, I CHOOSE

My needs must be taken with seriousness if I take myself seriously. I am tuned into my needs because I am important to myself, and so I listen to myself in all areas of my existence, and I hear and am in touch with who I am and what I need. This is in essence the nucleus of self-care. It is the opposite and the enemy of self-neglect. I never abdicate the chance to *tune in on myself* and my needs in favor of glorious martyrdom or in futile gestures of self-destructive sacrifice. My needs are never a source of embarrassment to me, because they spring from *me*, and no aspect of me is a source of embarrassment to me. How can it be otherwise if I do not ascribe to anything that is inhuman? I know that all that I am is human and can't be otherwise and this applies to that which I need. I do not have to justify my needs. My needing anything is justification enough because I accept myself and I am not beset by the self-doubt of pretense. My needs, I know, are not based on Godlike aspirations and do not require Godlike justification to be taken seriously. I need because I need, and that's good enough.

The same is true of my desires. I am their source. I trust in the human condition and in myself as representative of that condition, which makes my desires spontaneously acceptable. What I want may have nothing, little or much to do with what I need. Of course, in most cases I will want what I need, but not necessarily need what I want. I often want things and conditions for which I have no need at all, but I do not use need or intellectual rationale to justify my desires. That I want is enough.

I cannot permit myself to be embarrassed or to generate self-hate about any desire, however antithetical it may be to current mores or convention. I am entitled to want anything, anything whatsoever. Just as I refuse to deaden and refuse to exclude or cut off any aspect of myself, I refuse to blind myself to any desire, to feel less than or more than human about any desire, to allow any desire to be a source of embarrassment to me or to reject it.

I know that being human entails a vast variety of possible urges, thoughts and feelings and I expect any and all of them in myself, and an almost endless variety of appetites and desires ranging from the simplest and banal to the most complex, exotic, and, often, to what we are taught to look at as bizarre. But I also know that *most desires do not represent needs.* I also know the difference between a *thought* and an *action.* I can differentiate between a desire that can be fulfilled with constructive, enriching effects for self, and a desire that if fulfilled can impoverish and even destroy me.

The point is, that I compassionately accept and respect all my desires as mine and I do not repress them, because they do in fact spring from my very own self. But I do not attempt to *fulfill* all of them. As the chairman of the board and as my own benevolent parent, I listen to them all, but I choose among them for which ones I will attempt to fulfill and which ones I will not act on because they are exorbitant and even antithetical to my well-being, but which nevertheless do not embarrass me. For example, early in training I remember being in conflict about going into psychiatry or surgery or internal medicine, and for a while being buffeted about by a desire for all these options. I suffered from self-hate, which ensued when I contemplated the loss I would suffer as a result of giving up any two of these choices. But finally I assumed chairmanship of the board of my own life and decided on psychiatry, and refused to further entertain any recriminations based on either wisdom or fault inherent in the choice. I recognize that there is no possibility of fulfilling all my desires. *But,* cherishing myself, I do not generate self-hate in response to inability to fulfill a desire.

A state of grace includes benevolence and dignity toward human limitations as well as toward human ability and ingenuity. Thus, frustration springing from a desire I cannot fulfill, however much fulfillment may be within possibility and may be potentially constructive in its effects, brings even more compassionate benevolence rather than self-hate. This enables me to go on wanting and trying and succeeding and failing and experiencing and growing.

Many of us are so terrified by desire itself ("How can a nobody like me want anything?"), and by desires that seem inane, and by self-hate generated by inability to get what we want, which we view as failure, that we curtail and cut off our desires altogether. This prevents wanting, choosing and trying. It destroys the possibility of failing and also the possibility of succeeding. Through facing these options we experience, and it is through experience that we grow. We must be free to desire, free to differentiate which desires to attempt to fulfill and free to enjoy fulfillment and failure without self-hate. Otherwise, alive spontaneity must suffer ruinously.

I am reminded of children who when asked, "Why do you want it?" answer, "Because." We then sometimes ask, "Because of what?" or, "Because why?" and the child answers, "Because I want it." We then may go on and explain to the child, "But that's just another way of saying you want it. 'I want it because I want it' says you want it but doesn't tell me why." The child might say, "But that's why, I do want it because I want it."

This is not gibberish or a silly play on words. The child is saying she wants something, simply because she spontaneously does want something. The child's want needs no moral, cultural, logical, goal-directed justification for its existence. It springs from her self. For the moment unpressured, because she is a child, and not an adult trapped in a morass of culturally induced self-hating rationalizations, she needs no justification. Indeed, she resists entrapment and her response of "I want it *because* I want it" is resistance to in any way stilting her desire with any adult need for logic.

We are not children, and absolute spontaneity is not possible for us, and not wholly for children either, for that matter. But in our struggle to be increasingly compassionate with ourselves we can learn something from observing children. We can learn from observing their unembarrassed, undiluted commitment to their own ideas, feelings and desires. There is a facet of self-respect inherent in this attitude which is not only a function of *I want because I want*, but also delivers the message of *I am*. This, in essence, means that as a person *I* count, everything *in me* and *from me* counts, and this includes what *I want*. *I am* a person and I show it in all the ways a person shows it.

Choice has been called the prerogative of man, or the human prerogative. Many papers and books too have been written about choice. But I'm interested in choice here in the context of compassion. *Compassionate choice* is the prerogative of man and a human privilege, but only if that choice is *real choice*. Real choice always involves freedom from inner and outer coercion. Choice based on fear of recrimination and on what other people will think is pseudochoice and obviously springs from and contributes to self-hate. The real thing, *real choice, compassionate choice*, takes place in an atmosphere free of fear and free of anticipatory repercussions. The process of choosing, seriously choosing, through listening to my many feelings and coming to my conclusions and then making *my* choice, is extremely important regardless of the issue involved.

Of course, different issues warrant different expenditures of time and energy. Sustaining a realistic sense of proportion is in itself a function of compassion, but all choices, inasmuch as *I* make them, contribute to a very important process. In choosing, I always give something up. In effect I say, "I choose this and choose not to do or have that." This openly giving something up without fear of retaliation is an antiomnipotent and therefore anti-self-hating act. The inability to choose is most often based on the fear of giving anything up, based on the fear of mistakes and the fear of retaliation. This is converted into a desire to have it all, to satisfy all issues in a conflict, to be omnipotent (who after all can have it all, all the time, all ways?), and in so doing to destroy the need to choose.

I had a patient who wanted to buy many things but didn't want to spend any money. He wanted the omnipotent position of being able to get what he wanted while he kept his money. This would prevent an onslaught of self-hate following "mistakes." This inability to choose reverberated throughout his life in nearly all matters, as it almost always does. His "choices" were not choices at all, but rather wooden conclusions, having little to do with individual feelings and largely based on mechanical rationalized logic designed to cause him minimum trouble.

Each time we choose one situation over others we contribute to humility. As a human being I can't have it all because I am not omnipotent nor do I care to be. But even more important, each time I choose something and give up something else, I engage in the process of establishing a hierarchy of priorities.

In choosing, I constantly contribute to the establishment of my relative value system, to where things fit in in my life, and what degree of importance each assumes there. This process of choosing and establishing my priorities or hierarchy of priorities is extremely important in terms of self-assertion. It is the very nucleus of the self-asserting process.

I have had any number of patients who will manipulate in every conceivable way in order to avoid making a choice. Their last-ditch effort is to attempt to get someone else, particularly their therapist, to make a choice for them. They are trying to ward off self-hate, because they know about self-hate following choices made in the past. The self-hating autonomy wants perfect choices and decisions, and since no human choice is perfect, any choice they make will be looked upon as bad. *But,* the attempt to have others make a choice for us, to avoid making choices in any way possible, must always be viewed as an anti-self-feeling of global proportions. This invariably means that if I prefer to avoid the process of making choices in my life I am constantly functioning out of poor self-esteem and contributing to further obliteration of self. It means that I find my presence and myself to be a nuisance, an intruder and a stranger on the scene and that my actions and inactions are designed to ignore or even to obliterate evidence of my presence.

The words "I choose" immediately also mean "I prefer," indeed, they are almost interchangeable. These four words are both a function of and a contributor to the all-important process of self-assertion. Self-assertion is always a compassionate act involving myself. It is not aggressive. It does not put anybody else down. It is a continuing reaffirmation of my existence and it is born of my feelings for myself and from myself. Therefore, the act of choosing or preferring, in providing the central substance of assertion of *me*, is in fact providing compassionate substance of the first importance.

I AM WHERE I AM

I am where I am means I am the center of my world and also I am the center of the world. It also means I take myself wherever I go. I never abandon myself. Where, after all, is the center of the world? I am the center, as every person ought to be the center from his or her point of view. This is not a megalomaniacal point of view. Indeed, this point of view contributes to humanistic reality. It is antinarcissistic and anti what we have come to view as egocentric or egomaniacal. It is also antiprojective and antiphobic.

The individual who has no feeling for his center, and feels himself to be on the periphery of his own life, also feels that he is always on the edge of the world and that the central substance of the world is invariably at a great distance from him. When we feel this way, our sense of identity, solidity and balance is always fragile, highly precarious and tenuous. This contributes to an abdication of responsibility for ourselves. We become more reliant on other people's reactions for a sense of ourselves and in order to make decisions. This makes for projections in which we see others as the origins of our own feelings and ideas. This also makes for a chronic quest for narcissistic supplies, that is, for reassurance from *them*, from anonymous others, that we are all right after all. It also results in a synthetic blowing up of self, sometimes to megalomaniacal proportions in an effort to feel more adequate.

The loss of sense of central self and this self-hating shift of gravity, so that the center of our world is always distant, make us feel like strangers wherever we go, with other people and with ourselves. Each situation and each place becomes a strange situation and place, so that we become fearful and often develop symptomatic phobias as a response to this fear.

I recently terminated treatment of one of the members of a psychotherapeutic group I have been conducting for some years. The alarmed response from those in the group whose *center of the world* was not well established was immediate, and the anxiety generated almost palpable. They were at once concerned with what the new hierarchy of importance in the group would be. Who would be first, second, third now? Would it be based on intelligence, leadership, beauty? This was not a frivolous scramble for attention or for better status. It was rather a function of fear and an attempt to quickly re-establish a sense of self *vis-à-vis* the change of balance in that room now that someone had left the group. The people who experienced their centers as being within themselves felt no threat to their identifying structures. They were the same people before and after that member left the group. True, they were affected. They had feelings about her leaving. But these feelings did not include threats to the human substance that identifies us as separate, whole selves; these people know where they ended and others began.

If a person does not have a well-delineated feeling for a center and for one's own borders and separateness, one then feels only as part of the conglomerate mass of people. When identification is felt only as part of the mass "out there somewhere," any loss of the mass is felt as a loss of self. This in itself is a kind of megalomania in which one feels as large as the group of people with whom one identifies. It also makes for a megalomaniacal outlook in which we feel that every move we make will be of paramount importance, since as part of an extended and conglomerate humanity we feel we affect the mass in a highly exaggerated way. This can result in profound inhibition and even paralysis. It is part of an absorbing and being-absorbed process rather than a relating process, which can only take place between two whole and separate selves.

The group experience takes place constantly. If I enter a room and am immediately concerned as to where I fit in the pecking order, so far as money, looks, intelligence, sexual attractiveness, size, or any facet of the human condition is concerned, this is proof positive that the center of my world is not in me, where it ought to be, and I must make every effort to bring it home to where it belongs.

When I'm a whole and separate complete human being whose world's center is in myself, I know that I am in the best position to relate fruitfully to others. I have a real sense of self to relate with and I have no desire to shift responsibility for my life to *them*, to impose my ideas on *them*, to be absorbed by *them* or to absorb *them*. I am interested in an exchange and that exchange takes place between people who are whole people unto themselves.

Since the center of my world shifts with me, to where I am geographically, relative to other people, relative to work and to all other facets of the human condition, *I am at home* wherever *I am*. To whatever degree I have shed other than human attributes (martyrdom, saintliness, immortality, etc.) and have embraced the real human condition, I am still more at home. I find myself free of the need to establish who I am *vis-à-vis* others in a synthetic and frantic pecking order. I find myself free of pretentious maneuvers and cover-up embroideries. To whatever extent I am able to take responsibility for my feelings, choices, decisions and my life in all of its ramifications, *I am at home* and *my home is where I am.* I do not attempt to run from myself symbolically through either geographical or situational changes (seeking out other people, other jobs, other activities that mean little to me except that they are change, flight).

If I change situations it is because I want to. I know I can't run from myself and don't want to. On the contrary, I find the knowledge that *I am whoever I am* a great comfort since I am the best source of strength to myself and become more so as I am able to stand up to self-hate. People who can't stand being themselves are not being with themselves. They are being with self-hate, which has inundated them. This sense of being at home and being in the center of the world increases my sense of security as much as one can feel secure. Since I am not clinging to the periphery of the world, I am not constantly in fear of sliding off into oblivion. I am my center; I take myself wherever I go and I'm at home wherever I am.

The feeling of being at home in myself and being right at the epicenter of my world gives me a sense of compassionate inner safety that no cultural attainment, material possessions, power over others or saintliness can possibly provide. Thus, my ability to adapt to new situations is increased markedly. I can take constructive risks without fear and thus can enrich myself with new experiences in the service of my own healthy growth.

BE HERE NOW!

Be here now! is a compassionate directive to myself to live and to enjoy myself *as I am, where I am* and *when I am,* meaning *now.* I do not postpone living because I am not who I want to be. For example, as a medical student, I am not delaying satisfaction by living only for when I become a doctor. As a single person, I am not postponing my life or living in an anticipatory state of suspended animation in order to come to life only when I become married. Indeed, I am much more interested in *being* than I am in *becoming.* This does not preclude having goals and wanting to evolve and to develop intellectually, emotionally and professionally. But I do not permit goals, plans and ambitions to impoverish, let alone to destroy, any aspect of who I am currently. Utmost respect for who I am must precede and take precedence over who I may become. The same is true of who I have been.

Life is a continuum and I am the sum total of all I've been, but my vantage point and my largest interest is from the point I am at now. To *be,* means as *I am I* currently and this *I* must not be demeaned by either the past or the future. *Be* means to have full respect for who I am at any given moment and to live fully as I am. *Here* applies to whatever situation I am currently in, either geographically or situationally. This means relative to other people, to work, to current conditions, etc. Again, I do not permit other places or situations, past or future or imagined, to demean my current *here.*

If I am in New York in winter, I do not undermine my *here* with dreams of *Florida.* If I can go to Florida and decide to go, then I enjoy New York as much as I can until I go; I enjoy the trip to Florida as much as I can, and when I'm in Florida I don't ruin Florida by thinking of New York. If I can't go, I make as much use of New York as I can in my own behalf. I do not impoverish myself by demeaning where I am, what I'm doing, or what I've got. I use my current car until I get a new one and when I get it, I use that one. The one I'm using is more important to me than the one I do not yet own. If I'm working in my office I do not dilute the satisfaction derived from my work with fantasies of other activity which cannot be actualized.

The most important period from my point of view is the period defined by the time of my life. The most important time of my life is the present, the current now. Again, now must not in any way be denigrated by either fact or fantasy involving any other period of time. My *now* is sacred and I dignify it with serious care. This does not mean that I sit in constant judgment of how well I use time in the service of accomplishment. But I am concerned and involved in using my time in a satisfying way.

I do not deaden myself in this *now* of mine because I am impatient for tomorrow to arrive. I do not attempt through the use of any kind of stratagem, such as living in my imagination, to push the time of my life past me in an effort to actualize a future now and to get rid of this one. I do not waste the time of my life in futile recriminations about the past or worrying ruminations involving the future.

There is only *now*. The past is gone and the future is not yet here. I refuse to live this day as if it is the last day or only day of my life. This outlook is too pressuring and frantic. It has an aura of self-hate and I suspect is motivated by the need for self-hating, inappropriate and exorbitant accomplishment. I prefer to see this day as the first day. The first day is full of wonders and interests and this approach makes me the master of my time rather than the reverse, in which I become the slave of time.

While there is only *NOW, now is not forever.* This is not a paradox or a trick statement. It simply means that I enjoy the present as I can, with awareness of the possibility of change in other presents. In this way, I recognize my life as a continuing process rather than as a static entity.

How long is now? is an interesting question and I'm sure can lend itself to much philosophical discussion. In this connection I only want to say that with great repression, and an inability to tap our inner selves fully, *now* feels like tiny isolated segments. Life seems as if it is broken up into good and bad and all kinds of qualitative but for the most part impoverished and shortened *nows*. Self-acceptance, which contributes to greater consciousness, greater integrations of all aspects of ourselves, and greater ability to apply ourselves to perception of our world and our time, makes for a different feeling outlook. This particularly pertains to the feeling of *the present—the now* of our lives. *Now* is felt as a continuum and as such is felt as much more and much longer than an isolated, fleeting segment. It embraces all kinds of experiences, regardless of their particular value assignments (good or bad) as part of the process of living. The combined ability to tap one's whole self in perceiving, feeling and living *now* and to accept all occurrences and experiences of life as part of the human experience makes for a longer and richer *now*.

The application of *Be Here Now!* makes a valuable contribution to the fight against self-hating flights of fancy, recrimination for missed opportunities, and endless postponement of living. It aids immeasurably in *enriching life with what is available and possible*. It is the antithesis of resignation. The resigned, impoverished-feeling person expends all his energy in a desperate attempt to hold on to a status quo, to make static and to stultify. *Be Here Now!* enriches life so that it becomes an ever-evolving process of enriching changes.

THE PROCESS IS THE PRODUCT

Life is a process. It is a process in terms of biology, emotions, relating and all of human experiencing. Life is not a product. It is not static. It is ever moving, ever changing, and the most important process is that of my own life, my very own living experiences in all their ramifications. For my purposes, no matter what my age, I am smack in the middle of the living process all the time. Introductions, beginnings, endings and epitaphs have little interest for me. The middle is what interests me the most. The middle is the quintessential part of living.

What I am doing; what I am in the middle of; my current experiencing of my being *vis-à-vis* any activity— the process itself is not merely more important than the goal it fulfills or the accomplishment it produces or the product which results. It *is* that product. The product could not exist without the process and is only a representation of the process. If the process is the product, then accomplishment and lack of accomplishment, success and failure, good results and bad results, cannot rob us of either time or energy or self used by us in the time of our lives.

The process of writing a book is infinitely more important than the book that is completed as a result of the writing, let alone the success or failure the book may have after it is written. Without writing it, there would be no book. In writing it there is much more than a book, which is after all only a representative symbol of the writing that has taken place. In writing the book, I am living, I am growing, I am tapping myself, I am changing, I am synthesizing, I am struggling, I am producing. Yes, I am living, and I don't need a book or any other product and fulfillment of goals as evidence that I have in fact been engaging in the process of writing and living, because the process is indeed the product.

I think of the performing arts. The dancer who dances engages in the process regardless of whether or not the dance is recorded on film. The process is all. Now, you can ask, "Don't you care how the book is received after it is done?" Yes, I do. And my caring at that point is part of still another process—perhaps that of selling the book. Caring about the product—sale of the book during the writing or how the audience receives the dance during the dance— splits the artist and detracts from the process. To dance while observing audience reaction destroys total participation.

Investment *in the process rather than the product* is invariably compassionate and anti-self-hating in its effect. Process living is enriching in terms of plausible and available everyday pursuits. It does not require impossible and sustained highs in order to be viable and effective. It works against destructive competitive striving (making relating to others easier and happier), against efforts to attain impossible goals and the self-castigating attacks that follow falls from illusionary heights. It is one of the best antidotes for destructive and very painful mood swings.

Removing the judgment value that comes from *goal-directed living* (or *product living*) relieves us of destructive striving as well as self-hating consequences. It also frees us and encourages us to engage in here and now living and here and now real satisfactions. Process living neutralizes the depleting and impoverishing effects of chronically living in anticipation. Even when impossible goals occasionally are reached, satisfactions derived from them are invariably disappointing unless *the process* has given ample satisfaction along the way.

Process living blocks the gaff of unrealistic striving, blunts the sting of so-called failures, and enriches and strengthens the self as satisfaction is derived from every-day living.

I ALWAYS DO MY BEST

Yes, I do in fact always do my best. Whatever I do, is an expression of me at any given time. Therefore, whatever I do *is* one of my signatures, that is, a particular signature of me, at a particular time. It is *my* best because it *is* me at the time that I do it. In terms of myself and in my nonjudgmental, self-accepting, compassionate frame of reference, my heart is my best heart, my head is my best head, my thought is my best thought, and my action in this now of mine is my best action.

Indeed, best, worst, good, bad are qualitative words that are applicable only in a judgmental frame of reference applied from the outside to me. I refuse to judge me. I am happier assuming that what I do expresses me the best way I can express me in the moment. If my energy and time are spent observing and examining my thoughts, feelings, choices and actions, I do so not in the service of judgment or to assign value to performance. It is for the purpose of better understanding me so as to better help myself to still further self-acceptance.

My best may or may not be good enough for somebody else. Since life is not static, since I am always in process and in a state of change, I may be different tomorrow, and my best at that time may be a different best, too. If my best changes tomorrow, it is not because *it* has changed, but rather because *I* will have changed and therefore will express myself differently. If I exert more effort it will be because being different I exert more effort. If I exert less effort, this, too, is representative of a change in me which I accept and respect. Since nothing I do is worthy of self-hate, all that I do is easily seen by me as myself, or, if you will, my best.

This is in no way an attempt to escape or to dilute responsibility. Quite the contrary, self-acceptance is the epitome of responsibility, since it contributes to an integration of all aspects of self on a conscious level where responsibility functions best.

Seeing all aspects of self as being functions of self is practically a definition of being responsible for oneself and one's actions. If there are no judgments, there are no excuses or rationalizations. If self-accepting examination replaces castigation, responsibility is embraced rather than shunned. If we want to change the best we do, which is whatever we do, we must change ourselves. In important matters this usually involves changes in our hierarchy of values rather than a question of effort. In any case, constructive change is much more likely to take place when we feel we've done our best, since it now comes on a foundation built of self-esteem and dignity. "I always do my best," is a prime weapon against the onslaught of self-hate.

CONTRACTS, CONSISTENCY, CONGRUITY

As a human being, my psyche is full of incongruous and inconsistent feelings, thoughts, ideas and urges. Many of these inconsistencies and incongruities exist in close relationship to each other and include shades from the most simple and subtle to the most complex and blatant. To expect otherwise would be to expect the inhuman of myself. In fact, these very incongruities and inconsistencies identify me *as human.*

All other creatures on earth are infinitely more predictable, largely because they are highly consistent. My feelings and moods, compared to all other creatures, are capable of enormous complexity and changeability.

I contain hateful and loving feelings; possessive, generous, acrimonious, paranoid, open and altruistic feelings; jealous, envious and self-assured feelings, and many others. I contain them all at the same time. They exist side by side and they never exist in pure form. They are always there in combinations and patterns at least as complicated as the biochemical make-up of a molecule of life.

The complexity of my feelings is further enhanced by the myriad shades and nuances each represents. I can feel anywhere from imperceptible irritation to raw, raging hate. I can feel anywhere from a slight sense of ownership to utter possessiveness and bitter chauvinsim. The complexity of my inner psychic life and my life as a relating human being is further complicated by the fact that the people to whom I relate are as complex as I am. We do perceive each other, we do live within the matrix of the culture into which we were born and which constantly affects us as we in turn contribute to it. And none of what goes on in us remains static. Like the biological living cell, like the molecule of life, like the universe we live in, all is in a constant state of flux.

To demand congruity, consistency, fixed contracts, irrevocable decisions, clear-cut choices and ideas, predictable fixed behavioral patterns, purity of purpose and simple well-delineated feelings free of ambivalence and ambiguity in a world that becomes increasingly more complex every second is demanding a condition that is antithetical and foreign to the state of being a person. It is also asking for a death warrant.

It is true that human inconsistency and incongruity often get in the way of cultural rules and standards, and cultural demands make life nearly impossible for us, since they often demonstrate so little understanding or sympathy for the complexity we represent, let alone our enormous sensibility and vulnerability. But this very complexity of feelings, these very ambiguities and inconsistencies make it possible to survive and to survive as the most interesting relating and communicating creatures on earth, with all due respect to latter-day information regarding whales and dolphins.

Our complex, vast hodge-podge of myriad receptors, generators and transmitters of feelings are a burden, but they not only make us unique, they also make survival possible. Yes, they make for difficulty in arriving at choices and decisions; they make for struggle with ourselves and with each other—and these are sometimes destructive struggles—but they also make for survival.

In this enormous myriad of complexity we contain a vast storehouse of human substance capable of infinite combinations, which gives us unique flexibility. This makes us the symbolic reading and writing creatures we are. This makes us the unique inventors, creators and users of medicines, machinery and all the other materials we have developed as tools for living. This enables us to understand and to use abstractions.

In short, the very stuff that burdens us and produces

struggle (seeing many sides of an issue is more complicating and painful, but more realistic, too, than oversimplification) gives us enormous adaptative ability. The demands on us for adaptation have not yet even begun and our ability to adapt has not yet even been scratched. It is tempting to try to obliterate feelings and especially mixed, divergent ones, to polarize, to fragment, to compartmentalize in an attempt to avoid painful struggle. But it doesn't work.

Blinders are for horses and we use them on horses to prevent panic. In people, panic often ensues when unwanted feelings come up, sometimes in the form of peculiar thoughts or ideas that don't seem to fit and intrude on what seemed like a clear-cut position.

But this seeming mass of confusion is, in fact, the germinating ground for the creative efforts unique in man that make man so adaptable. Adaptability is the key to survival; without it we become extinct. When we attempt to oversimplify, overpolarize, overcompartmentalize, under the guise of smoothing things out and making things easier, the ultimate effect is stultification and paralysis.

Ultimate smoothness and lack of inner incongruity, total lack of inner conflict and lack of struggle, and constant adaptation only take place in death itself. This is not to say that inner conflict and turmoil cannot be reduced to relatively comfortable proportions. As the quest for utter inner peace and perfection and the attempt to have it all is reduced, relative comfort ensues. But comfort can only be relative. Knowing this is of immediate value in reducing self-hate born of impossible expectations. Whenever we aid the chairman of the board to make a choice and help him to surrender some of the desires involved in all choices without leaving a residue of acrimony, we aid the cause of comfort. By whatever means we aid compassion and resolve the conflict between it and self-hate, we are *enhancing* inner peace, but peace is *never* absolute.

When I speak of human inconsistency I am reminded of an experience I recently had. I was watching the news on television, a film depicting the plight of Arab refugees. I immediately felt most sympathetic for those suffering people. They then showed films demonstrating the great difficulty of Israelis living in bordering kibbutz sites, who were constantly being raided and killed by Arab guerrillas. I then felt great sympathy for them and rage at the Arabs.

In a few minutes this feeling subsided and I thought about the human condition, us, and the state of the world generally, and how much more advancement we need in the area of human communication and relatedness. Now I felt sad for the young Arab men who participated in these raids. I then asked myself whose side I was on and among whom I would be counted if the chips were down. I knew that I was on the side of the Israelis and that I would definitely be found in their camp, though I would continue to have all kinds of sad and mixed feelings and could at least in some measure understand the suffering of all concerned.

I did not polarize. I did not deaden and cut off unwanted feelings in an attempt to simplify my stance and to feel pure patriotic fervor for my side and hatred for the other. I did not destroy my quite human capacity for empathy in exchange for inhuman ideas of pure principle. Most importantly, I did not generate any guilt or any other form of self-hate or any feelings of disloyalty because my feelings were incongruous, impure, inconsistent and even changeable.

My acceptance of my feelings was not based on an

attempt to be particularly virtuous or saintlike. It was based on my knowing that being a person entails complexity and on an absolute refusal to perform a psychological lobotomy on myself by cutting off and deadening any aspect of myself and how I respond and feel in a given situation. This is a freedom which must be fought for against any self-hating inner coercion, or against pressure from an outside force that would dictate otherwise. This is the antithesis of Orwell's Big Brother's "double think" and thought control. This represents one of the most serious aspects of the freedom to be a person and constitutes a most important cornerstone of the compassionate nucleus.

As a person, I *must absolutely refuse to make any contract whatsoever that calls for consistency of feelings, purity of feelings or the promise that I will feel a particular way forever.* I know that such a contract would be at best a superficial and phony machination and at worst is antithetical to being a person and would lead to self-hate. It would do so because it immediately involves cutting off parts of myself and my human responsiveness. Changes in moods, feelings, yearnings, desires and goals are characteristic of the human condition, especially when a person is healthy enough to retain a good deal of aliveness. Also, the consistency contract must invariably be broken and breaks will surely lead to guilty self-recrimination and depression. The best decisions are based on feelings, that is, knowledge of how we feel. While respect for how we feel and decisions that are a function of how we feel are in order, we must not be bound down by these decisions. Feelings change, and that our decisions change accordingly is appropriate to healthy flexibility.

I must insist on the right to changes of feelings and even complete turnabouts in how I feel. I must insist on the human right to change my mind. This is not schizophrenic evidence of weakness or lack of commitment. It is evidence of being an alive, flexible, adaptable human being who constantly receives information, assembles and re-assembles it and feels many, many ways.

Of course, the chairman of the board eventually makes choices and decisions, and changeability used as a rationalization never to make a choice is destructive. But knowing that we sanction and approve of the right to change can, in fact, make choices and decisions easier and clearer since we are not then pressured by the terrible knowledge that each choice must be forever.

I insist on the right to harbor all kinds of nuances and mixtures of feelings, moods, certainties, uncertainties and confusions. I know that clinging to the stance of being immediately clear about things masks chronic confusion that is never clarified at all. I know that permitting myself, and even encouraging, confusion is the only route to real re-evaluation and real clarification. The former is an attempt to muddle through and to delude myself. The latter is allowing dissolution to take place so that real reassemblage and reintegration can follow. It is frightening to let go, to feel it and to feel confused, but this very process permits the kind of clarity that leads to real inner strength.

Many patients use the term breakdown when in fact they are going through a breakup of neurotic defenses and patterns, as I mentioned earlier. They can experience considerable fright and pain in such a process, but will eventually go through a strengthening, re-evaluating clarification of considerable merit. When we allow ourselves to feel it all, relatively speaking, of course, we are in fact engaging in this process constantly and thus often avoid the necessity of massive, painful breakups.

Our human demand for congruity creates unnecessary confusion and even terror. We become confused when we encounter the unexpected. Sometimes we become terrified because we encounter that which we have convinced ourselves is not supposed to be there. I believe such incongruities are the basis of successful horror stories and films. They count on the fact that we shut out incongruities and especially those situated in close juxtaposition to each other. By surprising those of us (and this means most of us) who insist that incongruous forces and characteristics do not meet, such stories and films produce a reaction of fright and horror. They openly mix ingredients that we have convinced ourselves never mix in human beings, which produce horror reactions in us as our own unexpected incongruities are stirred up. Thus they mix the living and the dead (we are not supposed to harbor very alive and relatively deadened feelings), the beautiful and the monstrous (who among us doesn't have both beautiful feelings and monstrous ones?), the innocent and the evil, the overwhelmingly powerful and the vulnerably helpless, etc.

But we do not need horror stories or films in order to go about in a state of inner terror on a chronic and devastating level. If we attempt to hold down and out of the way any feelings or ideas that are incompatible with our contrived notions of ourselves and the world, surely revulsion, horror, terror and even panic will ensue whenever these incongruities threaten to emerge. Repressed feelings are the ones that burst forth to produce unwanted and incomprehensible acts. To the extent that we honor all aspects of ourselves, we remove revulsion, self-hate, horror and terror from our lives. As whole human beings we are the creatures of the greatest complexity on this planet. Respect for this complexity includes our insisting on acceptance of the inconsistent and incongruous.

NO

I must have the right to say *"No."* Only I can give myself this right on a meaningful basis. Meaningful does not include an arbitrary *no* born of negativism without thought or the exercise of free will. My *no* is a function of some of the deepest compassionate feelings for myself. This *no* of mine represents whatever force I can bring against anything in me or outside of me which I recognize as being antithetical to my well-being. This *no* represents me at my most grown up. This *no* makes my *yes* meaningful.

Without this *no* I am without healthy, self-preserving defenses against infantile aspects of myself. These infantile aspects demand satisfaction of all impulses and desires, perfection in all areas of my life (perfect son, father, brother, doctor), satisfaction of all aspects of every conflict I find myself in, so that I have no need to make constructive and adult but painful choices. They result in demands for perfect relationships and a perfect world despite the incongruities and complexities of existence. They produce demands for omnipotence and omniscience, and all and every manner of childish, outrageous self-hating demand I make on myself.

Without this *no* I am indefensible against the demands

of other people and their desires, and even casual statements are often felt by me as demands. Because I can't say
no, then their demands become commands I must comply
with even in advance of anyone's request of me. Yes,
without this *no* I find myself in the untenable, chronic
condition of having somehow to please all aspects of my
complicated self as well as those of other complicated
people all at the same time. I am the prisoner of others.
Without this *no* I have no selective ability to accept or
reject requests arising in me or in people outside of myself.
I am buffeted about by all that goes on in me and cannot
develop a chairman of the board who can build a feasible
hierarchy of values, one based on what is humanly possible
and attainable. I play the role of Mr. Nice Guy with people
and function on a meaningless yes-man, sop basis.

None of us is perfectly mature, none of us destroys
self-hate completely, and none of us is completely able to
close off pressures from the outside. We all retain a certain
measure of infantilism. I have come to call this infant in us
"the omnipotent screamer," who wants it all (think of the
little boy who cries because he just finished his ice cream),
who cannot settle for choices and decisions that eliminate
certain possibilities in favor of others, and who never
forgives for decisions which turn out to be less than
perfect. Being able to say *no* to the omnipotent screamer is
of prime importance in establishing human dignity and
benevolence. This *no* becomes extended to a broader *no*
and to any forces destructive to my well-being.

No is my key to selectivity, choice and decision.

No is my key to a hierarchy of values that permit me to
function and to enjoy life reasonably.

No is my block and fortress to and against self-hate.

No is my stand against impossible demands wherever they come from.

No gives meaning to my *yes*, the yes that applies to choices and decisions I make and which I try to make, always doing my best. This *no* protects me from later recriminations and compassionately sustains me in the belief that I did my best when I made them regardless of how things turn out later. *No* prevents me from being a "yes-man." My *yes* to other people has meaning in terms of my own convictions.

PARTICIPATION AND PERFORMANCE

I say *no!* to performance. I refuse to perform! This applies to work, lecturing to an audience, sex, or any other area of my life or activity. Participate? Yes. I certainly desire and make efforts to participate in my life and in my life *vis-à-vis* other people and activities. Participation calls for my full involvement and my full contribution, and I see it as a compassionate contribution within my human means and limitations and without recriminating judgmental value. This applies to physical, intellectual and emotional activity. In participation I am *my whole self* and I am involved as my whole self, making self-consciousness and embarrassment virtually impossible.

Performance involves self-consciousness, self-judgment, fear of self-hate and fear of derision from other people. In performing I split myself into two people, the one doing the performing and the one watching the performance and also watching audience response, if there is an audience. Splitting, watching and judging not only prevent total, integrated participation of self, but also make for attacks of acute anxiety and impotence. Impotence, here, may be applied to sexual responsiveness in both men and women, as well as to whatever other activity may be taking place. This kind of consciousness of self can produce severe inhibition and stage fright in surgeons as well as actors, and is the stuff of phobias and paralysis.

If I refuse to dignify any demand for performance, but at most ask myself to be part of what's going on, I can enter into the situation as a whole person on a spontaneous level, free of the omnipotent screamer, whom I don't permit to sit on my shoulder.

As I mentioned earlier, my initial experience in lecturing was an ordeal. Until I realized the difference between performing and participation I used to get terribly anxious when I had to give a lecture of any kind. Indeed, I thought I'd have to stop lecturing altogether because the toll it took was becoming much too much. After I worked out the difficulty I was able to function in this capacity with relative ease. I asked myself, "Am I a performer? Do I expect my listeners to keel over in ecstasy having heard my impassioned, artful rendition?" The answer was no, but it came only after I asked the question.

Prior to that time my unconscious answer was yes. I expected a brilliant performance of myself and had a battery of self-hate waiting if I failed. Intense audience response and the narcissistic supplies they could give me would block or at least dilute that self-hate. Therefore, I was split three ways. One of me was lecturing; one of me was watching me; and one of me was watching the audience. Of course my destructive self-consciousness was enormous. Additionally, I was hardly in a position to whole-heartedly apply myself to my lecture. How could I when I was distracted by these divisions in myself and when I was also under such severe surveillance and demands as well? I struggled to give up the need for the narcissistic supplies that might ensue. I struggled against the self-hate in myself that was poised and ready and I struggled to re-establish a proper sense of proportion. I also struggled to re-establish my proper identity.

I told myself that audience response *would* be pleasurable but was essentially unnecessary to my true well-being and existence, and I believed it.

I also informed myself of another truth. That lecture, any lecture, was simply not that important. No lecture is as important as I am, and what I had been doing to myself and demanding of myself was grossly unfair. However the lecture went, there was simply no realistic crisis or catastrophe associated with it. But another aspect of a sense of proportion had to be established. I could fail and I had to have the right to fail. Indeed, I had somehow forgotten how many failures I had survived. I had forgotten that failure is no disgrace.

I had forgotten whatever humility I had and realized I had been identified with enormous vanity. I had forgotten that I knew very well that failure was not a disgrace or catastrophic but really an artifact manufactured by a culture *that has become ruthless and castigating in terms of its own humanity.* Our culture has forgotten that human experience is a cyclic affair made up of many bumps: the interpretation of this pattern as success or failure is a cruel, inhuman and unrealistic outlook. I took a little time to re-examine the whole business of success and failure and exorbitant expectations, and realized that in many ways I had become considerably more enriched on a human level through my so-called failures than my so-called successes, or at least what our culture would define as success. Failure experiences, thoughtfully, not pejoratively, re-evaluated, often brought me down to a human feeling level and were full of experiential richness. Success experiences often established unrealistic pride positions in me, from which falls and fright were always imminent. In thinking the matter over, I realized that many of the suicides I knew of, interestingly, took place among "great performers" and notable successes, that is, notable by our society's standards. I asked myself if I desired to become a fame-applause-notoriety-stimulation addict, and replied with a resounding *NO!*

Then I asked myself what I really did want to do in lecturing. In answering this question I re-established who I was. I wanted to participate in a teaching-learning-relating experience. I had something I wanted to tell other people about. I was going to try to convey to them the information I had and to participate in this give-and-take experience with them. I did have an area of expertise. I had information that I wanted to give them. I began to function in a position of reality, and my expectations for myself and the response of my listeners were markedly reduced. I also had rid myself of the illusion of the importance of attaining some kind of mythical success, as well as to rid myself of a sense of impending doom and catastrophe over mythical failure. Human participation is within my means and I approach lectures now with relative ease and leave them with a fair degree of good feelings and sometimes with considerable pleasure, too.

THE RIGHT TO DIE AND
THE RIGHT TO LIVE

By the right to die I am not talking about suicide. Except in rare cases involving unretractable pain I view suicide as a horrendous self-hating act.

By the right to die or the freedom to die, I'm talking about a psychophilosophical belief which in effect states that I want to live and as long as I live I live, and when the time comes for me to die I have the freedom and the right to die. This right to die invariably has the effect of freeing me in large part from the fear of death, and in so doing, enhances my right and my ability to live. How does it do this?

Some years ago I had a patient who complained bitterly that countless people depended on him. "I don't even have the right to die." As it turned out, he died of a sudden and unexpected heart attack during his course of treatment with me. Interestingly, I found out a short while ago, that the people who depended on him, and these included an extended family as well as business associates, went through a normal period of bereavement after his death and then got along very well. No one, not one, faltered along the way, although my patient was convinced, and had nearly convinced me, that without him at least several "would not be able to go on."

The right to die and the belief in human finiteness and death are more than realistic. They are psychophilosophical dynamics which mitigate against the ultimate omnipotent grandiosity of indispensability. They work against an unconscious pride investment in the belief that the world can't do without us. They remove the guilt associated with dying and the ultimate abandonment of responsibility. We must have the right to abandon all responsibilities in the moment of death, to let go without recrimination, in the real belief that the world will in fact go on without us. This establishes the fact that while each of us is the center of our world we are not the world, we are only part of the whole and as such can rest easy in the humbling but in no way degrading knowledge that we are replaceable and that the world can and will continue when we are gone.

Honest struggle to achieve the belief in our finiteness produces reverberations which are ultimately destructive to the megalomaniacal position generally and to the fear of cataclysm regarding our individual deaths specifically. In this humble and quite dignified position, in which death is viewed as applied to a human being rather than to a universe, the fear of death is markedly reduced because it has been brought down from cataclysmic to human proportions.

When the fear of death is reduced, contemplation of it does not bring on an attack of self-hate. The world goes on after I die. It does not die with me. Its continued existence does not depend on my continued existence. I can contemplate my own death without self-hate because my death applies to no one outside myself. Without the demand on ourselves for infinite existence, self-hate generated to produce illusions of impossible eternity (through magic or glorious memorials) serves no purpose.

Viewing death from the position of life can be horrifying, initially. We see death as a gangrene where dead tissue is in horrible juxtaposition to live tissue, as if after we are dead we will be able to see ourselves in helpless, putrifying paralysis for eternity. When this point of view is overexaggerated humanity frightens itself by imbuing symbols of death, such as skeletons, shrouds and ghosts, with evil powers. The life-death juxtaposition horror is sustained largely as a result of the omnipotent refusal to embrace the fact of our own finiteness. Real gut acceptance of this fact establishes death as a separate and different entity from life, and once established as different and devoid of horror, it can be accepted more objectively and realistically as another turn in the rich cycle of life. Dilution or removal of the fear of death and concomitant enhancement of a sense of human finiteness and humility give us the unencumbered freedom to live and to concern ourselves with that most important time, the here and now time of our lives.

LIFE IS TOUGH

Life is tough! How can it be otherwise? As people we are more than complex. We are also the most sensitive, vulnerable and aware creatures on earth. Our awareness keeps us in constant touch with the extremely tenuous aspects of human existence. More than any other creatures, we know and can anticipate and despite efforts to the contrary, do anticipate loss of loved ones and loss of ourselves. We call upon ourselves to be involved, to invest great emotion, to participate and to love life, and this is good. But our very love makes our losses that much more poignant and painful, and this, too, is part of the human condition in its natural and healthy state.

As human beings we are blessed with a capacity for communication and relating that is unique on our planet. But this very language ability contains its ambiguities and limitations, making communication breakdown common and even rampant. How many times I have seen two people whom I know to be in basic agreement arguing vehemently because of language misunderstanding. The very stuff of language makes for compassionate possibility and the most vindictive possibility.

Knowledge and fear of the finiteness of life and communication breakdown often make for great fear, paranoia, hunger for power and psychotic enterprises like war. Inability to express ourselves adequately, either because of personal limitations or situational difficulty, creates great frustration and rage. Knowledge of our species' superiority creates feelings and demands for omnipotence and eternal power, generating further communication breakdown. Too, often we use our considerable assets against ourselves and each other, making life even tougher than it has to be.

Despite these assets we never are adequately prepared for the onslaughts life brings us. Sickness, suffering and death cannot be avoided. At best we struggle to survive and to enjoy our lives as we can. But we have problems with ourselves and each other—we so need each other and yet, paradoxically, find it so hard to be with each other. We have problems making compassionate, functional and realistic use of our earth's resources.

Knowing that life is tough is an extremely valuable and compassionate process. Just knowing this and accepting it as part of the life process makes living easier and better. It cuts down inappropriate efforts and striving for nonexistent security. It helps us to appreciate our efforts and their results. It helps to soften disappointments born of expectations bred in the erroneous belief that life is easy or that an easy life exists but somehow eludes *us*, alone.

Reality is the best friend of compassion and the fact of

the toughness of life is a reality of prime importance. An important adjunct of reality is the fact that we human beings are pretty tough, too. If we have unduly fragile concepts of ourselves, this is to a large extent the result of an illusion that we are invulnerable and impervious. When we *feel* fragile we cut ourselves off from our real resources and strengths. Actually, we are tough. We are resourceful, and for the most part we manage very well.

There is much in life that will always remain imperceptible, unattainable, uncontrollable and unpredictable. We cannot climb every mountain and cross every river and anticipate every pitfall. We are sometimes right and often wrong. We must fight for the right to fail and to be wrong. In this way we don't make life tougher than it is and we become tougher and stronger by giving ourselves these human rights. These *rights* enhance our flexibility, and being able to bend, we don't break and crack because of rigidity.

At best, life still remains uncontrollable, unpredictable, finite. This is not a bitter, cynical, hopeless or depressing statement. It is only depressing if one retains imaginary Heaven-on-Earth illusions and uses them as comparison. It is a realistic fact, a compassionate fact; deep inner knowledge of it enhances our compassion and appreciation for ourselves, for our struggles, and for the human condition generally.

Compassion makes life easier, but is in no way a retreat from life nor is it an easy road to take. In establishing an increasingly realistic frame of reference, compassion has the effect of thrusting us into the very middle of ourselves and into the middle of life generally. With fewer and less devastating wounds, withdrawal and resignation become much less common. With increased satisfaction and less fear of recrimination, creative aspects of ourselves can be realized and used and we are much freer to move in the direction of increased involvement and participation in life's activities generally.

Developing compassion for ourselves inevitably results in developing compassion for our fellows and for the life process that we all share. Relating on a more realistic level to ourselves and to our fellows makes life easier and happier. The struggle for compassion is not easy. Like life itself, it is tough. Once engaged on a serious level, it goes on all of our lives, as we continue to grow all of our lives.

We never reach an absolute state of grace with ourselves, nor do we attain a compassionate psychophilosophy that functions without any dilution at all. The battle against self-hate is never complete. Being compassionate is not a static condition nor a status quo. Compassion is a life process and as such it is compassionate and realistic only if we view it on a relative basis. If we live in a state of compassionate struggle against self-hate and are developing a relatively compassionate psychophilosophy, we are realistically and constructively helping ourselves.

PART IV

On Human Terms

The Destructive Culture

The culture we live in comprises more than conventions and customs. It provides a value system, a frame of reference (of which we may have no conscious awareness), that in many ways defines the human condition in terms of both the individual and the world he lives in. Through language and ideas, through propaganda and the media we are pervasively and insidiously pressured and often persuaded into believing much that is erroneous about emotional and social human anatomy. The values of our society and culture have been handed down to us by our parents and their parents before them. But many of these cultural standards are antithetical to being a person. Living on those terms is often impossible. Many of these concepts contain erroneous ideas about human characteristics, human relationships and human expectations, which dictate a rigid, choiceless and self-destructive life-style. In setting puristic, extreme and conflicting standards, they obscure reality, denigrate the human condition, and produce a confused state, in which we forget what it is to be a person. In this way the culture provides a reservoir of material that is tapped and used in the service of self-hate. This mainly takes the form of disastrous illusions and terrible demands on ourselves and on the world at large, leading to bitter disappointment, hopelessness and despair.

We often are unaware of how inhuman, Godlike and impossible our terms for living and for self-acceptance have become. We usually have no idea that our aspirations are often totally inappropriate and incompatible with being human. Our culture produces many double-bind situations in which we are damned if we *do* and damned if we *don't*, and, even worse, damned if we *are* certain ways and at the same time damned if we *aren't*. For example, we are condemned as nonassertive if we are gentle, and as aggressively abrasive and braggarts if we are self-assertive. This surely provides a great fund for feeding the stuff of destructive illusions and forthcoming self-hate and stultification. Connections between our most malignant difficulties and the culture we live in are undeniable and constantly overlapping.

In this section I will discuss some of the most common concepts and symbols I have come across in myself and in patients, and will examine and comment on some of the more important emotion-laden stereotypes. There are many more and each of us must ferret out and be wary of those that are destructive in our own lives. *Standing up to and against cultural misinforming processes is invaluable.* It is vitally important to be wary and questioning about the absolutes dictated by the culture. We must especially examine them for lack of human compassion. Fighting against concepts which are basically inhuman is a way of humanizing ourselves and at the same time contributing to making our culture compassionate. Each of us is affected by, and ultimately has his effect on, the culture. To insist on living on human terms must have ameliorative repercussions on the human milieu generally.

PEOPLE, ANIMALS AND ANTS

Yes, it is true that ants live in social structures dictated by chemical or instinctual forces. Yes, it is true that animals other than people have intelligence. Yes, it is true that the species homo sapiens biologically falls into the category of animal. But to me people are much more than a mass of biological and instinctual stimuli and responses. People make cultures. People are capable of making choices. People are vastly different from any other creatures encountered up to this point. People may have limited abilities, but I do not believe they are limited and forever patterned in all respects, either by genetic structure or conditioned patterning of their first months of life. People can change and grow, however old and limited they may be at any given point.

COWARDICE, BRAVERY, COURAGE AND FEAR

I don't know exactly what cowardice is. I do know that our society uses the term pejoratively and alludes to it as a relatively rare and detestable condition. If fear is cowardice, then all normally sensitive people are surely cowards. To fear dangerous situations, including hazardous physical confrontations, dangerous relationships and entanglements, including those of a social, emotional and business nature, is self-preserving and often life-saving.

Our culture sees fearlessness as a virtue and particularly a masculine virtue. Fear is a natural and very valuable attribute common to all creatures of any intelligence on this planet. *To destroy the ability to be afraid is a guarantee of death and extinction.* To be afraid inappropriately and to the point of inhibition and paralysis may be the result of poor judgment either as applied to oneself or to a given situation. To be afraid inappropriately because of profound emotional insecurity and feelings of vulnerability surely asks for compassionate understanding; such feelings are not rare, and can and inevitably do occur at times in the lives of *all* human beings.

To fear war, which is a psychotic enterprise no matter what the ultimate rationalization or motivation, and to fear physical confrontations which can lead to death are appropriate life-saving reactions. The decision to refuse to kill and to chance being killed has genuine merit in the scope of human complexity, however devoted one may be to cause or country. Willingness to sacrifice one's life for a cause or for someone else is almost inevitably the result of severe self-hate, and dreams of a glorious nonexistent Valhalla or severely aberrated judgment. The exceptions, and these are not common, exist in those of us who have been unusually loyal to ourselves, so that there is no question of the presence of functioning self-hate. Self-sacrifice in this case may be a function of meaningful choice rather than neurotic need or compulsion.

Unusual bravery as promoted by our society is largely a myth and often serves as an impossible standard, producing much embarrassment and self-hate. Many so-called brave and self-sacrificing acts are born of impulses having little or nothing at all to do with love of one's fellow man. They are often the result of brain-washing, simplistic development and thinking, rage, poor judgment, poor impulse control, poor frustration tolerance, an enormous but usually hidden fund of raging self-hate, glory-seeking to compensate for feelings of rejection, compensation for fear about sexual identification, and psychopathy or sociopathy. The disquieting fact is that some of the so-called bravest acts are committed by people who are social misfits and borderline criminals.

The relatively well-adjusted individual is not famous for so-called heroic acts. Our culture demonstrates a preference on the part of most of us for peaceful and cautious behavior appropriate to fearful situations when it is called for, and then does a complete turnabout, condoning murder and suicide when national policy condones it. The well-adjusted self-saving individual cannot make this turnabout without severe repercussions because it involves behavior that is injurious to his development and evolvement as a compassionate human being. The maladjusted psychopathic individual, who hates himself and others to an enormous degree and who has deadened his sensibilities, can lend himself to both criminal violence or legal violence with equal enthusiasm. Many individuals dubbed as "brave" by our culture are feared and rejected once violent periods are passed because such "heroes" often make very poor adjustments to any kind of existence commensurate with compassionate sustaining of life *on a long-term basis.*

I think the bravest thing most of us do is to get up each morning and to face whatever life has in store for us. This is no small matter, considering our feelings, our sensitivity, our vulnerability and our awareness, however repressed, of how unpredictable and tenuous life and the world are. We are not aided by the considerable and ever-increasing complexity of the culture we live in.

The most courageously constructive thing we can do is to engage in the battle for compassion against self-hate.

This, after all, is the battle that dignifies man. This is the act that ultimately helps us to live better with ourselves and our fellows. It takes courage, real and constructive courage, to stand up against all kinds of inner and outer pressures. This is not easy; we must surely falter along the way, and during times of discouragement it is toughest of all to be compassionate, but we can try. Perhaps one day we will have parades celebrating the discovery of insulin and penicillin rather than commemorations of military exploits and conquests of human beings!

ARROGANCE, JEALOUSY, ENVY, PARANOIA AND GENEROSITY, HONESTY, OPENNESS AND TRUST

Our culture breeds and condemns arrogance, jealousy, envy and paranoia. We put great stock and praise on openness, trust, straightforwardness and even naïveté. We are also contemptuous of simplicity, honesty, openness and naïveté as childish and foolish, and secretly admire manipulation, duplicity, craftiness and suspiciousness. A culture that fosters and breeds suspiciousness, acquisitiveness and competition, and worships mastery and perfection, must breed fear. Arrogance and paranoia are the offspring of fear and especially fear of fear. If we are afraid of being afraid, we cover up with arrogance. If we are terrified of impending self-hate largely generated by "not measuring up," we project to others and become paranoid. Our paranoia is further fed by competitive suspiciousness, manipulation and duplicity, as our arrogance is fed by a culture that confuses arrogance with true inner strength.

Yet despite cultural condemnation and praise, all these traits and responses are human and exist ambivalently in each and every one of us. None of us lacks the ability to generate arrogance, paranoia—and trust, too—and we do so very often, all at the same time. In a culture that is constantly ambivalent about human characteristics, feelings and ways of relating, human beings cannot be otherwise. All of us not only have ambivalent feelings but often are ambivalent about each of the feelings that we have. Most of us have been at times jealous, envious, arrogant, suspicious, duplicitous, open, honest and straightforward, and we all have different feelings about these feelings at different times. These are not good and bad feelings especially reserved for good and bad people. These are human feelings, characteristic of all human beings and occurring in varying degrees in all of us as we interact with internal and external conditions.

Jealousy and envy are a function of insecurity and low self-esteem. They are not the results of some kind of basic human evil. Envy comes from feeling so deprived that it seems that everyone must surely have more than we do. Jealousy is born of feeling that we have so little to give compared to someone else. Fear of being left alone and empty leads to threatening ourselves that everything or everyone, or a particularly important person or thing, will be taken away from us. Jealousy and envy usually have a self-corrosive and depleting effect and as with all human ills require compassionate understanding rather than moral judgment, discipline or punishment. Since we are all insecure and suffer from bouts of low self-esteem, we are all susceptible to these feelings, just as we are to the common head cold.

Generosity, openness and honesty are fairly common.

But they never exist in pure form and no one consistently has these feelings and takes these positions purely and without dilution. The concept of good and bad people is a simplistic cultural concept with no basis in reality. We are in touch with different aspects of ourselves at different times and may present given sides of ourselves to different people at different times.

PREJUDICE

We all are victims of prejudice: fat people, thin people, bright people, beautiful people, redheads, homely people, maimed people, the bourgeoisie, racial groups, the poor, the rich, and, of course, as with all human conditions, there is always a question of degree. Society divides us into subsocieties or subcultures in which other subcultures are viewed as alien. This has a prejudicial effect. Yet, one of the important and destructive prejudices is against people *because* they are prejudiced people. Of course prejudice is destructive, and prejudice against ourselves for being prejudiced is just as destructive. Recoiling in horror and self-hate when we find prejudice in ourselves only sustains the vicious cycle. All human beings are prejudiced. The current structure of society dictates this fact. In dictating hate for ourselves for being prejudiced, the culture produces a destructive double bind.

The fear of the unfamiliar combined with any sense at all of vulnerability must produce at least some small, however minimal, prejudice. As with self-hate produced as a reaction to the discovery of self-hate in oneself, the punishment of prejudice for being prejudiced precludes change. This is promoted by a culture that preaches individuality and conformity at the same time, and paradoxically promotes the virtues of the safe and the familiar while it condemns prejudice produced by abhorrence, suspicion and fear of the unfamiliar.

WINNING, LOSING, STRIVING AND RESIGNATION

We must fight for the right to lose. If we don't accept the right to lose, then we so fear failure that we curtail realistic and attainable desires. This destroys the possibility of experimentation and risk and makes for resignation, inhibition and even paralysis. If we take any chances whatsoever in any of life's endeavors, then we must lose a bit and win a bit. Life itself is ultimately lost and this applies to ourselves and to loved ones. Therefore, each time we invest in love we must also, deep within us, to some small degree, anticipate loss. Relationships are broken. Loved ones die. Businesses fail. Examinations are failed. Succeeding or winning and losing are intrinsic parts of the life, death, rebirth and renewing cycle. They complement and supplement each other. We learn to be alive, to feel, to *be* through involvement in any and all of life's processes.

But despite this obvious reality, our culture stands rigidly against failure and loss and, lip service to the contrary, looks upon loss, failure and even the biological fact of death itself as an insult to the human condition. Fear and impossible demands produce personal resignation in a culture which at one and the same time demands constant striving for new heights while it abhors surrender and loss. Of course this position is untenable from a human point of view, and as a consequence we see much anxiety all about us.

There is a great difference between self-accepting the status quo and self-sinking into resignation. In the first state we accept contentment and the possibility of flexible choice and movement if and when desired. Resignation, on the other hand, is a function of paralyzing fear in which it is mandatory that we cling to a constricted position rigidly and compulsively.

For example, I knew an extremely intelligent and capable man who spent an entire lifetime working as a post office clerk. When questioned he answered that he really was content with the work. After twenty years in the post office, encouraged by his wife, he took a civil service examination for a much superior and interesting job. He scored higher than all other candidates. He immediately went into a deep depression from which he emerged only after his wife convinced him that he should resign himself to remaining in the post office job after all. Unfortunately, he was terrified of treatment and never did confront the underlying paralyzing self-hate that prevented real self-acceptance, growth and change. Had he been self-accepting rather than resigned, however content he may have been on his job, the possibility of change would not have produced panic and depression.

But resignation is often the only way out of a painful dilemma that dictates mountain-peak experiences on the one hand and intense self-hate for failure on the other. Entering a state of resigned anesthesia is after all an attempt to sustain life in a condition which is antithetical to life on a realistic basis. Fighting cultural admonition to the contrary and insisting on the right to lose and even to die is an important act in breaking resignation and in coming alive. If we struggle for the right to maintain a personally desired life-style against the dictatorial prod to climb higher and higher and still higher to ever more glorious peak positions, this struggle will immeasurably help us to restore a sense of inner personal richness and harmony.

Our culture in large part contributes to making us stimulation addicts. This is partially due to a fear of inner peace and to abhorrence of being content with ourselves. Contentment is confused with deadness and the deadening process of resignation, and is seen as stagnation. Stimulation addiction is a synthetic attempt to resist stagnation and to further enhance compulsive striving. This includes all forms of stimulation: constant entertainment, constant noise, endless new enterprises, compulsive sexual activity, hazardous ventures, and more.

Actually, contentment is the most fertile ground for growth, real growth of inner self, because it offers the possibility of the peace and energy necessary to listen, to hear, and to choose from one's own inner *I am I* life. In tapping, respecting and taking oneself seriously and taking care of oneself seriously, we are engaging in the constructive process of accepting the human condition on a reality basis. This includes the inevitability of loss and failure, taking risks and seeking further enriching experiences that make learning and growth possible.

COMPETITION, EQUALITY AND FAIR PLAY

Our culture extols the virtues of competition and fair play but decries opportunism. But the boundaries between fair play and opportunism are hazy and overlapping. Most of us are not entirely clear about the fine definitions that separate and describe "good, clean fun," "healthy competition," and "taking unfair advantage of the other fellow."

Unlike other cultural insights to the contrary, I believe that intense competition seldom brings out the best in us and often brings out the worst. It usually serves as a stimulus and goad that is often ruthless and destructive to our needs and well-being and the possibility of real cooperation with others.

Our culture pushes for equality and superiority at the same time, producing an impossible double bind. It simply is not possible to view people from a frame of reference based on a competitive hierarchy and at the same time to feel equal with them. Although the culture preaches the virtues of equality, it practices the opposite, and most of us, on a deeper emotional level, view equality as anathema. Cooperation is unconsciously felt as antimasculine by many of us, particularly the tradition-oriented American male.

Many men in our society grow up feeling that masculine life requires a pecking order and constant striving to outdo one's fellow man. I believe that a lot of this orientation is rooted in participation in competitive sports in early childhood. We organize small children into competitive athletic leagues from which they are supposed to derive "self-esteem" (although very few of them will grow up to be professional athletes). Instead of gaining true inner self-esteem, they learn, through parents, the coach, and the audience, that winning is much more important than enjoying the game and that losing is shameful. Many American men go through life feeling less than completely masculine or competent because they are not winners and, as irrational as it sounds, because they were not good athletes in their youth. This belief and feeling goes on despite the fact that their life's work has little or nothing to do with physical endeavor. It also contributes to the fear of real cooperation with one's fellows ("the opposite team") and to confused notions about what constitutes masculinity.

Our competitive society further emphasizes the differences between us by dividing the world into categories based on different value or privilege systems. One category, or world, is based on celebrity status or fame; another on old or inherited money; another on money earned per year; another on looks; another on professional standing and prestige; another on intellectual ability and degrees earned; another on physical prowess and skills; another on sexual conquests—and there are many more of highly unique and individual invention.

Pecking orders and hierarchies make for even more competitive feelings and further enforce a sense of alienation and separation from others and reality. Such false standards do not provide a climate of equality or fair play, but instead increase the pressure to achieve status at the expense of others, feeding suspicion, paranoid feelings and terror at possible loss of status. We must fight these social pressures constantly.

Yet our culture continues to insist on the constructiveness of competition in many insidious ways. We are constantly told that competition makes for self-assertion and creative inventiveness. This kind of rationale is a simplistic rationalization for acquisitiveness (in business, translate that into corporate greed), regardless of the ruthless and corrosive effects on self and others. Self-assertion requires development and use of self, the right to ask for one's rights, nothing more. Aggressiveness involves bullying and putting down the next fellow as a means of bolstering one's ego and masking one's sense of inadequacy and weakness.

In its pressure on us not only to compete but somehow always to win as well, our culture continues throughout our lives to provide an enormous bank of self-hate that we can draw on endlessly—if we let ourselves! If we all compete to win, and do this in all the smaller worlds I mentioned earlier (money, prestige, fame, beauty), then obviously there must be losers, too. Losing is feared and abhorred out of all proportion by our society. But it is not a disgrace if one has put forth one's best efforts—and if one's values are based on what is *one's own best*, rather than what society tells us "is best."

I see competition as a form of projection in which the development of self and *I am the center of my world* is abandoned in favor of beating the next fellow. In being more concerned with getting ahead of him, I use him as my measuring device and neglect my own real needs and feelings. This shifting of my internal frame of reference to the outside, so that my self-esteem is a function of how I'm doing versus other people, is perhaps the most destructive aspect of competition in terms of self. In this scheme I am no longer the center of my own life. It involves leaching other people for narcissistic supplies and involving them in sadistic maneuvers.

A shift to the values of others as our measuring stick and driving force is invariably linked to a compulsive, unhealthy need to be unduly admired (as apart from the simple need for mutual human appreciation of oneself and others). This invariably drains off enormous energy that otherwise could be used in the service of real self-development, evolvement and fulfillment. We are all in some way the victims of our society's processes. It behooves us to be compassionate with ourselves so that we are better able to stand up against this kind of cultural pressure and mythology and do what we can to reclaim ourselves.

BEING CHEATED, HELPLESSNESS, DEPENDENCY AND REJECTION

We are all partially helpless, dependent, rejected and being taken advantage of all the time, and sometimes to a large degree indeed. But some of us spend inordinate time and energy going about chronically feeling abused. Some of us even spend a lifetime guarding against helplessness, loss, dependency, rejection and being taken advantage of. Our culture contributes to these feelings through maintaining inhuman and untenable standards.

We are taught, propagandized and persuaded into believing that total independence is not only possible but must be attained at all costs. Any kind of dependency is viewed as terrible weakness, especially in men, where it is seen as lack of masculinity. This derogatory attitude toward dependency is paradoxically promoted alongside the opposite idea that we live in a complex society in which cooperation and interchange of talent and energy are necessary for survival. But it is the latter that is, of course, true.

We *are* dependent on each other, and while the *illusion* of dependency, which I described much earlier, is a function of neurosis, *interdependency of a healthy nature is appropriate to and necessary for human survival.* Our society, however, confuses the two. It asks for a degree of human independence that cannot be attained and which if attainable would destroy both cooperation and communication between people. We would function as isolates and cease to relate. *But* it is even more stringent and still more vindictive in its appraisal of human helplessness. This is a sin! Applied to men it is the sin of sins! Despite cultural rulings otherwise, it is simply impossible not to sin in this area.

We are born helpless and will continue to be helpless and to require help from our fellows throughout our lives, and we will require burial by other people after we die. The anticultural right to be helpless is a human one and one we must struggle against, cultural demands to the contrary, if we are to save ourselves from intense self-hate and severe anxiety.

I have encountered some of the most painful anxiety attacks in men who, finding themselves in a potentially helpless situation, were terrified of the self-hate that they knew would ensue. They had been virtually brain-washed into believing that "real men" are always independent, are never helpless, and never need help. To many of these men, coming to see me already had provided a terrible blow to their exalted position of never needing help. Coming down from this mountain top is not easy but is eventually enormously relieving and stabilizing. I have sometimes asked them, "Who are you that you shouldn't need help?" or, "Who are you that you shouldn't be rejected or cheated?" This usually produces immediate response and engagement in the humanizing battle.

What about rejection, or being taken advantage of, or even being cheated? None of us is happy about this. But if we do experience being rejected, or are cheated, or taken advantage of, are we at fault? Of course not! Strange as it may seem, we actually must fight for the right to experience rejection and being taken advantage of and even being cheated without feeling that we have in some way committed a grievous act or obviously have done something radically wrong or else things of this sort would not have happened to us.

I have described my patient Jean's reaction to rejection in the section on compassion. While her neurosis and reaction had intricate and complex origins and ramifications, our culture provides rich possibilities for self-hate in this area. Contrary to cultural belief, universal acceptance does not exist, not for anybody. There are times, many times, in fact, when we will be rejected by other people, even worthwhile people and friends. No matter what we do and no matter how we manage our lives, we will not be invited to all parties, all social functions, all organizations, or asked to take all jobs. Such a realization need not be an insult or an affront to our pride and dignity, nor need it bring on self-hate in any form whatsoever. This can only be if we do not insist on immunity from rejection, if we recognize that as people we are entitled to be rejected with relative equanimity and also are entitled to reject others as well. Our culture unfortunately dictates otherwise, making re-evaluation of our reactions to acts of rejection necessary until we are firmly in control of our responses to them.

Hypervulnerability and sensitivity to rejection are extremely destructive to morale but can only be reduced markedly if our acceptance of real self becomes compassionate enough so that acceptance of us by everyone else in the world is no longer a requisite for our happy existence. The same is true of "being taken." I have known men who have generated enormous misery and have expended huge talent and time in defense against "being taken" or cheated and in the hopeless pursuit of righting a wrong and for the so-called principle involved. Some of these men have had dreams of being attacked homosexually because they somehow permitted themselves to be used or manipulated in business—"like being raped," they've described it to me.

Unfortunately, being on top and in charge of every situation long has been equated by our society with masculinity. Promotion of this disastrous notion runs rampant in our population and produces considerable depression because each and every one of us, however manly, competent, mature, adult or in command of superb judgment, must at times be cheated, manipulated, out-guessed, out-foxed, and must also at times be out of control and even quite helpless. Yes, all of us at times must find ourselves in situations in which we are realistically helpless and realistically dependent and in need of other people's help. This may be the result of sickness, old age, the unexpected, or lack of expertise, but it will surely occur in all of our lives.

I've heard many people say, "I can't stand to be taken advantage of." My answer is, "Why not, aren't you a person? Give yourself the advantage of being able to be taken advantage of." I hear others say, "I couldn't stand to come to anyone for help—I'd rather die." The person who chooses death over asking for help is a person who has been dying for years. It is impossible to experience life fully in any reasonable degree if one is also living with the conflicting needs for *complete* control and total independence, at the same time expecting the rewards born of mutual cooperation. This person must engage in the painful, humanizing struggle to come down from this terrible cultural, privileged position to just plain Mother Earth. Although there are times when we are cut off from our resources, other times will always come when we can tap them again. We can use this deep, feeling knowledge to stand up against the cultural myths that would pressure us into straying too far from our real, compassionate selves.

RECOGNITION

Most of us are terribly concerned with ourselves. Admiration from others is important to many of us, and yet to what extent do we think of others and how much time do we expect them to devote to us? Sadly, our society pushes the importance of recognition to the hilt. Even when it is appropriate and we achieve recognition, invariably it is fleeting and quite limited in its therapeutic effect. Our society in its confusion over the value of modesty puts too little importance on the process of self-recognition. If we take *our*selves with enough appropriate and appreciative seriousness, this dilutes the compulsive and frustrating need for recognition from others. Self-recognition involves extensive knowledge and acceptance of one's assets and the ready ability to tap and use them in one's own behalf. This is the antithesis of feelings of inadequacy that lead to either self-effacing compliancy or compensatory grandiosity.

OPPORTUNISM

Our society hates opportunism but encourages self-hating recriminations if we miss any opportunity. Neglect of one's own talent is seen as absolute sinfulness. If all areas of ourselves cannot be developed in one lifetime, why can't we permit ourselves a choice of which we will and which we won't develop? Considering the complexity of human structure there will inevitably be thousands of areas of our lives that could never be fulfilled in a thousand lifetimes. It is impossible to take advantage of all inner resources and outside opportunities, but we must not permit condemnation for the attempts we choose to make and for "those that got away."

ACQUISITIVENESS

Our culture condemns acquisitiveness. We learn that there is really something wrong, selfish and tight-fisted about wanting to accumulate boundless material goods and money. At the same time our culture worships money-making ability and money itself and feeds us all kinds of illusions daily as to the magical powers of wealth. The double-bind situation involved is a source of considerable confusion and self-hate.

MILLIONAIRES

We are fed the illusion that each and every one of us can become a millionaire. To be a millionaire means more than merely having money. It implies Heaven on Earth. This pap drives us, depletes us, robs us of good judgment as to what is and isn't attainable and enjoyable.

BETRAYAL

We all betray ourselves and other people, at least in some measure, at times in our lives. To be loyal and to betray are human characteristics that are not the exclusive province of saints or traitors. Life is tough and sometimes fear is too great to uphold ideals that we can sustain and invoke during easier times.

SNOBBISM

We detest snobs and we are all snobs. How can it be otherwise in a society that insists on stratifying itself into myriad hierarchial competitive pecking orders?

SADISM AND MASOCHISM

I agree with Karen Horney that sadism and masochism are the result of feelings of inner deadness, and that they represent last-ditch attempts to stimulate ourselves into having feelings of aliveness. But we are all sadistic and masochistic to some degree. None of us is exempt, however destructive creating pain in ourselves and in others may be. Our culture promotes the value and pleasure derived from the attainment of vindictive triumph in films, television and novels, but is also ambivalently harsh and sadistic in its own attitude toward it. Sadism, especially of a blatant variety, requires compassion if it is to be overcome, but generally only brings forth additional sadism. Capital punishment—an eye for an eye, a killing for a killing, rather than the reacculturation of the offender toward a more compassionate way of life—is one way we act out this philosophy.

FOOLS

We despise fools. But all of us are at times fools, foolish, dumb and stupid, and need the human right to be less than wise and even downright ridiculous many times in our lives.

LOGIC, RATIONALE AND FEELINGS

Our culture is pro logic and rationale and often against feelings to the point of attempted obliteration. In this distorted application of values, a paradox is established, as well as a fear that *to feel is to be irrational*. As human beings, we derive much logic through encountering experience, using our feelings as receptors and as funds of information. Feelings in turn are supplemented by rationale and logic. One needn't preclude the other, and when they are healthily integrated they give information about ourselves and enhance the world at large.

We hear much about the value of cold logic and the

danger of intrusion of feelings in evaluating important circumstances. In most instances cold logic, without feelings, has limited value in providing a source of total and valid information. Contrary to cultural persuasion, if I find myself in a position where I think one way and feel another, I find I can trust in the logic of how *I feel* more than I can in *logical rationale.* This applies both to validation of reality and to how I should stand on most issues requiring choice and decision.

For example, let's say I am examining a potential candidate for psychoanalytical training. On a logical and rational level I see that his past training, grades and credentials generally are completely acceptable. *But* through our interview I feel that he is wrong for this kind of work. He gives all the "right" answers but my feeling about his "being wrong" for psychoanalytic work persists. Perhaps I feel he is not sensitive or emphathetic enough. I don't know with "logic" exactly what I feel but I am sure that I feel *it.* Then in my final decision I reject him for training. My perception of my reality and the choice I make which follows must be based on what I feel. This is not surprising, inasmuch as my feelings tend to represent all aspects of myself relatively free of diluting outside influences. My logical and thinking rationale often neglects aspects of myself that may currently run contrary to particular outside cultural influences. While I prefer to trust and to tap my integrated feeling and intellectual self, if they are at odds, I have learned that I do better in my behalf to listen to the music rather than the words. The music represents how I feel.

MOODS

I see moods as complex combinations of feelings and I see all moods as human and acceptable, even murderous moods. We are, remember, speaking of moods, not actions. We must permit and accept such varied moods as feeling lazy, full of vitality, happy, sad, sexy, repulsive, seclusive, charming, cold, luxurious, stingy, vulnerable, tough, fragile, irritable, abrasive, sensitive, nostalgic, lonely, ungiving, sentimental, beautiful, ugly, masterful, childish, loving, old, wise, dumb and many others, including great mixtures of all these moods, which are for the most part indescribable in mere words. Even art in all of its manifestations cannot capture the many moods that make up human existence.

I call these moods rather than feelings because as symphonies are composed of themes and many notes, these states are composed of many feelings and combinations of feelings, making for complexity beyond single feelings. Unlike characteristics or personality traits, they are never fixed and seldom can be accurately defined or correlated with particular "types" of people. They all exist in all of us. Moods seldom remain static for long. They keep changing as they respond to the vast admixture of feelings emanating from our own psyches and affected by stimuli from outside ourselves. Sometimes we can control or even change a mood, but this is relatively rare.

But our culture views certain feelings and moods as pejorative and even abhorrent and antithetical to the state of being human. I have seen so many people who say, "I don't know what is the matter with me, I feel so lazy" or "so vulnerable" or "so touchy" or "so dopy and childish" or "so lonely," and on and on it goes. This is largely a function of cultural prejudice.

Moods should require no justification whatsoever. As with little children who feel the way they feel simply *because*, we, too, must be permitted to feel because we feel. This especially pertains to very painful and chronically sustained moods involving loss of reality and inability to function. These, too, must not be viewed pejoratively but rather accepted with deep respect and sensitivity for the complex and powerful psychodynamics they spring from.

The urge to help a troubled patient immediately to escape emotional pain is easily understandable. But this urge can lead to vast oversimplification and destructive consequences. For example, a man whose mood can best be characterized as one of chronic depression must be viewed as at least as complex as a relatively happy person. To attempt to change his mood quickly with electric shock treatment, without analysis of his problem, may not only prevent growth but may eventually produce worse symptoms. It is important to realize that his mood, however painful, is part and parcel of many factors and forces in his life. His depression and the kind of anaesthetic haze it produces may be for the moment the only way he can cope with life as he perceives it. His perception of life and the world generally may need to be changed before we ask him to surrender his depressed mood. Otherwise, we can even precipitate suicide in a man whose mood, however painful, is his only means of self-preservation. We must respect his "painful mood" until we can give him better ways to cope. The approach to moods of all kinds must be a compassionate one, and especially to those where immediate change would seem to be desirable on the surface but needs to be analyzed very carefully.

But what about moods we consider socially reprehensible, like "feeling lazy"? We all have them and we are all entitled to them. A lazy mood can be a pleasant and relaxed state and a necessary respite for times when reverse moods are forthcoming. Loneliness often occurs when we are in the midst of friends and can be a way of tapping old nostalgic feelings for creative purposes. But in no case should we deaden, forego or see ourselves in a lesser light because stilted cultural judgment value tells us a particular mood or feeling is "not appropriate" or "not good." The more sensitive, alive, developed and evolved we are, the richer our range of moods will be. This wide range of feelings deserves human acceptance and dignity but never self-hate.

ANGER

Anger is probably the most maligned of all human emotions. Anger is seen as immoral, unhealthy, crazy, immature, primitive, rude, dangerous, etc. Anger is viewed as the antithesis of love and as a destroyer of love, respect, relationships and human status. Anger is therefore repressed more than any other emotion. Its repression and inevitable emergence produces anxiety, I believe, more than any other psychological mechanism we engage in. This in turn makes for a host of symptoms, all of which are forms of rage at oneself or self-hate. Despite cultural pressure and propaganda to the contrary, we human beings who are healthy enough to feel anything must generate anger many, many times in our lives.

Anger is a destroyer if it is repressed, so that it blocks other emotions and eventually comes out in explosive form. If it is given relatively free rein, it is one of the most human and warmest of emotions. It indicates that we care enough to feel and to voice displeasure. It also clears the air so that free exchange can take place. This includes the exchange of feelings of love which are blocked by repressed anger. Our society is particularly unrealistic regarding anger in children. It is considered good manners, appropriate form and natural for children to have even more control over their feelings, particularly angry ones, than parents. Children have undeveloped and unstable central nervous systems and control is much more difficult for them. In any case, our culture makes unreasonable demands regarding this most human of human emotions, and in a struggle for compassion the right to feel and to express anger is of paramount importance.

SADNESS

Our society views depression with particular abhorrence. In many quarters sorrow is regarded as a contagious and a dirty condition. It is considered necessary to be up and around, on one's feet and in good spirits all of the time, or at least nearly all of the time, regardless of circumstances that dictate otherwise. This often leads to our becoming depressed and self-hating *because we are depressed,* even though our primary depression may be completely appropriate. Many of us have particular difficulty because we do not feel jolly when our calendar dictates, "It is the season to be jolly." "Holiday blues" are *very* common. Responding to tragedy with sorrowful and appropriately depressed feelings is evidence of being alive enough to actively feel and to empathize humanly. Feelings of sadness and depression regardless of whether they stem from appropriate response to tragedy or are self-hating in origin are intensely human and deserve as much respect as feelings of joy and happiness.

OPTIMISM AND PESSIMISM

"Never say *can't.*" Why not? There are many situations that call for the right and ability to say, "I can't" without its being evidence of undue pessimism or a compulsive tendency to surrender without cause. Besides which, we are all entitled to feel pessimistic at some times and optimistic at others, and even to feel this way inappropriately in some situations. This is only human.

The words, "I can't," said to ourselves without recrimination, are ameliorative indeed when they represent standing up to impossible demands on ourselves. Unfortunately, many of us can only use these words constructively after we've suffered severe heart attacks, following years of over achieving, or have wreaked other irreparable, debilitating damage on our minds or bodies by imposing unreasonable demands on ourselves.

This kind of psychosomatic self-onslaught is sometimes a last-ditch move to block self-hate, and to use a massive attack to ward off painful emotional self-hating attacks such as depression, phobias and severe states of anxiety. Fear of death is sometimes the only blackmailing weapon that can produce an effective, "I can't" stand against impossible demands and standards. I have known a number of people who hoped for serious illness and hospitalization so that they could attain relief from impossible drives. Our society is enormously destructive in this regard and, despite some small propagandizing efforts made in behalf of the importance of taking care of ourselves, dubs us as negative people and pessimists if we in any way give up the quest for glory through all kinds of demands for increasing success.

DREAMS AND FANTASIES

We all dream, daydream and fantasize. Electroencephalographic studies indicate that we dream every night even if we don't remember our dreams. If we are awakened so that we can't dream, we build up a "dream deficit" and compensate for it on succeeding nights. It seems that our physiology requires this kind of continuing brain activity even during periods of rest. Our dreams have no need to be rational or logical in conscious waking terms when we let go, and our dreams and daydreams, too, are capable of vast and fantastic creative possibility. Sometimes with this kind of unfettered freedom of movement we work out problems in dreams that we can't resolve during working hours. *But* our culture demeans the dreaming process and often shuns it altogether. Again and again I hear people, especially men, boast about not dreaming. Why do we shun dreams? Is it because dreaming gets too close to our feelings, to our own inner poetry, and makes us uncomfortable? Perhaps it is also because people, and men particularly, are suspicious of any human output that is not immediately reduceable to controllable, logical, rational terms.

SECURITY AND HAPPINESS

Security does not exist in any aspect of life. *Life* is a process of change—it never stops dead and stays the same for a moment, let alone forever. Minute, relative security is possible but almost negligible in light of the complexities, unpredictable nature, and ephemeral quality of life. Our culture force feeds us Pablum about security, which creates vast illusions about the power of money and the possibility of perfection in human relationships. We spend an enormous amount of time and energy attempting to insure against all kinds of exigencies, when such insurance, unlike relatively simple maneuvers like buying an insurance policy, is to no avail. Our quest for security often produces ritual, stilted behavior and concentration on an anticipated anxiety-free life, which is never forthcoming. In search of mythical security through money, love, prestige, power, we often sacrifice spontaneous here-and-now living. The best contribution we can make to the attainment of a realistic sense of security is to realize and to embrace the human fact of insecurity. We live from moment to moment. Our lives are tenuous. We live in a state of flux, and accommodation to this reality makes it possible to live more fully and to avoid suffering born of impossible expectations.

Happiness, too, even of the realistic *just feeling good* variety, is at best ephemeral. Our society promotes all kinds of panaceas for the achievement of impossible peak kinds of happiness on a sustained, forever basis. But considering the vast complexity of the human psyche and the limitless feelings and moods that being a person encompasses, feeling good can only be relative as well as transient. Despite cultural myths to the contrary, this truth remains a human reality. If we accept insecurity and the transient nature of happiness as life conditions, we reduce illusion and false expectations, we make the here-and-now condition richer and more livable, and more intensely treasure our enjoyable moments as we live them.

IDEAL, PURE, ABSOLUTE AND PERFECT

There is nothing in the human condition that is pure, ideal or absolute! Death is perfectly absolute and a certainty, but once it is achieved the individual in question is no longer human. To any extent that our culture propels us in the direction of *purity* it pushes us either to unreality or to death or to both.

ENDURANCE, TOUGHNESS, FRAGILITY

People can endure much, and it's better if they don't have to. We are tough, and it's better if we don't have to be. We are fragile in many varying ways, some of us in one area, others of us in more than one, but fragility in any area should not be a disgrace at all. Our society stresses the importance of toughness and endurance, especially in men, although men are *not* tougher than women. It also condones tests in which toughness and endurance are evaluated—war, competitive sports and cut-throat career competition. While toughness may be necessary to get through rough situations, contrivances to prove toughness and the ability to endure are residues of childish dreams of glory and primitive simplistic outlooks.

INDEBTEDNESS

To be indebted or beholden to anyone, even a loved one, is a condition to be shunned at all costs, our society tells us. This is seen as the essence of humiliation and self-degradation. A good many people expend a great deal of effort trying to keep things equally balanced, trying to master the trick of walking a thin line between indebtedness and not being taken advantage of. A slight fall in either direction is usually ample reason to bring on attacks of self-hate. But we cannot relate to people on any level and have an absolute perfect balance of exchange, nor can we avoid indebtedness. We must all at times be indebted, and it is an inhuman cultural demand that makes us feel humiliated by indebtedness.

SUBSERVIENCE AND PASSIVITY

We are especially contemptuous of passivity and even more so of subservience. Yet none of us is exempt from feeling and needing to be passive in given situations; sooner or later circumstance will make it necessary for us to approach someone hat in hand. We may even have to polish the apple, too, to kow-tow, and to function as subservient supplicants. That this all-too-human occurrence still brings on vicious attacks of self-degradation is undoubtedly linked to impossible cultural demands that we somehow never permit ourselves to be in other than the on-top, in-charge, secure position. This has led to great suffering and even to deaths in prison camps and in other very difficult situations and may have served the cause of neurotic pride but not that of human need. Premature rebellious acts due to hurt pride rather than heroic, let alone practical, intervention have led to torture and death. The inability to accept what may be viewed as a lesser position often cements one into the very spot he hates. This is often seen in jobs where the rebellious employee spends time and energy complaining and sabotaging himself, when the same time and energy could have been used for learning and other practical, self-promoting activity.

AFFABILITY AND CHARM

Despite general admiration for the value of these commodities, we simply do not always feel or act affable or charming, and so must respect the grumpier expressions of our personalities, too, without fear of reprisal for acting contrary to cultural dictums.

SELF-CONTROL, RESTLESSNESS, ANXIETY AND INSOMNIA

Self-control is not always a virtue. There are many times when it is best to let go and get it out and clear the air. But even in situations in which it would be best, we often humanly lose control and must expect to. Nobody is free of anxiety, tension, restlessness and sleeplessness. No amount of attempted self-control, treatment or condemnation of these characteristics can obliterate them.

HUMILITY

Humility is preached and despised and is confused with humiliation. To be humiliated is not unusual. We are all humiliated at times, and this, too, is common to being a person and no cause for self-hate. But humility is not humiliation. To be humble enough to accept the human condition and its complications and limitations is one of the most valuable of human assets. Despite cultural confusion, feeling truly humble produces great strength and freedom from fear of falling off illusionary peaks. As I've said before, self-hate ceases to flourish in a state of humility.

TYPES AND CATEGORIES

Despite cultural attempts to type ourselves we continue to defy all typing and categorizing. We spill out into all categories. Beautiful people refuse to be dumb. Intellectuals insist on liking cowboy films and baseball. Simple men turn into chess prodigies. Depressed people refuse to be manic; the intricate, category-defying mélange is infinite, and human.

MATURITY

Few adults are equally mature in all areas; most of us are mixtures of maturity and childishness. There is a child in each of us who lives on in all the areas in which we somehow refuse to grow up. We must respect that child and, if possible, help him to grow. This means that if we find that he is out of step with society's needs and standards, that is no cause to hate him. Sympathy and understanding are in order.

It is even more self-hating and damaging to take orders from the screaming infant within ourselves, to be unable to say *NO* to immature, childish yearnings when we know they are going to be destructive to us. And how can we tell that? They are destructive orders if we are listening not to our true inner selves but to society's demands for perfection and ideals that feel uncomfortable to us.

CONFORMING, POPULARITY, MASTERY AND INDIVIDUALITY

A certain amount of conforming is necessary for survival. A certain amount of individuality is inevitable. Our culture exaggerates the virtues of conforming to achieve popularity while at the same time it demands nothing short of pure individuality of a virtuoso quality. Myths involving the rewards of popularity run rampant and are almost utterly without basis. It isn't possible to be completely popular and loved by all while pursuing aggressive mastery and power over all. It isn't possible to be a complete man of the people and at the same time to cater only to one's own individual needs.

We all have diverse needs and drives, but exaggeration of them produces internal conflicts, which in turn make for considerable anxiety and self-hate. Intense feelings of self-effacement and compliancy conflicting with intense and exaggerated needs for mastery, and subsequent withdrawal from the intolerable conflict between the two, are fed by a culture that overemphasizes the importance of each of these drives and at the same time expresses revulsion for them. We are told about the joys of being popular and loved by all. At the same time we know that contempt is leveled at conventional, conforming, milk-toasty sops. We are told about the rewards of being oneself purely, about expressing oneself straight out and open, being aggressive, grabbing what you can, but are kept in constant touch with the special contempt reserved for braggarts, arrogance, and pushy people generally.

Despite cultural admonitions pro and con we are all, as Karen Horney described, self-effacing, expansive and de-tached. We are as people conforming, compliant and individualistic. We are aggressive and we are retiring. While these characteristics in exaggerated form can be destructive, and while change may be indicated, they can never be completely eradicated, and human acceptance of human qualities is always in order.

INVOLVEMENT AND DETACHMENT

We live in a society in which we are told to get involved but not to make waves and to mind our own business. This is a double bind that puzzles many of us on an unconscious level. Although it remains unknown to us consciously, it nevertheless produces either paralysis or trepidation to the point of agitation and even panic when we do dare to get involved. Of course living a life of no involvement is impossible, and living one of minimal involvement is a self-hating bore. But to get involved without having any influence or impact is impossible. We simply cannot function as anything even resembling whole human beings without "making waves." We simply can't mind our own business, and society, incidentally, does not go to any great lengths in defining just where our own business ends and others' begin. There are times when we are more involved than at other times, but we must always be involved to some degree and we must contribute some ripple, however small. Our society also somehow delivers the message that less involvement is appropriate and even dignified in older age. This patent bit of nonsense often leads to untimely retirement, waste of some of our wisest citizens, terrible boredom and accelerated degeneration and early death. Involvement, making waves, making noise and impact are appropriate to all ages and are entirely human. It can't and should not be otherwise.

RESERVE AND GREGARIOUSNESS

We see reserve as a sign of wisdom, lack of personality, strength, stupidity, selfishness, independence and snobbishness. We are told that it is a sign of strength never to show feelings, but that we must, on the other hand, be feeling people. The gregarious person is seen as having personality, being kind, caring, trustworthy, nice, and—paradoxically—as being foolish, boasting and immature. Wanting to be alone is viewed as being antisocial. Wanting to be with people is seen as possible evidence of great dependency. These and an infinite number of other stereotyped concepts about personality characteristics are passed on from generation to generation. While we may lean in one or another direction, none of us is purely reserved or gregarious but we must give ourselves permission to be either or both, according to how we feel at particular times. If we are pressured into pretentious affectations by simplistic cultural notions, we inevitably deaden and cut off parts of ourselves.

PRIVACY

Privacy is important and even therapeutic. We are told that we are entitled to it and also that we are snobs if we guard our privacy too jealously.

TEMPTATION AND CURIOSITY

Our society preaches against succumbing to temptation or to curiosity. We are also taught that it is wrong to be tempted! This is impossible and works against the state of our being alive and feeling members of our species. As people we will be, and must expect to be, tempted in countless ways and situations every day. We must fight against any cultural dictates, regardless of what source they come from, that ask us to not be tempted, not to be curious or to stop breathing. Curiosity and temptation are not the special province of either sex or any age group. They are entirely human characteristics, born of intense feelings of aliveness.

HEALTHY NARCISSISM

At times we are all vain and ostentatious, and why not? We are told, "If you've got it, flaunt it," but, "Don't show off," yet, "Look and act your very best."

Ambivalently, our culture urges us to excell, yet forcefully condemns vanity and narcissism. A friend said to me recently, "It's not nice to feel about yourself, to talk about yourself, to let people know about your needs." Of course healthy self-assertion and loyalty to self must make for healthy good feelings about self and a willingness to talk about them, and to feel one's needs and to let other people know about them. Fear of being unduly narcissistic often results in damaging self-effacement, which in itself epitomizes self-hate. This kind of healthy narcissism results in a sense of aliveness and a capacity for enjoyment including enjoying relating to other people. Feeling for one's needs and assets makes us more receptive and awake to other people's feelings and needs as well, which is the antithesis of sick or exaggerated narcissism born of a sense of inadequacy.

UNIQUENESS AND ECCENTRICITY

Our culture seemingly condones and even encourages individuality, but this is usually within very constricted and conventional confines. Uniqueness, and especially any kind of eccentricity, is viewed with great suspicion and often with considerable disdain, contempt and even active hostility. People who are particularly individualistic, whether they are scientists, politicians or artists, must be prepared to fight for the compassionate *I am I* principle, against the popular and tenacious forces of conformity. The outrage of those with vested prestige and economic interests at anyone who dares even suggest "other ways of looking at things" can be murderous.

Most of us take a dim view of the unfamiliar and feel that uniqueness threatens any status quo resigned position we've sunk into. Coupled with cultural abhorrence of uniqueness, our own fear of the unfamiliar tends to make us reject any new or creative idea or feeling we may have. It usually takes considerable struggle against both inner and outer coercions to allow ourselves and others unique ideas and expressions, let alone actions and enterprises springing out of them.

POETS AND ARTISTS

Poets and artists are infinitely more suspect than mere eccentrics. They are all potentially unreliable, queer and peculiar to the point of being crazy and perverse, and, of course, homosexual. In many of us, this belief kills interest and involvement in art and particularly in our own artistic and creative proclivities. This is especially true of men in our culture, who are taught to view poetic interest as feminine. I believe this cultural prejudice springs from and feeds on fear of strong feelings. Art does, after all, have the potential to express and stimulate the strongest of human feelings.

ABILITIES

We are brought up believing that all human beings have *equal* abilities even if we don't have *the same* abilities. This simply is not true! This is cultural mythology, designed to promote fantasies of an ideal world, but it often produces futile competitive striving completely out of keeping with the possibility of satisfaction. We may, each of us, have one or another diverse capabilities and talents, and as people we have more in common than we do apart, *but* we are not equally capable. Some of us are more capable and have more assets and talents than others of us. This is a fact, and if the process living I have described replaces goal living, this need not be a cruel fact, because being a person is deserving of human respect and dignity, regardless of achievement.

PRIDE AND GREATNESS

Why must we strive for greatness? Why must we zealously guard our pride, feed it, fight and even die for it? Do pride and greatness make for happiness or an increasing sense of isolation, dehumanization and even paranoia? Is achieving greatness more self-satisfying than achieving self-acceptance and the ability to enjoy the commonplace? Does the drive for glory through the actualization of ever-increasing demands for greater perfection and attainment of more and more positions of special privilege make for sustained contribution to the betterment of life? Is a country great because it *is* "great," or is it a good place to live because its original premises are basically compassionate ones? Our culture in a large part feeds the neurotic need for pride positions and so-called greatness. This is probably its most destructive influence, and ultimately makes for an unreal, illusionary and destructive value system. It also contributes to emptiness and fragility, and assaults the humility from which real and useful human strength springs.

PROBLEMS, LIMITATIONS AND COMPASSION

We must be particularly compassionate about our problems and handicaps. We do not live in an altruistic, forgiving, enlightened society. We have improved in this regard but much is still lacking to make our culture one of compassionate consideration. Problems and handicaps, like old age, are still shunned and viewed with abhorrence. These include physical, social, economic and particularly emotional problems. Help for emotional problems is still viewed by most people as stigmatizing and degrading. Since nearly all of us suffer from serious problems at various times in our lives, our society, despite lip service to the contrary, supplies a ready fund of self-hate in this regard, if we want to avail ourselves of it.

I do believe that our world is more compassionate than ever before and that we are heading in the direction of compassion. But as yet the world we live in and the cultural value system we have developed is still exceedingly judgmental, and especially so to those of us who are for the moment particularly pained, vulnerable or incapacitated.

HEALTH, SICKNESS, PAIN, FRUSTRATION AND PATIENCE

False notions are constantly propagated that would have us believe that health and sickness are widely disparate processes, one of which precludes the other. They always exist in combination and in relative ratio to each other. None of us is perfectly healthy or perfectly sick. Only the state of death is perfect in its finite quality.

The same is true of emotional health.

The word "normal" is loaded with confusion and at best describes a fair degree of healthy function. No one alive is free from one or another kinds of emotional problems. Very few of us escape periodic attacks of anxiety, depression, phobic responses and other painful emotional disturbances. If we define normalcy as what happens to people in large numbers, then suffering emotionally at varying times in one's life would be the normal condition of people.

Cultural attempts to separate people into groups that are problem-ridden and those which are exempt lead to prejudice and self-hate. Nearly all human beings are problem-ridden. Problems are an intrinsic part of being alive.

I view psychoanalysis as the best modality to help people to help themselves emotionally. But while analysis can help to resolve problems with great efficiency and constructiveness, it cannot *end* problems. They continue as they must in all people as long as we live.

We are also told that different people have greater or lesser tolerance for pain and frustration. Studies have indicated some degree of difference, but for the most part very few of us tolerate pain well. We hate pain, and there is no virtue in liking it or encouraging it. It is entirely

human to avoid pain and to attempt to relieve it constructively and prudently, however we can, as rapidly as
possible.

Very few of us do well with frustration. Higher self-esteem, increased richness of experience and wisdom, can
raise one's frustration tolerance somewhat. But despite
cultural exhortations, most of us do not have much
tolerance for frustration, and few human beings are
particularly patient. Patience may be worthwhile and our
culture may rightly preach its virtues, but the "hurry-up,"
success-oriented world we live in is not nourishing to the
attainment of patience. While it may help us to be patient,
especially with ourselves, we must also try to be tolerant
with our impatience. We must guard against self-hate
following impatience or the results of impatience.

AGING

Our zeal to destroy established institutions and to knock
down old buildings and landmarks is a demonstration of
our phobic obsession with age. Aging is viewed by our
society as an insulting, dehumanizing process and, of
course, aging can only be avoided by dying. As we get
older, we lose self-respect, and as those around us get older
we become contemptuous of them. Even worse, we
separate ourselves from them, often unconsciously feeling
that aging is a contagious, destructive disease to be
shunned at any cost.

Many people make all kinds of futile attempts to arrest
the aging process, including physical interventions and
emotional maneuvers as well. There's something quite sad

in viewing the obvious self-hate in people of advanced age who dress, talk and act like people a third their age in an attempt to turn back time. Much of this makes for a youth-worship cult of vast proportions, in which young people are seen as fonts of wisdom, creativity and experience.

Our culture, and especially our spokesmen in advertising, continuously pound home *the crime* of looking and feeling one's age, let alone older. The process of getting older is accompanied by self-revulsion. Self-hate directed toward aging is particularly destructive because aging cannot be altered. The dawn of each day becomes a further insult to impossible demands to arrest time and continually brings on renewed attacks of self-hate.

On minimal investigation, many aging people reveal that they chronically feel as if they suffer from a malignant, insidious disease which not only increasingly robs them of physical function but dignity as well. In our culture this is largely true. People who are more than competent but who are also highly experienced, full of wisdom and *still* certainly capable are viewed with increasing suspicion, lack of trust and even contempt because they have not somehow remained young.

Of course if we are to live we must age. If we are to grow we must age, and growing and aging must not be passively acceptable sources of self-hate. It is imperative to fight this detestable, antihuman, cultural stance on aging. We must not become swamped by ridiculous illusions about the insight and judgment of youth. We must do what we can to dignify the process of getting older, to continue to tap the wisdom, usefulness and resources born of evolvement and development, which can come only of age and in so doing dignify the human condition and the life process itself.

SURRENDER AND RESPITE

Surrender is a very important reality of human existence. It should be accepted and even cherished. This applies to intrapsychic issues involving only ourselves, as well as encounters with other people and the world at large. Our society views surrender with revulsion and would like to strike it out of the human vocabulary. It encourages false, Godlike aspirations always to be right and always to win.

The fact that we are all losers and winners remains an abrasive insult, and leads to confused notions about honor and perseverence even unto death. We see this demonstrated when people refuse to surrender an idea, however much it is stripped of merit or lacks validity. I think our recent policy in Vietnam was a case in point.

This pride in nonsurrender of ideas and fixed positions renders us stubborn, rigid, constricted and impervious to learning and to growth. Unfortunately, it is confused with "allow yourself to be heard" and "stand up for your ideas and rights." There is simply no virtue in holding to ridiculous positions unless rigidity unto death is our goal.

For most of us the inability to surrender can be destructive in our daily lives; it often occurs without our awareness. I had a patient who moved to the suburbs and became increasingly miserable. It turned out that she despised every aspect of non-city living. But she went on living there until she realized that she was doing so only because she felt it would be a sign of weakness if she succumbed to having been wrong in her preference. When she was able to surrender her need to have been right and to surrender to her inability to adjust, she was free to move back to the city. People refuse to surrender to exhaustion and to engage in a period of respite even though continued activity may cost them their lives. Every good fighter understands the value of taking the count, recouping strength and perhaps trying again.

CONVALESCENCE

We are not machines. Sometimes we cannot bounce back after great hurt, pain and sickness, and we should not have to demand this of ourselves. There are many times in our lives when we need a period of convalescence. This need deserves utmost attention and is an antidote to ruthless machine-like striving that results in blunting of the senses and sometimes early death. Convalescence as a prophylaxis is not a commonly recognized device in our society. But if we can recognize the need to take it easy, to take especially good and loving care of ourselves even before it is absolutely required, we are engaging in a process that can save us from considerable mishap and difficulty, while at the same time dignifying the human condition.

SOCIAL ROLES AND RELATIONSHIPS

We are none of us ever perfect husbands, wives, children, professionals, teachers, students, employees, employers, fathers, mothers or friends. We are humanly limited in all these social human roles despite pressures to the contrary. Therefore, all relationships are limited. Perfect communication, agreement and equal satisfaction, balance and reciprocation are never possible or forthcoming—never! If we have created an illusion of a perfect relationship in any area, chances are that both individuals involved are enormously disloyal to themselves. Some controversy is inevitable in a healthy relationship in which two people *are loyal to themselves*, even though every relationship involves some capitulation and give and take on the part of all concerned.

FRIENDSHIP

Friendship is not forever, self-sacrificing, selfless, utterly loyal, free of jealousy, envy and manipulations, ideal in relating and communicating. Friendship is invariably full of problems, bumps in the road, limitations and satisfactions, too. Satisfaction is only possible if impossible expectations and claims do not spoil it with grievous disappointment, feelings of being abused, and the subsequent attacks of cynicism, bitterness and withdrawal that follow. Our society promotes expectations of friendship that are rarely forthcoming. But this need not denigrate the satisfaction derived from realistic but limited relationships. People, however close or well they relate, do not and must not expect themselves to meld into single two-headed monsters. Each person in a relationship functions as a separate human being, and much as one exchanges and cares about another, it is entirely human to place top priority on oneself and to maintain enough distance to sustain separate identities.

SEX

Since our sexual lives are a mirror of how we feel and relate generally, that this is an area of maximum confusion to many of us is no surprise. But our culture contributes an enormous amount of sexual misinformation, impossible standards and dehumanizing dictums. Each generation is told the correct way to think, feel, and to act as a man or a woman. One generation of women is told not to have orgasms, while another is told that only multiple orgasms of cataclysmic and explosive proportions suffice. Pressures in this area continue to sustain the battle of the sexes, which deserves to become an inappropriate anachronism.

Obviously, sex is an exceedingly sensitive and important area of our lives. While it is infinitely more compassionate to feel ourselves as human beings first and as either men or women secondarily, sexual identification plays an enormous role in our lives. Sexual activity is after all the way we procreate and continue our species and our future representation. Therefore, it is impossible not to be concerned with changing definitions of masculinity and femininity. Let me explore some of the current malignant sexual mythology that plagues many people by blasting some of the myths that currently inhabit us and should be dispelled as much as possible:

People are sexually arhythmic. This means that, however much they are in love, they usually do not have equal appetites at equal times and therefore accommodation to each other's needs is always necessary.

Men are neither less nor more interested in sex than women.

Men are neither less nor more logical and rational than women.

Men are just as sentimental, jealous, envious, as women, but unfortunately are concerned about and threatened by softer feelings, such as love.

Men need as much affection as women.

Women gossip as much as men and no more.

Fear of homosexuality is not evidence of homosexuality but is most often due to exorbitant sexual demands and exorbitant standards in behavior and performance generally. It is often connected to situations involving helplessness.

Prostitutes do not have hearts of gold.

Prostitutes are not experts about sex.

Women's frustration tolerance is as poor as men's.

Men and women are equally creative.

Men and women are equally predisposed to being neurotic. It is easier for women to seek help because getting help is supposed to be antimasculine.

Men and women are equally dependent and equally harbor illusions of dependency.

Men and women have equal potential in their ability as parents.

Women have as much potential to be engineers, doctors, architects and electricians.

People are attracted to people other than legal mates, however much spouses love each other. Exclusivity of sexual attraction is not evidence or a requisite of love.

Size of genitalia and breasts are not proportionate to sexual drive or ability.

All small children have sexual feelings and appetites we

later come to think of as perverse. All of us retain at least some of these appetites; therefore, our thoughts, fantasies and actions, too, sometimes do not fall within culturally defined lines of acceptability. These include: homosexual feelings, masochism, voyeurism, exhibitionism, fetishism and incestuous feelings.

Men and women are equally capable of aggression.

The culture insists that in a heterosexual relationship the man must be more intelligent than the woman. This is simply patent nonsense, and if there is difficulty in this area it is because our culture manufactures it.

There is no special peak sexual excitation that exists at the beginning or midway in a relationship but rather there are the possibilities of all kinds of variations in intensity of feeling within a relationship.

Both sexes can be equally petty or magnanimous.

Both sexes are equally capable of vanity and narcissism.

Aggression and ambition in women is not evidence of repressed homosexuality.

Preference for one coital position over another is not evidence of repressed homosexuality.

There is no correlation between hair color, beard growth, beauty, nose length, foot size and sexual appetite or ability.

Sexual feelings and satisfactions can be associated with loving feelings of deep relatedness, and on the other hand can take place between complete strangers where relatedness plays almost no role at all.

Masturbation is common to both sexes at any age, and occurs in married people, too.

Both sexes are equally curious and inventive and both have early histories of having played "doctor."

Pornography attracts and stimulates both sexes. Differences in taste are largely due to cultural pressure and orientation, so that men prefer starker, more mechanical, visual stimulation, while women find romantically oriented stimulation more exciting. This difference has no origin in biological differences.

Homosexual men are not more talented than heterosexual men. But heterosexual men often repress sensitivity and talent fearing that they are evidence of femininity and homosexuality.

Sex is not always an expression of love. It also can be an expression of anger, a way of dissipating anxiety, a means of getting closer, a means of maintaining emotional and communicating distance by keeping things purely physical, an attempt to dominate, an expression of creativity, an attempt at self-sedation, and a combination of any and all of these possibilities.

Mutual sexual interest is not enough to sustain a marriage but it helps enormously.

Both sexes are equally capable of promiscuity.

Hysterectomy does not cause frigidity.

Prostate surgery does not lead to impotence.

Individual tastes, differences, proclivities and preferences are exceedingly diverse and inventive in both sexes.

To date, no sexual life-style has been demonstrably proven to be better than any other.

HOMOSEXUALITY AND SEXUAL PURITY

Homosexual is still one of the dirtiest words in the language and still represents terrible stigmatization. Fear of being homosexual is still exceedingly prevalent in men, and homosexuality is equated with being relegated to the most degrading of human conditions. This fear is particularly in evidence in men who suffer serious hurt to their self-esteem. Business reversals, loss of a loved one, rejection, often bring on fear of being homosexual. This fear is also fed by mythology—there are rigid characteristics, feelings and interests men are supposed to have or to be exempt from.

Interestingly, most men equate homosexuality with asexuality and perhaps their underlying fear is related to castration and impotence (not only sexually but in the broadest sense involving being helpless and without power) as well as to general cultural stigma in this area.

I believe that homosexuality is also abhorred by men because it is felt by them to represent confused, poorly defined and poorly delineated boundaries of what constitutes so-called normal male feelings. Homosexuality, the word and the symbol, threatens masculine gender identity, and identity generally, because it is felt as potential eradication of safe limits and borders within whose confines we can rest easy and sure of what and who we are supposed to be and what we are supposed to feel.

Women are not nearly as concerned about homosexuality or feelings society may call antifeminine. This is not because of our culture's greater altruism toward women, *but is largely a result of deep sexual prejudice, in which it is believed that women are relatively asexual and childish, so that whatever they feel or do isn't that important.* This applies to homosexuality and to perversions generally. I believe that today, just as much as fifty years ago, women are still seen either as pure, virginal, idealized goddesses who must shun "excessive sexual interest," or as immoral, promiscuous, sexually insatiable, man-digesting temptresses. This cultural compartmentalization makes for much sexual conflict and self-hate in women, often blocking any possibility of sexual enjoyment. Such cultural pressure, along with male fear of homosexuality and female purity and falls from ideal grace, make for highly disturbed relations between the sexes, much self-hate and mutual recrimination.

BATTLE OF THE SEXES

Little boys are made to feel like sissies if they play with girls, or if they like cooking, sewing, or knitting. Later on, as young adults, they are seen as "queer" if they are afraid of girls. Girls are called boy-crazy if they openly like boys. Both groups are teased by their peers if they express feeling for or interest in one another. Yet, paradoxically, conquests are encouraged in both groups. Unconciously, they are prejudiced against one another and taught to fear one another, thereby stunting their facility for developing friendships. Such tactics on the part of peers are assumed to be natural and even amusing. Quite the contrary. They are sado-masochistic, and dilute and even destroy mutual respect, and eventually produce self-hate when mutual attraction can no longer be denied.

Teasing and putting down shared feelings serves to maintain the distance between the sexes and to sustain the illusion that vast differences exist between men and women. Actually, boys and girls and men and women have much more in common than they have apart. It would be helpful if parents promoted this truth. Given the right kind of sociocultural milieu, the sexes would naturally develop more friendships between them, both casual and deep and long-lasting, in which sexual attraction would not be a necessary component. But for the most part this is not the case, and lack of friendship between sexual partners is only too common.

As a consequence of this conditioning, later on many people find themselves trapped in a battle between the sexes in adult life. Some people even go through life feeling that mutual enmity is the only possible way for the sexes to comport themselves and relate, not realizing that they actually are caught in a deceptive and destructive cultural bind. Our adult society, on almost every hand, emphasizes the idea that social communication between adults of opposite sexes, without any sex involved, is impossible. Imagine the social effect if Mr. A. chose to take out Mrs. Neighbor B. for lunch and a long, purely platonic discussion about a topic of mutual interest—simply because Mrs. B. is unusually well informed and interesting to talk to on a subject of deep mutual concern. Mr. A. may be truly in love with his wife, have no interest in Mrs. B. beyond what he would have in a male colleague who shared a mutual interest—but society would not readily believe this. This attitude means that roughly half the population is prevented from having and enjoying social contact with the other half except under the most stringently prescribed cultural rules.

Interestingly, men and women involved in the arts tend to break this social taboo and often do have enriching and enduring friendships with someone of the opposite sex. Literature is full of examples of such relationships. Most likely this is due to the writer's or artist's or composer's or dancer's break with convention generally and is an extension of his or her proclivity toward individuality. Unfortunately, though, many potential good and enriching friendships in the general population are destroyed or never begin because the people involved happen to be members of different sexes.

LOVE AND MARRIAGE

Our culture, through every conceivable device and media form, propagates all kinds of nonsense about love and its vast powers. Love is important indeed, but the belief that pure love can be achieved and that love remedies all human problems inevitably leads to disappointment, self-hate, cynicism, and a breakdown in relationships that otherwise could have been humanly satisfying.

Our culture promotes the notion that being loved is all-important. While being loved has some therapeutic effect, *this is not nearly as effective as loving.* Loving, the active process of loving self, others, causes, activities, mobilizes people in a constructive, self-evolving direction. Illusions about the pure power of love received bringing happiness in marriage are equally disastrous. Many people are severely traumatized when they realize that love and marriage do not result in immediate perfection.

Adaptation to marriage is at best difficult. Many people have no idea at all that living in close relationship with another human being, however much love is shared and exchanged, involves considerable accommodation and struggle. As noted earlier, initial difficulties are often viewed with horror, as evidence of lack of sufficient love, and are followed by impulsive divorce.

PARENTHOOD

Ideal parents do not exist, despite cultural propaganda to the contrary. Publications on child rearing and child education abound. Many of them imply that parent-child ideals are attainable, which produces highly intellectualized, stilted behavior in worried parents, who would otherwise act with spontaneity born of considerable natural wisdom.

We all have problems, and our children must have them, too. We are all the victims of victims, and this fact must be accepted if we are to be realistically compassionate with ourselves, our parents and our children.

Becoming parents does not resolve personal problems or remove human limitations. All of us are capable of, and at times feel angry at, jealous and envious of, and even murderous toward our children. We are capable of feeling incestuous toward them, too. There are times when we feel more concerned about our own welfare than about them. There are times we wish they didn't exist. All these and many more feelings, thoughts and actions, which are viewed with abhorrence by our society, are nevertheless common and natural to the human condition.

Generally, we are better parents to our children as we are able to be better parents to ourselves. Self-nourishment leads to a healthier relationship with them. Self-neglect and chronic self-sacrifice produce much repressed hostility toward them and sicker relating to them.

It must be remembered that children are very complicated people, too. How they behave is not purely a function of parent-child relationships. They, too, are subject to their own internal and external pressures.

To any extent that the culture promotes the myth of

ideal parenthood it promotes self-hate. The same is true of promotion of the idea of exclusivity of function. I have seen a number of mothers in consultation over the years who honestly believed that motherhood prevented the possibility of any other interest or activity. Indeed, some of them felt that they would be "bad mothers" if they still had other interests, enjoyed sex, wanted to go on vacations (especially with their husbands and without their children). This kind of concept was very destructive to themselves, to their husbands and especially to their children. For a child to have to bear the burden of being the product of exclusive interest and perfect parenthood is a terrible pressure. I have known a number of people whose greatest resentment to their parents was stimulated by the statement, "I only live because of you. You are my whole life." No child should be burdened with the need to provide motivation for another human being's continuing life, and every parent needs a life that is much fuller than that of parenthood. Satisfaction of one's personal needs outside of parenthood, contrary to cultural beliefs, contributes to a sense of well-being and contentment, which aids parenthood and mitigates against self-hate and the destructive influences of striving for ideal parenthood.

DEPENDENCY ON CHILDREN

Our culture views dependency on children with utter horror. "Better I should die than have to come to my children for help" is not an uncommon statement. But cultural pressure along these lines is antihuman and contrary to normal biological evolvement. As we get older we need our children. If for nothing else, we often need their presence, friendship and warmth. This is most natural and in keeping with the emotional investment we make in them over the years. Since we feel so much for them, it is only human that we would need their presence and attention as we grow older. That these attentions are not always forthcoming may well be a reality for which we are better off if we don't have exorbitant expectations. But to deny this desire and need is usually false.

As we grow older, and if we live to a very old age, it is entirely possible that our children will be like parents as we become like children and require their help. This is only a disgrace in a culture that builds inappropriate and ruthless pride in independence, regardless of age or infirmity. This position is devoid of compassion and is the essence of the antihumanistic attitude. That children need parents when they are young, and that parents should need children later on, is entirely appropriate to the life cycle of compassionate human beings.

STATUS QUO AND CHANGE

We talk about change and the value of change, but our society, largely in fear of the unfamiliar, detests change and clings tenaciously to status quo situations. While we envy our innovators and explorers, we are threatened by them and despise them almost as much as our poets and artists.

We are told to hold fast at any cost and to maintain the status quo. We are told not to be sticks in the mud and to move and change and go ever forward. We are fed constant excitation and told not to be stimulation addicts. We are told to take it easy and to get going. Neither status quo nor change should be a function of cultural pressure, but rather a question of free choice based on whichever decision makes for more happiness in a given situation or point of time.

WORK

Work is considered godly and—ambivalently—as the ultimate stupidity. Of course, it is neither, and we are entitled to feel different ways about it appropriate to our moods.

KNOWLEDGE AND STUDY

We put great stock in study and knowledge but at the same time feel that there is something not quite right about "knowing too much" and "being grinds" and "egg heads." Ignorance is confused with honesty, straightforwardness and simple virtue, despite the fact that ignorant people also are entirely capable of being devious, crafty, duplicitous and cruel. I repeatedly hear students boast about how much they don't know and how little they studied to acquire what they do know. It is almost as if they must apologize for their interest and effort, let alone their struggle in the acquisition of knowledge.

PLEASURE AND SERIOUSNESS

Despite conscious arguments to the contrary, many of us still suffer from the residual influences of a puritanical Anglo-Saxon culture, which views pleasure with much suspicion. I still encounter any number of people who are embarrassed about saying they have had a really pleasurable time somewhere. This is not true only of masochists but also is common among those of us who unwittingly have been led to equate pleasure, especially deep and sustained pleasure, with superficiality, shallowness, foolishness, frivolity and a general lack of maturity and responsibility. Yet our culture is confused enough also to view seriousness and intellectuality as peculiar, queer, egg-headed, bird-brained and untrustworthy. Of course it is possible to be serious, intellectually inclined, individualistic, responsible and pleasure-oriented all at the same time, but only we can grant integrated acceptance of these quite compatible characteristics to ourselves.

DECISIONS

We are taught to believe that decisions are inevitably important and indeed fateful and eternally binding. The fact is that very few decisions are of the Rubicon-crossing variety. Most decisions in our daily lives involve issues that are not of life and death magnitude and most can be rescinded if necessary, *if we feel free to do so.* Our society dictates against this freedom. It feeds the pride position of irrevocability of decisions and supports the notion that to re-decide otherwise is evidence of weakness of character and unreliability. I have heard people say, "Once I decide, I decide!" My question is, Why? If factors, feelings and ideas change, isn't the ability to decide otherwise evidence of flexibility, adaptability and strength? But our culture continues to confuse rigidity and stubbornness with strength.

We are told that decisions must be made at once. In most cases they can be postponed, and many times it is appropriate to postpone them to gather more adequate information. The pressure our society puts on us always to make decisions immediately and irrevocably contributes greatly to our mass tendency to anxiety. However, we must not confuse the pause to make a wise decision with postponement used as a form of self-hate, which I described earlier.

We are also taught that only one decision of all the possible ones is the best and correct one. In most issues there are no best ways and many correct ones.

What if we do err? The realization that we can make a so-called wrong decision without having to castigate ourselves and suffer fear and self-reprisal will lead us into a state of self-acceptance that can make our full resources available to us. This contributes to our increased ability to make better decisions.

We should not flagellate ourselves with self-hate expressed in second-guessing and recriminations for decisions made in the distant past. "Going to court with ourselves," ostensibly to examine the wisdom of a past decision, is itself a form of treacherous self-hate in which we surely will come out the losers. I simply refuse to go to court with myself about any decision made years ago, which I couldn't affect today. I know that "going to court" at all is a form of self-hate.

PAIN AND PAIN-KILLERS

Our society views sustaining pain for pain's sake a virtue. It is seen as evidence of strength of character, ability to endure frustration, and as a talent for tolerance. Any effort to reduce pain is viewed with suspicion and contempt and as weakness. This applies to psychotherapy as well as the use of drugs. I do not condone the indiscriminate use of drugs for any purpose, but it is sad indeed to see people writhe in pain because of confused notions involving pain and its relief through constructive means such as therapy.

Chronic and sustained pain does not build character and in no way enhances the ability to perceive reality and human realistic limitations: it simply is not one of the experiences that leads to maturity or wisdom. On the contrary, it often leads to withdrawal and resignation. Suffering, whatever its source, often has a debilitating effect emotionally as well as physically, and leads to the production of fantasy and to an aberrated view of life generally. This results in limited insight and poor judgment. The struggle to grow and initial confrontations with reality often are fraught with unavoidable pain. The value of struggle and growth must *not* be confused with the draining effect of pain.

ALCOHOL AND TOBACCO

Our culture abhors alcoholism and is terrified of cancer, but continues to use tobacco and alcohol as integral devices in social relating. Both alcohol and tobacco are part of the cultural mythology relating to maturity, peer acceptance and sexual identification. Advertisers know this and make ample use of this knowledge in selling their products to young people as entrance portals to adult life and sexual flowering.

POLITICIANS AND LEADERS

We continue in a futile search for men of altruistic, pure and ideal vision and purpose. Politicians and leaders are people, and very often they are people who suffer more than others from a compulsive need for power. This need does not usually augment altruism. We insist that our leaders be great performers who will beguile us into voting for them and at the same time active participants in being able to administer and govern with professional skill. These characteristics are seldom shared by the same person. We can certainly ask for more than we've got, but we must be prepared to get less than we ask for.

JUSTICE

My purpose here is not to provide any kind of legal or philosophical discussion of justice. My only aim is to describe justice as a possible base for self-hating, which can be turned to a more compassionate point of view.

Justice is not a natural state of being or a biological production of nature. Justice is a human invention and largely imperfect, and at some times, places and circumstances it is impossible to achieve. Personal claims for *perfect* justice must lead to grievous disappointment. Claims for personal justice are sometimes very subtle and quite inappropriate in terms of reality. A patient of mine, soon after having a gall bladder removed, developed a hernia. He said, "It's not fair. It's just not just. I was sick and I recovered. It's not right that I should have trouble again so soon." True, this poor fellow did feel a bit like Job, but he was miserable on two scores, one appropriate and the other inappropriate to being alive and human. Yes, he was upset about being sick again. But his upset about lack of fairness and justice indicated a claim for a natural kind of justice, for someone up there to make sure that things balance out, but life doesn't work this way. Perfect justice in terms of self, such as the claim for health, simply does not exist.

Justice in almost all areas of personal life is a terribly haphazard affair. The cultural myth about its existence always produces disappointment, abused reactions, injustice collecting, cynicism, bitterness and self-hate. Justice between people and groups of people in a world in which communication is still very limited and complicated can be very elusive and often impossible to attain.

Until we achieve a much higher degree of compassion than we have so far, a social structure without law, and the machinery to attain justice, however limited or aberrated, is unthinkable in any kind of civilized context. Indeed, justice is a step in the direction of compassion, compared to a primitive world in which might makes right. While it is not an adequate substitute for compassion, this man-made construct is a kind of compassionate expedient. When I say expedient, I mean that in our culture there is little and even no attention paid to causes and possible cures for the social malaise that generates the problems that call for the exercise of justice as we know it.

Our society gives a much higher priority to weighing guilt and innocence, and rendering punishment, than to examining the roots of difficulties. This is still a more compassionate process than utter lawlessness and ruthlessness. A society in which punishment is to any degree humane is better than one in which cruel and unusual punishment are common. Thus, lacking a better, less expedient and more permanent system, we are grateful to pursue justice in our society, no matter how imperfect it may be. But we do not have to translate this to mean that we must demand perfect justice for ourselves. This demand has no validity at all. Viruses, bacteria, accidents and chance know nothing of man-made institutions.

We do not have to bring questions of guilt, innocence and punishment into the picture at all in relating to ourselves. Instead, we can struggle to go a step further than our society does on issues in which confrontations with ourselves are involved. We can employ the compassionate approach by asking ourselves what? where? and how did I go wrong or do wrong?, and how can I better understand and help myself?, rather than imposing judgments of guilt or innocence or choosing what may seem like appropriate punishment in the form of self-hate.

NEW BEGINNINGS AND CONTINUUMS

We are exhorted and indeed come to believe that we can and should make "fresh starts," "to begin all over again," and "to do it better next time around." We must accept mistakes, impurities, and blows to pride positions as a natural part of our lives so we don't always need fresh starts and *can* feel better without having to "do it all over again." This usually is an illusionary desire to do it *perfectly* this time around, without any trace of human mistakes. Interestingly, people suffering from schizophrenia sometimes attempt suicide, feeling that in dying a rebirth will be possible, in which they can begin all over again unsullied by past impurities. Of course this is the height of self-hate. If we accept the human condition, and this includes the many human mistakes and indiscretions that exist, we lose the desire to wipe the slate clean and to be reborn. In accepting our human fallibilities we see life as a continuum of all kinds of experiences and we refuse to surrender any segment of that continuum. If we could and did begin again each time we erred in any way, we would kill all possibility of experiential wisdom. We would remain pure, unsullied, bland—*and blank.*

THE GREAT REHEARSAL

We are given to believe that life is a great rehearsal for another life, that a score-keeper will straighten it all out, anyway, later on and will see that each of us gets our rewards. Yet, as a friend of mine said, "This is no rehearsal! This is it! This is your one and only life!"

CHANCE AND CIRCUMSTANCES

Chance plays a big role in our lives. This is inevitable. Despite conventional wisdom to the contrary, there is much that happens over which we have little or no control. We are not Godlike and our worlds can never be perfectly ordered, predictable and our safe bailiwicks. Contrary to traditional social and cultural beliefs, we cannot create favorable circumstances for *all* occasions. Accidents, real accidents, having nothing to do with unconscious motivation, occur in the life of each of us. We must stop blaming ourselves for what we cannot control.

ADAPTATION, ACCOMMODATION, ADJUSTMENT, GROWTH AND EVOLVEMENT

Our culture is geared to rapid change, as I have observed earlier, but the human psyche is not. We have come to expect instant growth and evolvement as well as immediate adjustments and accommodations to new situations. As people, we are the most adaptable living creatures on earth, but even we need time to grow, to evolve and to acclimate. There are also situations when adjustment is not possible. Time to grow, to change, to learn, to adjust, is a human necessity, usually neglected and even held in contempt by a materialistic, computerized technological society. People have come to believe that something is wrong with them if anything less than instant orientation takes place.

Instant full-blown relationships and friendships simply

do not occur. We need time and struggle to establish meaningful relationships. This applies to relationships to people, to situations, and to activities. This is particularly applicable to marriage. In our society people unfortunately have come to expect instant adjustment to married life. This is impossible, since any "new situation" invariably calls for struggle to adjust, and expectations for instant accommodation often lead to disappointment.

Expectation of instant adjustment to school (especially to nursery or kindergarten and first-year college and to first-year professional school) and to new jobs also leads to disappointment, hopelessness and depression.

The pressure to accommodate immediately can make life tougher and more cruel than it has to be. I have, with sadness, seen parents of small children admonish them for not instantly adjusting to new situations, such as first experiences at school and at camp. If we expect very young children to adjust instantly to new circumstances, we contribute to low self-esteem, more than usually difficult adjustments in later life, and considerable disappointment with self, leading to attacks of self-hate. If we learn the lesson of compassion very early in life, this makes for a wonderful reverberation throughout an entire lifetime. The time and effort a child expends in his struggle to adapt to successive new situations teaches him compassion. This lesson is invaluable because he will use it to treat himself compassionately when adult situations call for patience and accommodation to change.

CRISIS AND DISASTER

Our culture participates in a mass masochistic enterprise in which each generation convinces itself that it is witnessing the worst of times, the most acute crisis and disasters, galloping deterioration and imminent world destruction. This kind of disaster orientation functions as a stimulating sadistic goad and is a component of mass addiction to stimulation. Unfortunately, it has the cumulative effect of producing vast confusion, disorientation, and great distortion.

Yet despite continuing and serious problems, mankind is making progress. There is less overall cruelty in the world, less dehumanization, even less war, less ruthlessness and more conscious caring and growing awareness of the need for compassion than ever before. We continue to grow. But when we pull down the world, put down our fellows, our country, and, more, we put down *ourselves*—and that is truly unfair and destructive.

Of course our country and our world have enormous problems. We are a complex species. Our country is no small experiment. It represents the largest cultural attempt at compassion to date. It is, after all, attempting to bring together people of many cultures, colors, races, and kinds, to live in relative harmony with one another. This experiment is not unlike the compassionate one we attempt in microcosm when we try to bring diverse aspects of ourselves into acceptable harmony. This kind of compassionate work and struggle requires considerable time. Our species is still young. Our country is still very young indeed. Here, too, our discouragement is largely a function of unrealistic expectations.

We do not live in a world of glorious, constant peak experiences in which people live happily forever after. We, the people, are not consistently brave, pure, ever-loving, selfless, deserving and just. We do not climb every mountain, ford every river, or make the impossible dream come true, and we must not expect these inhumanities of ourselves. We are not idealized sea gulls or dolphins. We are people.

We live in a world of people who are a vast mixture of inconsistent feelings and moods, who try, who falter, who get tired, who get discouraged, who are lazy and energetic, who laugh and cry, who accept and reject, who are kind and cruel, who are uncaring and altruistic. We live in a culture that is ambivalent in its values and we, the people, constantly have ambivalent feelings. These are the human terms. To be alive and human are the only terms on which we can compassionately flourish.

In a state of grace with ourselves we immediately, as part of the human condition, contribute to a more compassionate culture. Compassionate self-acceptance invariably makes for better relating to ourselves and our fellows. Inner peace makes peace with others a possibility. Once the struggle for a compassionate life is engaged it continues all of our days. This is the essence of healthy human growth. This is the stuff that enables us to feel like people, real people, who are able to dignify and enjoy the richness of daily possibilities. I am reminded of an incident involving my daughter and son when she was four and he was seven. They were getting on the school bus. My son said to the driver, "Wait, another person is getting on." She looked around and realized that no one else was there and that he meant her. She glowed with wonder for days, repeating over and over again, "I'm a person. He called me a person." Yes, to be a person, a real person, not an idealized fabrication, is no small matter. The human condition remains the most interesting, challenging and promising one on this, our earth.

Index